THE AMBASSADOR OF CHRIST.

BY

JAMES CARDINAL GIBBONS,

Archbishop of Baltimore.

AUTHOR OF "THE FAITH OF OUR FATHERS" and "OUR CHRISTIAN HERITAGE."

" For Christ we are ambassadors,
God as it were exhorting by us."
II. Cor. v. 20.

JOHN MURPHY COMPANY
PUBLISHERS

BALTIMORE,   MARYLAND

RESPECTFULLY DEDICATED

TO THE

Venerable Prelates and Clergy

OF THE

UNITED STATES.

PREFACE.

A PIOUS, learned, and zealous priesthood is the glory of the Church of God. By our personal holiness, we work out our own salvation, and edify our neighbors; by our erudition, we enlighten them; and by our zeal, we make them partakers of the precious heritage of Christ.

I do not think that any age or country ever presented a more inviting field for missionary labor than that which the United States exhibits to-day.

"The word of God is not bound," or shackled here, as it has been elsewhere. No military satrap or State functionary is permitted to enter our churches in the capacity of an official censor, to arrest, fine, or imprison a minister of the Gospel for his conscientious utterances in vindication of social morals, and in denunciation of official corruption.

The Catholic pastor is sure to be heard with reverence, sympathy, and adhesion by the members of his flock; and many even of those that are not of the household of the faith, will often be attentive and respectful listeners, especially on extraordinary occasions.

The periodical whirlwinds of bigotry that sweep over the land soon subside, like the upheavals of nature, after spending their force. Nor are they an unmixed evil; they serve some useful purpose. They purify the moral atmosphere; they clear the spiritual skies, and give observant men a better insight into the uncreated world. They are winnowing winds separating the wheat from the chaff. They are storms that try men's souls. They help to render the members of the Church more loyal to their religion, and they awaken in serious and honest minds outside her pale salutary reflections, often resulting in their conversion.

Indeed, it has frequently been observed that periods of violent hostility to our religion have been, also, seasons of notable accessions to the Church, of which there are some shining examples around us. Institutions, as well as men, that have stood unmoved amid the raging billows, have always commanded the admiration and homage of mankind.

It may also be observed that rabid bigotry is not a plant that flourishes on Columbian soil. Those ebullitions of unreasoning hatred toward the Catholic Chuch, are not congenial to the American character. They are generally aroused and fomented by aliens as yet ill-acquainted with our Constitution, which guarantees to all freedom of conscience, who bring with them, and who would fain perpetuate, the intolerant spirit unhappily prevailing in the countries from which they came.

Besides these spasmodic outbursts of religious fanaticism, we are confronted, also, by the steady and unceasing tide of opposition on the part of a considerable number of our fellow-citizens who, without any malice or ill-will toward us, sincerely regard with dislike or suspicion the religion that we profess. Their animosity is no evidence of their hostility to Catholic doctrines, but rather to what they erroneously conceive to be such. They are the unconscious heirs of traditional prejudice, which is not easily eradicated.

This unfriendly attitude, however, should not discourage us. An earnest antagonism, prompted by honest, though misguided, zeal in the cause of Christianity, is far preferable to a spirit of apathy which springs from religious indifference.

There is more hope for the sick man who winces under the application of the lancet than for a patient who is insensible to the surgeon's scalpel. The former shows signs of vitality; the latter excites fears of approaching dissolution.

Of the thousands of Americans that annually embrace the religion of Christ, the most exemplary and conspicuous are often found among those that had been, at one time, the most pronounced opponents of the ancient faith. The most formidable zealot of the primitive Church afterward became the great Apostle of the Gentiles.

Americans are fundamentally a religious people. They who characterize them as a nation so absorbed in trade and commerce, in agriculture and politics, as to give scarcely a thought to eternal truths, judge them not correctly.

A people having little regard for Christianity, would not spend millions annually in the erection of churches, and in the maintenance of home and foreign missions, as Americans are known to do.

Within twenty years after the Civil War, twenty-two millions of dollars were contributed by Northern Protestants for endowments of educational institutions in behalf of the negroes of the South, all these institutions being strictly religious. In 1895, the Presbyterians spent $927,000 for American Home Missions, besides vast sums for Foreign Missions.

According to a statement apparently authorized, the five leading denominations in the United States, contribute annually $88,000,000 for the support of their respective churches and missions.[1] And these contributions are not exacted as a compulsory tax, but are bestowed as voluntary offerings.

The American people possess, also, in a marked degree, the natural virtues that are the indispensable basis of supernatural life. They are gifted with a high order of

[1] H. K. Carroll, in *The Forum*, May, 1896.

intelligence; they are self-poised and deliberate; they are of industrious and temperate habits; they are frank, manly, and ingenuous. They have a deep sense of justice and fair play; they are brave and generous; and they usually have the courage of their convictions.

They are, withal, a law-abiding people. At the close of the Civil War, when hundreds of thousands of Federal and Confederate troops were disbanded, they laid down their arms, and quietly resumed the civic pursuits of life, submitting without constraint to the constitutional laws of the country. They eloquently disproved the ominous predictions uttered abroad that a soldiery suddenly released from the restraints of military discipline, would be a standing menace to the peace and industry of the country by their acts of violence and sedition; and that, after having once acquired a taste for blood, they would still thirst for more.

During a Presidential campaign, we find both great parties fiercely striving for the mastery. A stranger observing the passions and animosities that are aroused, the vehement denunciations poured out by the contending forces, and the dire disasters predicted by each side should the other triumph, would imagine that we were on the eve of a bloody revolution. But he would soon discover that the conflict did not occasion the loss of a single life. It was a bloodless revolution, effected not by bullets, but by ballots.

Each side spends colossal fortunes, and impresses into its service the best talent of the nation in the hope of securing the coveted prize.

The highest office in the gift of the people, the enormous patronage attached to it, the exultation of victory, the glory of presiding over the destinies of the country, are all involved in the issue. And yet on the morning after the election, the defeated party bows to the will of the majority.

A people that yield so ready and loyal obedience to human laws, will not set their face against divine revelation when its imperious claims are clearly and cogently set before them.

O if those "olive branches" that were rudely broken from the parent stem by the destructive tornado which swept over Northern Europe in the sixteenth century, were "ingrafted and made partaker of the root and of the fatness of the olive-tree"[1] of Catholic and Apostolic faith, they would grow into fair and majestic proportions, abounding in the fruit of Christian virtues such as few nations ever produced!

While the Catholic religion accommodates itself to every form of government, it has a special adaptability to our political system and to the genius of the American people.

We are happily living under a government of constitutional freedom. Our citizens enjoy the largest measure of liberty that is compatible with law and order. They are justly impatient of arbitrary coercion, and chafe under any undue restraint that might be imposed on their personal independence. This individualism is, indeed, a healthy stimulus to legitimate activity and honorable emulation in the various walks of public and private life.

But there are multitudes of others who give vent to the freedom in which they revel, by disseminating the most utopian and impracticable schemes affecting the religious, political, social, and economic world.

This centrifugal force should be counterbalanced by a corresponding centripetal power, which is found in the religion of Christ. The Catholic Church is the great conservative element of society, as all reflecting men are ready to avow. The Mistress of truth, she pursues a middle course, avoiding the extremes of undue severity and excessive laxity She

[1] Rom. XI.

holds the balance of even-handed justice between the rights of capital and the claims of labor. She teaches that all antagonism between the employer and the employed is suicidal and abnormal, and that the same harmony should subsist between both as exists between the head and the members of the body.

She is eminently the Church of the people. She exercises a wholesome influence on the masses. While always in sympathy with genuine progress, and the lawful aspirations of the toiling millions, she knows how to curb their excesses. She appeals to their enlightened self-interest and moral sense, and she endeavors to control them by religious sanctions.

In fierce political and social convulsions, what voice is more potent than hers in assuaging the storm, and saying to the troubled waters: "Peace, be still!"

Our mission is twofold: 1. To the members of the Church; 2. To the hosts that are outside her pale, "who are Israelites," glorying in the title of Christians: "who are our kinsmen according to the flesh," descended like us from the same family of nations, "to whom belongeth the adoption of sons and the glory, and the covenant,"[1] for God is their Father as well as ours, and Christ Jesus died for them as well as for us: who speak our language, and enjoy with us the heritage of the same constitutional freedom.

Let our hearts go out to them; let us yearn for them; let us appeal to them and importune them till, by our untiring patience, force of argument, and gentle persuasion, we "compel" as many of them as we can, to enter "the one fold of the one Shepherd."

This little volume, with all its imperfections, has cost the author much labor, expended amid many interruptions. The motive that impelled him to undertake the work, is his sincere affection for his devoted and venerable fellow-

[1] Rom. ix.

laborers, the clergy of North America, and his desire to see
the kingdom of Christ extending its spiritual empire far and
wide throughout our beloved country.

If the book will contribute in some small measure to
inspire the noble band of learned and self-denying professors
with fresh zeal in the execution of their sublime and arduous
calling, so essential to the welfare of the Christian Commonwealth; if it will quicken students with more reverence and
gratitude for their teachers, and with more diligence in the
pursuit of knowledge; if it will animate our clergy with
renewed ardor in the cultivation of piety and science, and
with increased earnestness in the work of the ministry, it will
not have been written in vain.

FEAST OF ALL SAINTS,
    1896.

CONTENTS.

xiv   CONTENTS.

THE AMBASSADOR OF CHRIST.

CHAPTER I.

EXCELLENCE OF THE CHRISTIAN PRIESTHOOD.

"HONOR is he worthy of whom the King (*of kings*) hath a mind to honor."[1] God is never imposed upon by the din of popular praise. He estimates a man at his real worth. His verdict is the standard, the criterion of genuine excellence, and the patent of true nobility. He crowns merit only and the dignity which springs from virtue.

We know in what honor and esteem God, in the Old Dispensation, held His prophets, who were the teachers and expounders of the Law, the vindicators of Jehovah's rights and dominion among the people, and the watchmen on the towers of Israel. "Let us praise men of renown," says the inspired writer, "and our fathers in their generation, men endued with wisdom, showing forth in the prophets the dignity of prophets, and by the strength of wisdom *instructing* the people in most holy words. All these have gained glory in their generations, and were praised in their days. Their bodies are buried in peace,

[1] Esther VI. 11.

1

and their name liveth unto generation and generation. Let the people show forth their wisdom, and the Church declare their praise."[1]

The Almighty gave them prerogatives such as were not bestowed on earthly rulers and conquerors of nations. He lifted up the veil, and disclosed to them a clear vision of futurity. In response to their prayers, He suspended the laws of nature, and enabled them to work miracles. He proclaimed their persons sacred and inviolable, so that he who touched them, touched the apple of His eye. "Touch not," He said, "My anointed, and do no evil to My prophets."[2] Sometimes He inflicted summary chastisement on those that offered personal violence to His consecrated servants. King Jeroboam raises his arm to strike one of the prophets, and his hand instantly falls withered by his side.

John the Baptist, the great preacher of the desert, stands on the confines of the Old and the New Law. He is the connecting link between the Synagogue and the Church. He is the morning star ushering in the Sun of Justice, and disappearing at His rising. He points out with his finger Him whom the prophets beheld in spirit at a distance: "Behold," he says, "the Lamb of God who taketh away the sins of the world." So precious is the Precursor in the sight of God, that he is sanctified before his birth; he is called "the friend of the Bridegroom," and Christ pronounces his eulogy in these words: "Amen I say to you, there hath not risen among them that are born of women one greater than John the Baptist."[3]

[1] Ecclus. XLIV. 1–15.   [3] Matt. XI. 11.
[2] I. Par. XVI. 22.

✓ The Apostles, who announced the new law of grace, are the legitimate successors of the ancient priests and prophets in offering sacrifice, in proclaiming God's name, and in extending His kingdom among the nations of the earth. Christ manifests His predilection for them in the three most signal ways that a chief can honor and recompense his followers: He cherishes them by His personal friendship; He exalts them by associating them with Himself in the final judgment of men; He rewards them with eternal beatitude in His heavenly kingdom.

Now, the anointed preacher of the New Law inherits the office of the prophets and the Apostles; and, as he continues their mission, he shares in the dignity and prerogatives conferred on them so long as the integrity of his private life corresponds with his sacred calling.

I will even affirm, on the authority of St. Paul, that the priest is as much more exalted than were the prophets, as the New Covenant is more glorious than the Old. "*God*," says the Apostle, "hath made us fit ministers of the New Testament, not in the letter, but in the Spirit; for the letter killeth, but the Spirit giveth life. Now if the ministration of death engraven with letters on stones was glorious, how shall not the ministration of the Spirit be more glorious? For if the ministry of condemnation is glory, much more the ministry of justice aboundeth in glory." [1]

St. Leo the Great thus addressed the laity of his day: "Acknowledge thy dignity, O Christian, and having become partaker of the divine nature, do not return to your former vileness by degenerate conversation. Be

[1] II. Cor. III. 6–9.

mindful of whose Head and of whose Body you are made
a member. Remember that you were delivered from the
power of darkness, and translated into the light and kingdom of God." If Christians are thus exhorted to recognize their spiritual dignity even as laymen, how much
more profoundly should you be impressed with a sense
of the exalted rank to which you have been raised as a
minister of Christ?

"What is man," says the Psalmist, "that Thou art
mindful of him, or the son of man that Thou visitest
him? Thou hast made him a little less than the angels,
Thou hast crowned him with glory and honor; and hast
set him over the works of Thy hands."[1] But how much
is this earthly dominion of man excelled by the spiritual
power of the priest! May we not exclaim in joyous
wonder: What is the priest, O Lord, that Thou art
mindful of him, or Thy anointed minister that Thou
visitest him! Thou hast invested him with prerogatives not given to Thy angels. Thou hast made him the
custodian and dispenser of Thy heavenly treasures.

"Ye are no more strangers and foreigners," says St.
Paul, "but ye are fellow-citizens with the saints, and of
the household of God, built upon the foundation of the
Apostles and prophets, Jesus Christ Himself being the
chief corner-stone."[2] If it is a great distinction to be
a private citizen of the Christian Republic, how much
greater to be one of its magistrates? If it is a mark
of divine predilection to be a member of God's household, how much more to be one of His chamberlains?
If it is a privilege to be a living stone in the spiritual

[1] Ps. VIII. 5, 6.   [2] Eph. II. 19, 20.

Jerusalem, how much greater to be one of its shining columns?

St. Peter addressed these words to the Christian people of his time: " Ye are a chosen generation, a royal priest-hood, a holy nation, a purchased people."[1] If it is a divine favor to be selected from countless millions of souls, and adopted as children of the Christian family, how much more precious the grace to be enrolled among its chieftains? If Peter congratulates the faithful on being consecrated priests in their baptism, that they might offer on the altar of their hearts and in the sanctuary of their homes, the spiritual sacrifice of praise and thanksgiving, how much more fervent would be his felicitations to you who are made a priest according to the order of Mel-chisedech, that you may offer the spotless Lamb in God's holy temple?

But we cannot adopt a better method for showing forth the dignity of the priest, than by enumerating some of the principal titles by which he is honored in the Sacred Scriptures.

He is called *the Salt of the earth.* " Ye are," says our Lord, " the salt of the earth. But if the salt lose its savor, wherewith shall it be salted?"[2] As salt pre-serves meat from corruption, so is the priest placed among the faithful that he may preserve them from moral taint and defilement by the wholesome influence of his example and precepts.

He is called *the Light of the world.* " Ye are the light of the world. A city seated on a mountain cannot be hid."[3]

---

[1] I. Pet. ii. 9.   [2] Matt. v. 13.   [3] Ibid. v. 14.

Jesus is the Sun of Justice. He is "the true light, which enlighteneth every man that cometh into the world." [1] After He had descended below the horizon of the tomb, the Apostles and their successors were set in the firmament, to shine by His light during the dark night of this world, until "the Day-star, from on high, would arise" and illumine His saints during the never-ending day of eternity.

As a city, built on a mountain, is a guide to the wayfarer, so is God's minister placed in a conspicuous position in the Church, that "to all by whom he is seen and heard, he may be an exemplar of celestial life." [2]

The prominence of a priest as a moral guide was beautifully expressed in his own figurative and poetic language, by *Old Wolf*, a Cheyenne Indian chief in Montana : " In the land of the Cheyennes, there is a mountain higher than all the mountains around him. All the Cheyennes know that mountain ; even our forefathers knew him. When children, we ran around wheresoever we wanted. We were never afraid to lose our way so long as we could see that mountain, which would show us home again. When grown up, we followed the buffalo and the elk ; we cared not where we pursued the running deer, so long as the mountain was in sight ; for we knew he was ever a safe guide, and never failed in his duty. When men, we fought the Sioux, the Crows, the white men. We went after the enemy, though the way ran high up, and low down. Our hearts trembled not on account of the road ; for as long as we could see the mountain, we felt sure of finding our home again. When far away, our

---

[1] John I. 9.   [2] Pontificale Romanum.

hearts leaped for joy on seeing him, because he told us that our home came nearer.

"During the winter, the snow covered all the earth with a mantle of white; we could no longer distinguish him from other mountains except by his height, which told us he was *the* mountain. Sometimes dark clouds gathered above. They hid his head from our view, and out of them flew fiery darts, boring holes in his sides. The thunder shook him from head to foot; but the storm passed away, and the mountain stood forever.

"This mountain is the Black-robe. His heart is as firm as a rock. He changes not. He speaks to us the words of truth. We are always sure of our path, when we look to him for guidance. He has taught us in the summer of his days. And even now, when his head is whitened by the snows of many winters, and his face is wrinkled by the storms of life, we still recognize him as our spiritual chief. He is the mountain that leads us up to God." And surely the admiration of the Indian Chief was well grounded. For if the world justly honors the explorer who has discovered a new continent or an island on our globe, what reverence is due to him who guides men by the unerring light of faith to the realms of eternity?

The priest is called the *"Man of God,"* [1] just as Antichrist is called " the Man of Sin," the popular leader is called a *man of the people,* and as the votary of fashion and pleasure is called a *man of the world.* This title the priest shares with the prophets of old, because his mission like theirs is divine, and because he is exhorted to resemble God in holiness of life.

[1] I. Tim. vi. 11.

He is named the "*Servant of God*,"[1] "whom to serve is to reign." The most honorable title claimed even by the Pope, is: "The servant of the servants of God." After Jonas the Prophet had embarked for the port of Tarsus, in Cilicia, he fell into a profound sleep. Meantime, a fearful storm arose, which terrified the mariners. The shipmaster awoke him, and eagerly asked him: "Who art thou? and whither goest thou? or of what people art thou?" Jonas replied that he was the servant of "the Lord of heaven, who made both the sea and the dry land;" therefore, he feared not the storm. He regarded this prerogative of *Servant of God* as more sublime than that of monarch or conqueror. Well did the Royal Prophet exclaim: "Better is one day in Thy courts above thousands. I had rather be a door-keeper in the house of my God, than dwell in the tabernacles of sinners."[2] For the dignity of the servant is enhanced by the exalted rank of the Master whom he serves.

The priest is the "*Friend of Christ*." "I will not now," He says, "call you servants, for the servant knoweth not what his lord doth; but I have called you friends, because all things whatsoever I have heard of My Father, I have made known to you."[3] In becoming the friend, he does not, indeed, cease to be the servant of Christ. But his is the service of a cherished companion and not of a hireling.

"A faithful friend is a strong defence, and he that hath found him, hath found a treasure. Nothing can be compared to a faithful friend, and no weight of gold and silver is able to countervail the goodness of his fidelity."[4]

[1] Tit. I. 1.
[2] Ps. LXXXIII. 11.
[3] John xv. 15.
[4] Ecclus. VI. 14, 15.

If such is the value of an earthly friend, how inestimable is the privilege to be like John the Baptist, "the friend of the Bridegroom!" Friends confide to one another the secrets of their hearts. This is one of the chief characteristics of true friendship. Our Lord manifested His attachment to His disciples by revealing to them the mysteries of the kingdom of heaven, which had been locked in His own breast, or only partially disclosed to others in parables.

The more we love our Lord, the more desirous we are to commune with Him; and the more we resemble Him in our dispositions and aims of life, the more intimately will He manifest His friendship for us by communicating to us His heavenly secrets: "If any one," He says, "love Me, My Father will love him, and We will come and will make Our abode with him." [1]

He is the *Brother of Jesus*. After His Resurrection, our Lord sent by Mary Magdalen this touching and gracious message to His Apostles: "Go to My Brothers and say to them: I ascend to My Father and to your Father, to My God and your God." [2] In addressing them by this endearing name, He wished to reassure them of His abiding love for them, and of His entire forgiveness of their abandonment of Him.

The priest bears the tender name of *Father*, a title which he shares with his eternal Father, "from whom all paternity in heaven and on earth is named." [3] "For if you have ten thousand instructors," says the Apostle, "yet not many fathers, for in Christ Jesus, by the Gospel, I have begotten you." [4] He becomes the spiritual father

[1] John xiv. 23.   [3] Eph. iii. 15.
[2] John xx. 7.   [4] I. Cor. iv. 15.

of his flock whom he has brought forth to a new life
in the regenerating waters of baptism, and whom he
nourishes with the Bread of heaven. What filial love
and confidence does not this beautiful name inspire in
the hearts of the faithful ! For there is no relation more
close, more potent, and more honorable than that which
binds the child to the parent. The priest renounces all
carnal fatherhood, that his affections may be concentrated
on his spiritual offspring.

✓ The boatman on the Lake of Geneva used to address
St. Francis de Sales with great familiarity, by the title of
Father. The Bishop of Belley, who happened to accompany him one day, instructed the boatman to call the
saint *My Lord*. St. Francis rebuked the prelate, saying :
" Let them call me their father, and indeed they love me
as such. O how much more good they do my heart,
than those who call me *Monseigneur !* "

Some days before his death, Archbishop Bayley, in one
of his soliloquies, was heard saying : " Father Bayley,
Bishop Bayley, Archbishop Bayley. I prefer the title of
Father Bayley."

But of all designations given to a minister of religion,
the title of *Priest* is manifestly the most sacred and honorable. The essential office of a priest is to offer sacrifice :
" For every high priest taken from among men, is ordained for men in the things that appertain to God, that
he may offer up gifts and sacrifices for sins." [1] As the
most sublime act of Jesus Christ was His sacrifice on
Calvary, so the sacrifice of the Mass, which commemo-
rates the bloody immolation of Christ, is the most august
act that can be performed by a human being. " No act,"

[1] Heb. v. 1

says St. Thomas, " is greater than the consecration of the Body of Christ." The priest brings down on the altar, he holds in his hands, and partakes of the same flesh that was born of the Virgin Mary. Thomas Carlyle, though far from being partial to the Catholic religion, says : " Higher task than that of priesthood was allotted to no man ! wert thou but the meanest in that sacred Hierarchy, is it not honor enough therein to spend and to be spent ? " [1]

The true priest has the noblest mission on earth, not only because he offers up the Lamb of God on the altar, but also because he immolates himself on the altar of duty and charity in behalf of his fellow-beings. His whole life is a perpetual sacrifice, and self-sacrifice is an evidence of a magnanimous soul.

He is also called by St. Paul, " *a Dispenser of the mysteries of God.*" [2] He is the custodian of the Blessed Sacrament, as Joseph in Egypt was the guardian of Pharaoh's treasures. The words of Proverbs may be justly applied to him : " He that is the keeper of his master, shall be glorified." [3]

As steward, he is also charged with the office of dispensing the Bread of Life to those worthy of receiving it. Like the foster-father of Jesus, he has sometimes to carry his Lord among a hostile or an alien people, and to shield Him from irreverence. " Who (thinkest thou) is the faithful and wise steward whom his lord setteth over his household, to give them their measure of wheat in due season ? Blessed is that servant whom his lord when he shall come, shall find so doing. Truly I say

[1] Sartor Resartus, B. 1. Ch. x.   [3] Prov. XXVII. 18.
[2] I. Cor. IV. 1.

to you, he will set him over all his possessions." [1] Where is the diligent pastor that distributes the Bread of heaven to the Christian family? Blessed is he, for his Master will have him reign with Him in heaven.

The priest is *the Minister of reconciliation.* "All things," says the Apostle, "are of God, who hath reconciled us to Himself by Christ, *and hath given us the ministry of reconciliation.*" [2] The priest has jurisdiction not only over the natural Body, but also over the mystical Body of Christ, which is composed of the members of His Church. After the power of consecrating the Body and Blood of our Lord, the highest privilege ever conferred on man, is that of pardoning sin in the tribunal of penance. This prerogative is clearly expressed in the following passages: "Verily, I say to you, whatsoever ye shall bind upon earth, shall be bound also in heaven, and whatsoever ye shall loose on earth, shall be loosed also in heaven." [3]

"As the Father hath sent Me, I also send you. When He had said this, He breathed on them, and He said to them: Receive ye the Holy Ghost. Whose sins ye shall forgive, they are forgiven them: and whose sins ye shall retain, they are retained." [4]

So wondrous is this faculty of forgiving sins, that when our Saviour exercised this merciful prerogative, the Scribes exclaimed: "Who can forgive sins but God?" For hitherto this was an exercise of jurisdiction delegated by the Almighty neither to prophet, priest, nor angel. Kingly authority affects only the outward acts of man. Sacerdotal authority penetrates into the sanctuary of the

[1] Luke xii. 42.
[2] II. Cor. v. 18.
[3] Matt. xviii. 18.
[4] John xx. 21–23.

<u>soul</u>. Earthly judges punish crime, even though the criminal abhors his guilt; it is the priestly privilege to pardon the repentant sinner. The sentence of the earthly judge is restricted to the temporal life of man; that of the Lord's anointed extends into the regions of eternity.

The priest is styled the *Physician of the soul*. " Is any man sick among you," says St. James, " Let him call in the priests of the Church, and let them pray over him, anointing him with oil in the name of the Lord : and the prayer of faith shall save the sick man, and the Lord will raise him up : and if he be in sins, they shall be forgiven him." [1]

The priest of the New Law discerns between sin and sin, as the priest of the Old Law discerned between leprosy and leprosy. But he exercises the functions of a soul-physician, not only by his sacramental powers, but also by administering the medicine of consolation to the sorrowing, and by prescribing salutary remedies to the victims of moral diseases. In his daily visitation, the compassionate minister of God brings sunshine into the house of mourning. He staunches the bleeding wounds of the broken-hearted, cheers the disconsolate, heals domestic dissensions, and assuages the fever of anger, cupidity, and voluptuousness.

He is called *an Angel*, or *Messenger of God*, because like the angels he is the bearer of messages between earth and heaven, and is " sent to minister for them who shall receive the inheritance of salvation." [2] Like the angels, also, he should be the exemplar of truth, sincerity, and chastity.

[1] James v. 14, 15.   [2] Heb. i. 14.

" The lips of the priest shall keep knowledge, and they shall seek the law at his mouth, because he is the angel of the Lord of hosts." [1] The prelates appointed to preside over the seven churches of Asia, are called angels.[2] When St. John prostrated himself at the feet of an angel, that he might worship him, the angel forbade him, saying that they were both the fellow-messengers and servants of the Lord: "And I fell down before his feet to adore him; and he saith to me: See that thou do it not, for I am thy fellow-servant, and of thy brethren who have the testimony of Jesus." [3]

The priest is like those angels whom Jacob saw in a vision, ascending and descending by a ladder, which reached from earth to heaven. He ascends, bearing to the throne of God the petitions of the people; and he descends, bringing to them benedictions from the Lord in response to their prayers.

Like Moses, he is a *Mediator of intercession* between God and man, as Christ Jesus, our Lord, is the Mediator of redemption. As the official advocate of the people, he pleads in their behalf for mercy: " Between the porch and the altar the priests, the Lord's ministers, shall weep and shall say: Spare, O Lord, spare Thy people, and give not Thine inheritance to reproach, that the heathen should rule over them." [4] " Every high priest, taken from among men, is ordained for men in the things that appertain to God, that he may offer up gifts and sacrifices for sins: who can have compassion on them that are ignorant and that err, because he himself also is encompassed with infirmity. And therefore he

[1] Mal. ii. 7.
[2] Apoc. ii.
[3] Ibid. xix. 10.
[4] Joel ii. 17.

ought, as for the people, so also for himself, to offer for sins."[1]

The priest is the *Ambassador of Christ.* "For Christ, therefore, we are ambassadors, God as it were exhorting by us."[2] As there is scarcely any public office more honorable or more expressive of a sovereign's esteem and confidence than that of ambassador, so there is hardly any title in the hierarchy which conveys with it more dignity and responsibility than that of Christ's legate. The envoy of Jesus Christ upholds and vindicates the rights and prerogatives of God among the people to whom he is sent, just as a minister plenipotentiary of the civil government sustains the power and majesty of the nation that he represents. He is furnished with the credentials of a divine embassy, and is empowered to prescribe the conditions on which men may enter into a treaty of reconciliation and peace with the King of kings.

He is a *Co-laborer with God.* St. Paul says: "We are laborers with God."[3] The priest is, therefore, more than an ambassador of Christ: he is also His coadjutor in the moral government of the world. He not only represents Christ, but he *personates* Him, and becomes identified with Him in his ministerial functions, as far as two personalities can be considered identical. There exists between Jesus Christ and His priesthood, not only a succession and continuity, but an identity of ministry. The priest not only acts with Christ, by the authority of Christ, in the name of Christ, but his official acts are Christ's acts. His words are the echo of Christ's voice: "Behold," He says, "I am with you all days, even to

[1] Heb. v. 1–3.   [3] I. Cor. iii. 9.
[2] II. Cor. v. 20.

the end of the world." [1] "He that receiveth you, receiveth Me, and he that receiveth Me, receiveth Him that sent Me." [2] "He that heareth you, heareth Me, and he that despiseth you, despiseth Me; and he that despiseth Me, despiseth Him that sent Me." [3]

If the priest addresses to heaven the prayers of the faithful, Christ presents them to His eternal Father. If he sows the Gospel seed, Christ giveth the increase. If he confers the Sacraments, Christ imparts the grace that makes them fruitful : "Though Peter baptize," says St. Augustine, "it is Christ that baptizeth. Though Paul baptize, it is Christ that baptizeth." The priest absolves the penitent on earth, Christ ratifies the sentence in heaven. If the priest offers the adorable Sacrifice, Christ is invisibly present, the High Priest and Victim. In a word, "The priest is another Christ."

Our Lord, in His gracious condescension, thus associates us with Himself, as partners and colleagues in the work of the apostolate. It is by virtue of this coöperation that the merits of His sacrifice on Calvary are applied, and the light of His Gospel is diffused throughout the world.

In short, if the Church is an army, the priests are its captains ; if it is a sheep-fold, they are its shepherds, leading the flock to healthy pastures and refreshing streams. If the Church is a city, they are its appointed magistrates ; if it is a vine, they are the branches clustering around the parent stem, from which they draw their vitality and support ; if it is named the holy city Jerusalem, they are placed as guardians and defenders on its

[1] Matt. xxviii. 20.   [3] Luke x. 16.
[2] Ibid. x. 40.

watch-towers. "Upon thy walls, O Jerusalem, I have appointed watchmen all the day, and all the night; they shall never hold their peace."[1] If the missionary world is a sea, they are its fishermen. If it is a field, they are the sowers of the good seed, without whose labor the land would be a barren waste. If Christ compares His Church to a kingdom, the priests are its vice-gerents, governing their subjects according to the law of God, and enforcing obedience by religious and moral sanctions: "Thou hast made us a kingdom and priests to our God, and we shall reign on the earth."[2]

The dignity of the priest as a spiritual king and leader of the people is beautifully expressed by Carlyle: "The priest presides over the worship of the people; is the uniter of them with the unseen Holy. He is the spiritual captain of the people; he guides them heavenward, by wise guidance through this earth and its work. The ideal of him is that he be what we call a voice from the unseen heaven, interpreting even as the prophet did, and in a more familiar manner, unfolding the same to men. He is the prophet shorn of his more awful splendor, burning with mild radiance, as the enlightener of daily life. This, I say, is the ideal of a priest. So in old times, so in these, and in all times. A priest who is not this to all, who does not any longer aim or try to be this, is a character of whom we had rather not speak in this place."[3]

May we not exclaim with St. Ephrem: "O glorious miracle! O ineffable power! O tremendous mystery of the holy and sublime priesthood, most venerable and

[1] Isaiah LXII. 6.   [2] Apoc. v. 10.   [3] Heroes and Hero Worship.

2

without blemish, with which Christ, coming into this world, has vouchsafed to clothe His unworthy creatures! On bended knees, with sighs and tears, must I beg the grace to comprehend this celestial gift, a treasure, indeed, to those who guard it worthily and holily. Truly is it a tower of strength, an indestructible wall that reaches from earth to heaven. The priest pauses not at the celestial gates; he penetrates even the heaven of heavens. Behold him in the midst of the angels, in company with the angelical host. Even as those bright spirits does he enjoy the intimacy of the Lord, the Creator and Source of all light; he has but to desire, and he instantly obtains by right, so to speak, all that he asks." [1]

God has honored you, my Brother. Be it yours to say with St. Paul in grateful homage: "As long, indeed, as I am the Apostle of the Gentiles, I will honor my ministry." [2]

-----

[1] Oratio de Sacerdotio.   [2] Rom. XI. 13.

CHAPTER II.

DIVINE VOCATION TO THE SACRED MINISTRY.

HOW sublime is the vocation to the sacred ministry, and how privileged the candidate upon whom this mark of predilection is bestowed! The Lord Himself is the Master in whose service he is enlisted; he is the dispenser of the word of God and of the Bread of Life; the kingdom of heaven is the special object of his thoughts, the goal of his ambition.

Vocation to the priesthood is a providential act, by which God selects some persons in preference to others for the work of the ministry, and confers on them particular graces for its faithful execution.

Hence, there are two elements in a divine vocation: God's free choice of His elect, and the outpouring of His grace to enable him to discharge the sacred duties assigned to him.

It is in accordance with the economy of Divine Providence that, whenever Almighty God calls a man to a position in life beset with difficulties and dangers, and requiring an extraordinary exercise of virtue, He favors him with special gifts to accomplish his mission, and inclines his heart toward the worthy fulfilment of the obligations confronting him. But it is obvious that the office of the Christian priesthood is most arduous and formidable, and demands the practic of the highest

19

virtue; therefore, the worthy candidate may confidently rely on the supernatural help needful for him.

The necessity of a vocation to the priesthood cannot be gainsaid. It is clearly affirmed in the Sacred Scriptures, and intrusion into the sanctuary without evidences of a divine call, is denounced by the voice of Revelation as not only a usurpation, but a sacrilege.

Among the twelve tribes of Israel, God selected that of Levi for the exclusive service of the altar : " The Lord hath chosen you to stand before Him, and to minister to Him, and to worship Him, and to burn incense to Him."[1]

St. Paul declares that Christ Himself did not assume the dignity of High Priest till He was called by His eternal Father : " *No man* taketh the honor to himself, but he that is called by God as Aaron was : so Christ also did not glorify Himself that He might be made a High Priest, but He that said unto Him : *Thou art My Son, to-day have I begotten Thee.* As He saith also in another place : *Thou art a Priest forever according to the order of Melchisedech.*"[2] Who can presume to undertake the functions of the ministry without the sanction of a heavenly call, since the great High Priest Himself did not do so until He was commissioned by His eternal Father?

Christ utters the following denunciation against those that enter the sanctuary by a forbidden and tortuous route : "Amen, amen, I say to you : He that entereth not by the door into the sheepfold, but climbeth up another way, the same is a thief and a robber. But he that entereth in by the door, is the shepherd of the sheep. To him the porter openeth; and the sheep hear his voice."[3]

[1] II. Par. xxix. 11.   [2] Heb. v. 4–6.   [3] John x. 1–3.

In the law of grace, the Apostles were expressly called to the service of God by their Divine Master. As Jesus was walking by the Sea of Galilee, "He saw Simon and Andrew his brother casting nets into the sea (for they were fishermen). And Jesus said to them : Come after Me, and I will make you to become fishers of men. And immediately leaving their nets, they followed Him. And going on from thence a little farther, He saw James, the son of Zebedee, and John his brother, who also were mending their nets in the ship. And forthwith He called them. And leaving their father Zebedee in the ship with his hired men, they followed Him." [1]

"And after these things, He went forth and saw a publican named Levi, sitting at the receipt of custom, and He said to him : Follow Me. And leaving all things, he rose up and followed Him." [2]

Soon after the call of Matthew, or Levi, our Lord chose the twelve Apostles. "It came to pass in those days, that He went out into a mountain to pray, and He passed the whole night in prayer to God. And when day was come, He called unto Him His disciples ; and He chose twelve of them (whom also He named Apostles)." [3]

And in His last discourse, He solemnly reminds them of their special election, of their mission, and of the fruit which they were expected to bring forth : "Ye have not chosen Me, but I have chosen you, and have appointed you, that ye should go, and should bring forth fruit, and your fruit should remain." [4]

[1] Mark i. 16–20.   [3] Luke vi. 12, 13.
[2] Luke v. 27, 28.   [4] John xv. 16.

Matthias, also, was called to the apostolate by the direct agency of the Holy Ghost. When the Apostles had determined to select a successor to Judas, "They appointed two, Joseph . . . . and Matthias, and praying, they said : Thou, Lord, who knowest the hearts of all men, show whether of these two *Thou hast chosen* to take the place of this ministry and apostleship, from which Judas hath by transgression fallen. . . . And the lot fell upon Matthias, and he was numbered with the eleven Apostles."[1]

Paul's miraculous conversion, and the subsequent vocation of himself and Barnabas are graphically told in the Acts of the Apostles. When Ananias hesitated to approach Paul, because he had hitherto been a persecutor of the Church, "the Lord said to him : Go thy way, for this man is to Me a vessel of election, to carry My name before the Gentiles and kings, and the children of Israel. For I will show him how great things he must suffer for My name's sake."[2]

Later, *as the Apostles* "were ministering to the Lord, and fasting, the Holy Ghost said to them : Separate Me Saul and Barnabas for the work whereunto I have taken them. Then they, fasting and praying, and imposing their hands upon them, sent them away. So they, being sent by the Holy Spirit, preached the word of God."[3] St. Paul, from a profound sense of gratitude for his extraordinary election, refers to it frequently in his Epistles.

In his Epistle to the Romans, he insists on a divine vocation as an indispensable charter for the official heralds of the Gospel : "How then shall they call on Him in whom they have not believed? Or how shall they believe

[1] Acts I. 23–26.   [2] Acts IX. 15, 16.   [3] Ibid. XIII. 2–5.

Him of whom they have not heard ? And how shall they hear without a preacher ? And how shall they preach unless they be sent ?" [1] This commission is not from kings or civil magistrates, but from the Lord Himself, either directly or through His lawful representatives.

In fact, there are few transgressors more sternly denounced in the sacred text than they who presume without a call from God, to become the self-constituted and misleading heralds of His law : " The prophets prophesy falsely in My name. I sent them not, neither have I commanded them, nor have I spoken to them : they prophesy unto you a lying vision, and divination, and deceit, and the seduction of their own heart." [2]

" Son of man, prophesy thou against the prophets of Israel that prophesy. And thou shalt say to them that prophesy out of their own heart : Hear ye the word of the Lord. Thus saith the Lord God : Wo to the foolish prophets that follow their own spirit, and see nothing. . . . They see vain things, and they foretell lies, saying : The Lord saith : Whereas the Lord hath not sent them. . . . Therefore thus saith the Lord God : Because ye have spoken vain things, and have seen lies, therefore behold I come against you, saith the Lord God. . . . They shall not be in the counsel of My people, neither shall they enter into the land of Israel." [3]

Indeed, it is scarcely necessary to produce these proofs from the sacred oracles, in order to be convinced that we must be empowered by a call from God, and fortified by His grace, before presuming to undertake ministerial duties and obligations, formidable even to angels. So weighty

[1] Rom. x. 14, 15.   [2] Jer. xiv. 14.   [3] Ezech. xiii. 2–9.

are our responsibilities, so immense the sacrifices we are called upon to make, that many sincere people outside the Church, imagine that we are not in reality what we profess to be, and that it is even impossible for us to fulfil the vows we take at our ordination.

The candidate for Orders places his hands between those of the officiating prelate, at the foot of the altar, and solemnly promises a life-long obedience to his bishop. He must be ready to go to any part of the diocese to which he may be sent, and to assume any duties that may be imposed on him.

He becomes the servant of the faithful to whom he is assigned. He ministers to them every morning at the altar, and preaches to them the word of God in season and out of season. He responds to their summons night and day. He is to be a light to those that are in darkness; he is food to the hungry, a refreshing fountain to those that thirst after righteousness, a guide to the wayfarer, a physician to the soul-sick, and a father to the whole congregation.

He makes a vow, not of conjugal, but of virginal chastity; he must be pure not only in body, but in mind, heart, and affection also. He must be "a pattern of the flock from the heart." It behooves him to maintain an unsullied reputation before an observing, critical, and unsparing world.

He is obliged to move daily in the poisonous atmosphere of sin, without breathing its infection. He will, so to speak, have to touch pitch with unsullied hands. He must be prepared to minister to the victims of pestilential diseases, at the risk, and even, if necessary, at the sacrifice of his life.

In a word, He is expected to be in the world, though not of the world, and all these tremendous responsibilities are assumed, not for a term of years, but for a lifetime. The armor of God, with which he was clothed on the day upon which he was enrolled among the Christian leaders, is laid aside only at the hour of death.

Surely, the soldier that engages in an unremitting campaign of this kind, without an express command from the great Captain and without the shield of grace to protect him, will be confounded as was Saul when he followed the counsels of human prudence, rather than the oracle of Heaven.

Many doctors and saints of the Church, notwithstanding their extraordinary abilities and their predilection for an evangelical life and apostolic labors, hesitated to enter the ranks of the priesthood from a profound sense of the holiness it required and the duties it imposed.

St. Ambrose fled and hid himself; he yielded only to pressure before he could be prevailed upon to be ordained. St. Augustine avoided episcopal cities, lest he should fall under the eye of a bishop, who might be desirous of promoting him to sacred Orders. St. Jerome, though eminent for learning and merits, resisted Paulinus, his bishop, for a considerable time before consenting to have hands imposed on him. So deeply was the humble St. Francis of Assisi penetrated with the spirit of reverence for the sacerdotal character, that he would never aspire to the priesthood, but lived content with deacon's Orders. The same may be said of the glorious St. Benedict, Patriarch of the Western Monks. The contrast between these men of God and others (happily, very few) who stride toward

the sanctuary with eager and irreverent steps, is well
expressed by the poet :

> "Fools rush in where angels fear to tread."

✓ If a man is justly regarded as an intruder and an incu-
bus on any civil profession, whose ranks he enters without
calling or capacity for it, what an insult does he offer to
God, what an injury he inflicts on religion, and what
disorder on Christian society, who thrusts himself into
the ministry without a divine vocation and, consequently,
without the grace and aptitude indispensable for its sacred
functions !

The mischief occasioned by an unworthy priest would
be more endurable if, after an unsuccessful trial, he could
return to secular avocations. But he is debarred by his
sacred profession from worldly pursuits, and whatever be
his demerits (unless he is to be a burden on the diocese)
he must hold some position of trust. He thus becomes
the sterile occupant of a field in which another would
produce rich fruit, like the barren fig-tree, of which our
Lord said : "Cut it down, therefore, why cumbereth it
the ground ?"[1]

There are some candidates who may enter the seminary
and continue there for a protracted period, without seriously considering the burdens and responsibilities inseparable from the ministry. They are influenced principally,
if not solely, by the temporal advantages supposed to be
attached to it. They may be dazzled by the glare which
their youthful and vivid imagination throws around the
priestly state, or attracted by its honors and emoluments,

[1] Luke XIII. 7.

or allured by the ease and comfort which, according to their fancy, clergymen enjoy. They resemble a certain youth who, when questioned as to his vocation by the bishop to whom he had applied for adoption, frankly answered that he had a strong prejudice against work, and that, therefore, the ministry suited him very well; or they may be impelled by an inordinate ambition to seek in the Church a preferment which they would despair of compassing in secular life.

✓ Does it not sometimes happen that a student who has entered the seminary in obedience to parental wishes, hesitates to return to the world, even after he is conscious that he is not called to the ministry, because he fears to incur his parents' displeasure, or perhaps, because he has a certain vague and superstitious dread that "having put his hand to the plough, he should not look back?"

Such a youth should remember that, by ceasing to aspire to a profession to which he is not called, far from deserving a stigma of reproach, he is pursuing a prudent and honorable course; that salvation is not confined to the priesthood; and that a man who would be an indifferent clergyman may make an upright and exemplary layman.

When Matthias and Joseph appeared before the apostolic College, the former alone was chosen for the ministry. And yet we have no reason to doubt that Joseph served the Lord in the private walks of life not less faithfully than Matthias in the work of the apostolate.

But it would be manifestly unjust, as well as ungrateful, to refer even incidentally to the interested motives of some parents, without recording our admiration for the host of Christian mothers of America to whom, under God, the

Church is indebted for so many of her most zealous and devoted levites. Almighty God, who usually employs secondary agents in the choice of His ministers, often selects pious matrons for moulding the character, and directing the steps of their sons toward the sanctuary. If some have been actuated by motives of temporal consideration, like the mother of the sons of Zebedee, hundreds could be named, like the mothers of Samuel, of Chrysostom, and of Augustine, who sacrificed parental affection to the interests of heaven, and inspired their sons with the loftiest and holiest conceptions of the Christian priesthood.

In calling us to the service of the altar, God has due regard for our free-will; hence, our hearty coöperation is necessary to render our vocation efficacious.

By resisting the divine call, a true vocation may be lost or made void, as happened to the young man mentioned in the Gospel: "Jesus looking on him, loved him, and said to him: One thing is wanting unto thee. Go, sell whatsoever thou hast, and give to the poor, . . . and follow Me. Who, being struck sad at that saying, went away sorrowful, for he had great possessions." [1]

Some, without ever being ordained, may lose their vocation by habitual contempt of seminary rules, by leading a tepid life, by spurning the inspirations of Heaven, and by daily conduct incompatible with the sacred profession to which they aspire. Perhaps they allow their first fervor to cool, and yield to dissipation of mind and heart during the annual vacation, which is intended to be a period of healthful recreation for soul and body; or they may have sullied their soul by grosser vices totally at variance with the sanctity of the priesthood. By a

[1] Mark x. 21, 22.

compulsory or voluntary withdrawal from the seminary without receiving Orders, certainly a less evil befalls them than if they had undergone the imposition of hands.

That many priests who had an undoubted vocation to the Sanctuary, have been wrecked in faith and morals, is attested by melancholy monuments along the highroad of history, even in the golden age of the Church. Judas was chosen for the apostolate by Christ Himself, and yet he fell. St. Paul thus pathetically laments the apostasy of a fellow-laborer called by himself: "Demas hath left me, loving this world."[1] St. John, in his Apocalypse, denounces the Bishop of Laodicea for having abandoned the spirit of his vocation by a life of luxurious indolence. "Thou sayest: I am rich, and have need of nothing, and knowest not that thou art wretched, and miserable, and poor, and blind, and naked."[2]

But, alas! what need is there of citing such examples of remote history? Are we not shocked in our own day by the sad spectacle of degraded ministers of the Gospel who have not only soiled their sacred garments, but unblushingly glory in their shame before the world; who have not only forsaken the Mother that reared them, but who insult and vilify her, who hire themselves for a price to the enemy?

How were these lights extinguished? How did these ambassadors of Christ perish? Very probably, their downward course began in the seminary, where they led an indolent and tepid life, without betraying, however, any evidence of glaring delinquencies. The day of ordination was contemplated by them, not with salutary dread on

[1] II. Tim. IV. 9. [2] Apoc. III. 17.

account of the new yoke it imposed, but rather with joy
as emancipating them from seminary restraints, and in-
augurating a reign of mundane freedom.

In the ministry, they lived without order or method.
They prayed without devotion. Their official duties were
irksome and oppressive, and were performed in a perfunctory manner. The studies congenial to the ecclesiastical
state became an intolerable bore. They lived on the
excitement of the hour. They were, at first, sustained by
amusements which were harmless. When these began to
pall, they indulged in more stimulating and dangerous
pleasures.

Meantime, God's grace was less abundantly bestowed
on them; their conscience became blunted; their intellect
clouded; for "the sensual man perceiveth not these things
that are of the Spirit of God." [1] Those divine warnings
which before had stung the soul, were brushed aside as
weak-minded scruples. To every fresh attack of temptation, they offered a more feeble resistance, till, at last, they
fell easy and willing captives to the tempter. It may be
remarked that the two rocks which have occasioned the
greatest number of wrecks, are intemperance and impurity.

The relative proportion of those ordained with a supernatural call, to those that receive Orders without a vocation, God alone can reveal. St. Alphonsus was of the
opinion that a considerable percentage of priests were
ordained without a divine election.[2] St. Chrysostom and
others seem to take the same view. The impressions of
these learned and apostolic men are worthy of most serious
consideration; but they wrote, of course, for their own age

---

[1] I. Cor. II. 14.   [2] Homo Apos. Tract. VII. No. 47.

and country, and their estimate was influenced by the circumstances of the times and the environments in which they lived.

Some old and experienced superiors and directors of seminaries in this country, have informed me that the number of those who are raised to the priesthood without a vocation, in the institutions under their charge, is in their judgment comparatively small.   In the United States there are no benefices, and very few patrimonies to tempt the unworthy aspirant to Holy Orders; while on the other hand, there are many attractive and lucrative fields of labor in secular life to excite the laudable ambition of our young men, and to remove from them the pretext of entering the ministry from sordid considerations.

But instead of indulging in this speculative question, the solution of which cannot affect you personally one way or the other, I would rather recall to your mind what Jesus said to Peter, when the latter was curious to know the destiny of John: "What is it to thee?   Follow thou Me;" and I would exhort you in these words of the Prince of the Apostles: "Labor the more, that by good works you may make sure your calling and election.   For doing these things, you shall not sin at any time.   For so an entrance shall be ministered to you abundantly into the everlasting kingdom of our Lord and Saviour Jesus Christ." [1]

---

[1] II. Pet. I. 10, 11.

CHAPTER III.

Marks of a Divine Vocation.

SINCE no man can assume the duties of the priest-hood, unless he is called by God, as Aaron was, and since the candidate is not now chosen, as were the Apostles directly by the voice of Christ, he must be furnished with some marks or signs, which will give him a practical assurance of his divine vocation.

✓ The first and the best criterion of an election to the Sanctuary, consists in a heavenly attraction toward the service of the Lord and His Church.

But not every attraction is a proof of a call from God. It may have for its object the essential duties of the ministry, or its mere accessories and appendages.

By the accessories of the ministry are understood those external circumstances which constitute the situation of a priest in a Christian society, and which imply a certain degree of authority, respect, honor, influence, temporal gain, ease, and comfort.

The acceptance within reasonable limits, of the honors and emoluments incidental to the ministry, cannot be unlawful, as they are the legitimate tributes attached by Christian usages to the sacerdotal state, and St. Paul says: "Let the priests that rule well be esteemed worthy of double honor, especially they who labor in word and

doctrine . . . and *the laborer is worthy of his reward.*"[1]
"They who work in the holy place, eat the things that
are of the holy place; and they who preach the Gospel,
should live by the Gospel."[2]

We may occasionally pluck the fruits of honor along
the roadside, if they hang in our way, but we are not
to cross the fence to reach them, still less are they to be
our sustaining food.

The day on which Bishop Verot was consecrated for
the See of St. Augustine, after receiving with quiet dignity the honors and congratulations bestowed on him by
his friends, I heard him remark: "To-day the ox is
wreathed in garlands; but to-morrow the sacrifice of the
victim begins." And, surely, his whole episcopal life
was a sacrifice well-pleasing to the Lord. The homage
of reverence justly paid him, he did not disdain; but his
heart was in the work which lay before him.

But if the aim which impelled us in aspiring to the
priesthood, were solely or chiefly the desire of its dis-
tinctions and emoluments, such an incentive would not
only clearly indicate the absence of a divine election, but
would be positively sinful.

✓ The real indication, then, of a heavenly call to the
service of God, is found in an attraction for the priesthood with the view of procuring His glory and the
salvation of souls, and in a relish for the functions and
duties by which this two-fold object is to be attained.

If God ordinarily gives men a taste for the civic pursuits of life in which they embark, He will not fail to
incline the heart of the levite to the sacred profession

[1] I. Tim. v. 17, 18.   [2] I. Cor. ix. 13, 14.

3

to which He calls him. Happy is he in whom this tendency is sweet, strong, and constant ! He takes delight in his work, he has an abiding assurance that the Lord is with him.

This inclination embraces an honest desire, an earnest good-will, to perform with purity of intention the work of the ministry, though the details of that work may be as yet only imperfectly understood. The generous novice is filled with the sentiments of Saul, when he exclaimed : "Lord, what wilt Thou have me to do?"

It is worthy of remark that our Saviour never sought to allure His disciples to the apostolate by setting before them the dignities, honors, or temporal advantages that might be associated with their ministry. His practice was rather to inure them to its hardships by frequently representing to them the privations, the trials, and the sacrifices to be endured in His service. Forewarned, they were forearmed, and the adversities they were actually to encounter, became not only less formidable, but were even joyfully borne, after they had habitually confronted them in imagination, and looked on them as their earthly portion.

On the occasion particularly of the disciples' election to the work of the ministry, Jesus minutely portrayed the self-denying features of their mission. He braced their energies and cheered their hearts by the influence of His own example, and by reminding them that they were constantly under the sleepless eye of their Heavenly Father, without whose knowledge and permission a hair of their head would not be disturbed.[1]

[1] Matt. x. 30.

He revealed to Peter the martyrdom that was to crown his earthly labors.[1]

Of Paul, He said : " I will show him how great things he must suffer for My name's sake." [2]

✓ The sons of Zebedee He gently weaned from their thirst for earthly distinction, which had marred their zeal for God's glory, by telling them that their mission was to suffer, and that they should partake of His chalice.[3]

The conduct of these two Apostles ought to serve as a comfort and an admonition to the ingenuous disciple of Christ. It teaches him not to be disheartened, nor to question his vocation, if he finds the flame of his zeal mingled as yet with some smoke of selfish considerations; but rather to labor day by day at eliminating the dross of worldly desires from the gold of a pure intention, and to consider as addressed to himself what our Lord said to the Bishop of Laodicea : " I counsel thee to buy of Me gold fire-tried, that thou mayest be rich " in divine charity, " and mayest be clothed in the white garments " [4] of an unsullied priesthood.

The attraction for the ecclesiastical state is not always very *sensibly* felt. It may even co-exist with a dread of its responsibilities, and with a natural repugnance for some duties of the ministry. This repugnance will be gradually overcome by the sweet unction of God's grace, by the consciousness of good accomplished, and by frequent repetitions of the same acts.

A judicious director of one of our seminaries advised some of the more advanced theological students to habitu-

---

[1] John xxi. 18.   [3] Matt. xx. 23.
[2] Acts ix. 16.   [4] Apoc. iii. 18.

ate themselves to the more distasteful occupations of missionary life by visiting and instructing the inmates of an institution most of whom were repulsive in appearance, coarse in manners, and little acquainted with even the rudiments of religion. The ordeal was, at first, a trying one; but after a while, when they realized the gratitude of their untutored congregation, and the rich fruits resulting from their labors, the exercise became delightful. No pleasure is more keen than that which springs from the tangible evidence of the happiness we communicate to others.

I was, also, acquainted with a clergyman who had deferred his ordination for one or two years, on account of the aversion he felt to the office of hearing confessions. But shortly after having embraced the priesthood, it became his most congenial and cherished occupation, being made sensible of the peace and comfort he brought to others in the tribunal of Penance.

✓Innocence of life and integrity of moral character is another mark of a divine vocation, or rather a sign of one's fitness for the ministry, and an indispensable condition for its adequate fulfilment. It is self-evident that the standard-bearer of Gospel holiness should be conspicuous for moral heroism; his life should be the sweet perfume of the doctrine that he preaches. "Lord, who shall dwell in thy tabernacle, or who shall rest in Thy holy hill? He that walketh without blemish, and worketh justice: he that speaketh truth in his heart, who hath not used deceit in his tongue, nor hath done evil to his neighbor, nor taken up a reproach against his neighbors." [1]

[1] Ps. xiv. 1-3.

" Be ye clean," says Isaiah, " you that carry the vessels of the Lord." [1]

" Whosoever of thy seed throughout their families, hath a blemish, he shall not offer bread to his God; neither shall he approach to minister unto Him." [2] " By blemish," says St. Thomas, " all vice is understood." [3] If moral defilement excluded the priests of the Old Law from offering bread to the Lord, it ought certainly to debar the priests of the law of grace from handling the Body of Christ in the Holy Sacrifice.

" Purer than any solar ray, should be the hand which divides the flesh (of Christ), that mouth which is filled with spiritual fire, that tongue which is purpled with that most awful blood." [4]

" To the sinner, God hath said: Why dost thou declare My justices, and take My covenant in thy mouth? Seeing thou hast hated discipline, and hast cast My words behind thee." [5] Even the world which is so tolerant of sin, has no patience with the hypocrite or the libertine who announces the Gospel with polluted lips.

St. Paul thus rebukes the religious instructor whose example does not correspond with his words: " Thou, therefore, that teachest another, teachest not thyself. Thou that makest thy boast of the law, by transgression of the law, dishonorest God." [6]

St. Alphonsus teaches that a higher degree of sanctity is required for Sacred Orders, than for the religious state, and that the virtue of a priest ought to bear some

[1] Isai. LII. 11.
[2] Lev. XXI. 17.
[3] Supplem. Quaest. 36.
[4] St. Chrysostom.
[5] Ps. XLIX. 16, 17.
[6] Rom. II. 21–23.

proportion to the excellency of his vocation, and the
responsibilities of his charge.[1]

The priest should be adorned with innocence preserved,
or, at least, with innocence regained by true repentance
and long-tried virtue. Some, indeed, of the most eminent saints had grievously sinned before they undertook
the work of the ministry. Who committed more flagrant
offences than Peter and Augustine? And yet they became
shining lights, and the greatest pillars of the Church.
They amply atoned for their transgressions by extraordinary humility and solid virtue. ✓ Their examples are
given, that they who have erred by youthful delinquencies should not despair of being raised to the priesthood.
Such examples, however, are few, in order to remind us
that blameless youth is the ideal nursery of the Sanctuary. It is much easier to abide in virtue, maintained
from youth, than to recover and preserve it after it has
once been lost. "It is good for a man," says the prophet,
"when he hath borne the yoke from his youth."[2]

Hence, the Church desires that religious safeguards
should, in early youth, be thrown around those that
exhibit a tendency for the ministry; and she strongly
recommends the establishment of preparatory seminaries,
in which the morals of young men may be sheltered from
the incursions of vice, and their pious aspirations fostered
and developed.

Another requisite element in a divine vocation, is a
capacity for the work of the ministry. "God fits the
back to the burden." St. Paul, speaking of himself and
his fellow-Apostles, says: "*God* hath made us *fit* ministers

[1] Homo. Apos. [2] Lamen. III. 27.

of the New Testament;"[1] intimating that they were not
only called to the apostolate, but that they had the ability
to perform its duties. If capability is needed for the
proper fulfilment of any civil occupation, it is preëminently demanded of those that aspire to the most exalted
and exacting of all professions.

Hence, a student who has a call to the priesthood, will
obviously have a taste for the cultivation of the sciences
suitable to his state of life, and that will enable him to
discharge its functions with credit and ability.

Of course, all students are not gifted with the same
degree of talent. Every candidate cannot hope to be a
Cyprian or a Chrysostom, a Jerome or an Augustine.
" Every one," says the Apostle, "hath his proper gift from
God."[2] "To one He gave five talents, and to another two,
and to another one."[3] One student may be endowed with
brilliant acquirements, and another with solid judgment.
It does not always occur that these two gifts are conspicuously combined in the same person.

Experience shows that solid judgment with moderate,
though sufficient, attainments, is far more serviceable to
religion than brilliant talents combined with a deficiency
in practical sense. The occasions for the display of
genius are rare; the opportunities for the exercise of
mother-wit and discretion occur every hour of the day.
Whenever a student applied for adoption into the arch-
diocese, Archbishop Spalding was accustomed to make
this inquiry regarding him : " Has he common sense?—
which," with a touch of humor he used to add, " is not so
very common a commodity."

[1] II. Cor. III.   [2] I. Cor. VII. 7.   [3] Matt. XXV. 15.

And, indeed, a lack of prudence and tact usually exposes a diocesan priest to more serious blunders than similar defects would occasion a religious. A member of a Religious Order generally leads a community life. His judicious superior assigns to him special duties suitable to his capacity; but a secular clergyman frequently lives alone. He is constantly thrown into relations with persons dissimilar in disposition and avocations of life; he is charged with pursuits of a most varied character. He becomes all to all, that he may save all.[1]

If the foregoing qualities of mind are supplemented by earnestness of manner, by force of character, strength of will, tenacity of purpose, and by a serious view of the path of duty that lies before him, the devout student will have a well-grounded hope to become "a fit minister of the New Covenant."

It may be observed, however, that the last two notes, namely, innocence of life and capacity for ministerial duties, are to be regarded as negative rather than positive marks of a vocation. They are evidences of fitness for the work of the ministry, rather than proofs of a supernatural election; for there are in the world hosts of upright men, versed in sacred lore, and to whom theological studies are congenial; nevertheless, with all these gifts, it cannot be said that they have a divine call to the priesthood.

The fourth mark of a vocation is the official call to Sacred Orders announced by the bishop through his legitimate representatives, the Faculty of the seminary. A man may be endowed with the martial spirit of a soldier, yet he cannot be enrolled among the defenders

---

[1] I. Cor. ix. 19.

of his country till he is enlisted by his superior officer. Another may possess legal acumen of a high order, and a judicial frame of mind, but he cannot assume the ermine and ascend the bench till he is lawfully elected.

Neither can the aspirant for the ministry put on its robes and exercise its functions, unless duly summoned by the living voice of authority.

God rules the Church as He governs the world, through subordinate agents. As He regenerates souls in Baptism, absolves from sin in the Sacrament of Penance, and proclaims His Gospel by the lips of men, so in the election to the Sanctuary is He represented by His established delegates.

The conscientious and faithful levite will, therefore, unfalteringly recognize the voice of his director as the voice of God.

Matthias, who was chosen to the ministry through the agency of the Apostles, was as much assured of his divine election as was Peter, who had been called by the living voice of Christ Himself.

But how profoundly should the directors of seminaries be penetrated with a sense of their responsibility, when they reflect that they are the final arbiters to determine the selection of the successors to the Apostles!

Jesus Christ, before choosing His Apostles, spent a whole night in solitary supplication on the mountain. Surely, His judgment had no need of being enlightened by prayer. But His protracted communion with His Father was to serve as an admonition to every director charged with the training of young evangelists that, before deciding on their vocation, he should seek light "from the Father of lights."

The leaders of the Church had recourse to prayer before the election of Matthias,[1] and to prayer with fasting before the vocation of Saul and Barnabas.[2]

St. Paul gives the following solemn charge to Timothy: "Impose not hands lightly upon any man, neither be partaker of other men's sins, "[3] by assuming without investigation, the fitness of the candidate for the service of the altar. If this admonition was given at a time when conversions were growing apace and missionaries were few, how much more imperatively is circumspection in superiors now required when applicants for the priesthood are daily multiplied?

The director is, however, but human. With all his insight and discernment, he is liable to err unless you disclose to him your heart with child-like simplicity, sincerely manifesting the motives that prompt you to aspire to the Sanctuary, as well as the weak and vulnerable points in your character.

But, above all, you should have recourse to God, who "searcheth the heart and the reins" of men, that He would deign to guide you in the momentous step on which your future destiny so much depends. Say to Him with the prophet: "Make known to me the way wherein I should walk, for I have lifted up my soul to Thee. Teach me to do Thy will, for Thou art my God."[4]

Then, if your own enlightened conscience is in accord with the decision of your director, in calling you to Orders, you may with humble confidence assume the

[1] Acts I.
[2] Ibid. XIII.
[3] I. Tim. v. 22.
[4] Ps. CXLII. 10.

yoke of the priesthood, and accept the announcement as the voice of God. You may devoutly regard as repeated to yourself what Christ said to His Apostles: "I have chosen you that you should go and bring forth fruit, and your fruit should remain."

But it behooves us to remember that "we have this treasure (of apostolic grace) in earthen vessels, that the excellency may be of the power of God, and not of us." [1] We know, alas! too well, that the vase may be shattered, and the treasure may be lost.

Every day, from the morning of our ordination, our watchword should be: "The night is passed, and the day is at hand. Let us, therefore, cast off the works of darkness, and put on the armor of light." [2] We should, in the language of St. Paul, "be renewed in the spirit of our mind, and put on the new man who, according to God, is created in justice and holiness of truth." [3]

"Neglect not," says the same Apostle, "the grace that is in thee, which was given thee with imposition of hands of the priesthood. Meditate upon these things, be wholly in these things, that thy profiting may be manifest to all." [4]

Filled with the gratitude which animated the Apostle, we should often say: "I give Him thanks who hath strengthened me, *even* to Christ Jesus our Lord, for that He hath counted me faithful, putting me in the ministry." [5]

On being invested with the office of the ministry, you should mark out for yourself a practical rule of life

---

[1] II. Cor. IV. 7.
[2] Rom. XIII. 12.
[3] Eph. IV. 23, 24.
[4] I. Tim. IV. 14, 15.
[5] I. Tim. I. 12.

which ought to be neither too elastic nor too rigid. "Let all things be done decently, and according to order."[1] "Order is heaven's first law." It is the economic distributer of time, the guardian of peace and tranquillity.

A fixed hour should be set apart, as far as possible, for the customary duties of each day. It is not wise to burden or bewilder yourself with too many religious exercises; but you should endeavor to perform well those that a judicious director and your own conscience may prescribe.

A meditation every morning, though it be brief, should rarely be omitted. It is a refreshing and purifying spiritual bath, preparing you to appear with a clean heart before the great King at the Sacrificial Banquet, and invigorating you for the work of the day.

By the daily oblation of the Holy Sacrifice, in a spirit of faith and thanksgiving to the august High Priest, and by going "with confidence to the throne of grace, you will obtain mercy, *and find* grace in seasonable aid."[2]

Recite the Breviary with recollection and devotion. Its prayers are authorized by the Church and consecrated by universal usage. If said in a hasty and listless manner, it becomes an irksome task, instead of being a stimulus to piety. A story is told of two clergymen reciting the Divine Office together during a fearful thunderstorm. One of them remarked to the other: "Let us suspend the Office and say our prayers." He did not advert to the fact, that the devotion in which they were actually engaged, was the most salutary of religious exercises.

---

[1] I. Cor. xiv. 40.   [2] Heb. iv. 16.

It is most profitable to spend at least fifteen or twenty minutes each day in spiritual reading. The books should be few, but well selected. The perusal of a great variety of religious books is apt to dissipate the mind without making a deep or lasting impression. St. Francis de Sales happily illustrated this truth by saying that "the bees make less honey amid the abundance of early spring flowers than later on, because they delight to roam about amid the general abundance, and do not pause long enough to gather the precious juices with which they fill their comb."

I would recommend *The Following of Christ*, *The Spiritual Combat*, *The Lives of the Saints*, especially of those who were engaged in the apostolic ministry, and above all, the Sacred Scriptures, which have an unction and authority exclusively their own.

Devote an hour or more each day to the serious study of subjects connected with your state of life.

Consecrate yourself without reserve to the work of the mission assigned you in all its details, fulfilling each duty, not with the perfunctory routine of the hireling, but with the diligence and zeal of a faithful steward.

A visit every day to our Lord in the Blessed Sacrament, dissipates the worldly mist that may have enveloped you, and brings you nearer to the God of light. It sobers the senses, moderates the abnormal activity of the mind, calms the passions, sweetens the labors, lightens the burdens of life, and diffuses around you a spirit of heavenly peace and tranquillity.

Let your night devotions always include an examination of conscience. Of all spiritual exercises, this examen is, perhaps, the least agreeable, though the most profitable.

It is worthy of remark that some of the greatest Pagan philosophers, such as Pythagoras, Plutarch, Seneca, and Epictetus, have recommended this personal scrutiny. It is the best means of preventing us from drifting with the tide, and of stimulating us to ply our oars in stemming the current of our own downward tendencies.

Like a faithful steward, you should balance your account with your Maker every night, and study your profit and loss.

Examination of conscience is the complement of the morning meditation. In the morning, you reflect on your range of duties, and resolve to acquit yourself faithfully of them. In the examen, you inquire whether and how you have discharged them. In the morning, you survey the field before you, and determine to advance with steady steps. At night, you look back, and contemplate how much ground you have covered. Happy are they whose time is thus regulated. "Full days shall be found in them."

After having invoked the mercy and benediction of your heavenly Father by fervent prayer, you can say with the confidence of the Psalmist: "In peace will I both take my rest, and sleep, for Thou, O Lord, specially makest me dwell in safety."[1]

---

[1] Ps. iv. 9, 10. St. Jerome's Version.

CHAPTER IV.

On the Duties of Preceptors toward their Scholars.

PLUTARCH, in a letter to his former pupil, the Emperor Trajan, says: "I am sensible that you sought not the Empire. Your modesty, however, makes you still more worthy of the honors you had no ambition to solicit. Should your future government be in keeping with your former merit, I shall have reason to congratulate both your virtue and my own good fortune on this great event; but if otherwise, you have exposed yourself to danger and me to obloquy; for the faults of the scholar will be imputed to the master. Only continue to be what you are. Let your government commence in your breast; and lay the foundations of it in the command of your passions. If you make virtue the rule of your conduct and the end of your actions, everything will proceed in harmony and order. I have explained to you the spirit of those laws and constitutions that were established by your predecessors, and you have nothing to do but to carry them into execution. If this should be the case, I shall have the glory of having formed an Emperor to virtue; but if otherwise, let this letter remain a testimony to succeeding ages, that you did not ruin the Roman Empire under pretence of the counsels or the authority of Plutarch."

From the words of Plutarch we may draw this important lesson, that the moral precepts of the teacher will exercise but little influence on the scholar, unless they are enforced by his own example. But if his life is in harmony with the instructions which he inculcates, they will make a deep and lasting impression on the heart of his disciple. For if the edifying demeanor of those whom we casually meet in the walks of life, is a stimulus to virtue, how potential for good, and how enduring is the exemplary conduct of the professor who is the official guide of our susceptible youth !

Every one admits the truth of the Horatian axiom, that persons are more deeply affected by what they see than by what they hear. If this maxim can be affirmed of all men, how much more forcible is its application to the impressionable scholar !

The pupil's character is almost unconsciously formed after the model of his instructor. The impression produced on the youthful mind, by the tutor's example, has been happily compared to letters cut in the bark of a young tree which deepen and broaden with time.

Of our excellent teachers, we can say in the words of John Sterling :

> " Ever their phantoms rise before us,
>   Our loftier brothers, but one in blood ;
>   By bed and table they lord it o'er us,
>   With looks of kindness and words of good."

The institution in which a man studies, is supposed to exert so dominant an influence in moulding his character, that his *Alma Mater* is as sure to be mentioned by his biographer as the parents from whom he sprang.

So close, indeed, and tender and far-reaching are the relations subsisting between the teacher and his pupils, that the master feels honored by the virtuous and distinguished career of his scholar, while he has a sense of personal humiliation, should the pupil's record prove dishonorable and scandalous.   Harvard or Yale, Princeton or Georgetown, is eager to claim as her son the statesman, the jurist, or the man of letters who chanced to have drunk at her fountain of knowledge.   Oxford would have gladly erected within her walls a monument to her peerless son, Cardinal Newman, had she not been thwarted by unreasoning bigotry.   In like manner, our ecclesiastical colleges and seminaries refer with commendable complacency to their alumni who have distinguished themselves as priests or prelates in the paths of science and virtue.   As Cato, in his old age, pointed with pride to the widespreading trees that his hands had planted in early manhood, so will the venerable teacher contemplate with admiration every fresh blossom and fruit that enrich the living tree reared and cultivated in his nursery of learning.

But while the preceptor enjoys the reflected honor that beams on his favored scholar, public sentiment makes him share, in some measure, though often unjustly, the odium attached to a pupil whose public life has been stained by unworthy conduct.   The good name of Quintilian was marred by the vicious conduct of some of his scholars.   The reputation of Seneca suffered on account of the crimes of Nero, his former disciple.   The reproach seems, however, to be unmerited, for, as long as the young prince followed the instructions and counsels of his preceptor, he was loved by the Roman people; but

4

when he fell into the hands of other masters, he became
the shame of the human race. The exterior gravity and
propriety of Seneca were a continual censure on his
pupil's vices.

The professors of our colleges and seminaries should
be profoundly impressed with the dignity and grave
responsibility of their position. They are the constituted
guardians of their pupils *in loco parentis*. It should be
their constant aim that the lustre of the jewels confided
to their keeping be not dimmed by neglect, but that they
reflect more and more the brightness of the Sun of Justice. "What is more noble," says St. John Chrysostom,
"than to form the minds of youth? He who fashions
the morals of children, performs a task, in my judgment,
more sublime than that of any painter or sculptor." In
contemplating the magnificent works of art exhibited in
the churches of Rome, we extol the great masters who
produced them, and we know not which to admire
more, the paintings and statues which adorn St. Peter's
Basilica, or the temple itself in which those masterpieces
are enshrined. But the teacher, in moulding the character of the youths committed to his care, is engaged in
a pursuit far more worthy of our admiration. He is
creating living portraits destined to adorn, not only our
earthly temples, but also the temple of God in heaven
"not made by hands."

The professor who would aim at shaping the character
of all his students according to one uniform ideal standard,
would be attempting the impossible, because he would be
striving to do what is at variance with the laws of nature
and of nature's God. In all the Creator's works, there
is charming variety. There are no two stars in the firma-

ment equal in magnitude and splendor, "for star differeth from star in glory;" there are no two leaves of the forest alike, no two grains of sand, no two human faces. Neither can there be two men absolutely identical in mental capacity or moral disposition. One may excel in solid judgment, another in tenacity of memory, and a third in brilliancy of imagination. One is naturally grave and solemn, another is gay and vivacious. One is of a phlegmatic, another of a sanguine temperament. One is constitutionally shy, timid, and reserved; another is bold and demonstrative. One is taciturn, another has his heart in his mouth. The teacher should take his pupils as God made them, and aid them in bringing out the hidden powers of their soul. If he tries to adopt the levelling process by casting all in the same mould, his pupils will become forced and unnatural in their movements; they will lose heart, their spirit will be broken, their manhood crippled and impaired.

"I will respect human liberty," says Monseigneur Dupanloup, "in the smallest child even more scrupulously than in a grown man; for the latter can defend himself against me, while the child cannot. Never shall I insult the child so far as to regard him as material to be cast into a mould, and to emerge with a stamp given by my will."

Instead of laboring to crush and subdue their natural traits and propensities, he should rather divert them into a proper channel. The admonition which would be properly administered to a sullen or obstinate youth deliberately erring, might be excessive, if given to one of an ardent or sensitive nature acting from impulse or levity.

One day, an abbot of some reputation for piety, was complaining to St. Anselm about the boys who were being educated in the monastery. "Though we flog them continually," said he, "yet they become worse." "And," queried St. Anselm, "how do they turn out when grown to be young men?" "Stupid and dull," answered the abbot. "At that rate," exclaimed the saint, "the system you employ is a model one for stunting intellectual growth. My dear abbot, suppose you were to plant a tree in your garden and shut it in on all sides so that it could not shoot forth its branches, what might you expect save a twisted, tangled, and worthless trunk? Now, by enslaving the spirit of children, by leaving them no liberty of action, you foster in them narrow, vicious, and wicked propensities, which, growing stronger day by day, resist every effort to change and eradicate them. Finding, moreover, that you are neither kind nor amiable, they will put no confidence in you; they will believe that you are moved by motives of dislike and envy. These inclinations increase with their years, and their minds and hearts grow bent to vice. Devoid of Christian charity, their views of the world and of life become utterly distorted. Now, tell me, were you in the place of these boys, would you be pleased with such treatment as you give them?"

The abbot threw himself at the feet of St. Anselm, admitted his lack of tact and discretion, and promised amendment.[1]

Jesus Christ is the model Teacher. His conduct toward His disciples is the best example to be followed. He did not attempt to quench their natural spirit, but

[1] Rohrbacher, Vol. xiv. p. 465.

He purified and sanctified it in the fires of Pentecost. After Peter had graduated in the school of his Master, he remained the same ardent man that he had ever been. His vehement energies were expended, however, not in defending his Saviour's Person with the material sword, which he had formerly used in cutting off the ear of Malchus, but in wielding the sword of the Spirit in the cause of righteousness. The sons of Zebedee were ambitious of glory. Ambition is in itself a magnanimous sentiment; therefore, Christ did not smother it in their breast, but He ennobled it by directing it to higher and holier ends. He taught them to aspire to a heavenly, instead of an earthly kingdom.

Paul, after his conversion, retained the fiery zeal that had marked the youthful Pharisee, though it was now transformed into a zeal tempered by charity, and it found vent in evangelizing the world. Instead of dragging Christians before civil tribunals, as he was wont to do, we now find him arraigning Jews and Gentiles before the tribunal of conscience. Our Saviour did not blame Thomas for opening his mind and expressing his honest doubt upon the fact of the Resurrection; but He gently reasoned with him, and removed that doubt by a palpable argument. In the same way, should the professor study, as far as possible, the individual character of his pupils, and adapt his instructions and admonitions to the capacity and temperament of each.

Regarding the discipline to be observed in our colleges and seminaries, the Third Plenary Council of Baltimore lays down the following judicious rules: " Let the discipline for regulating the whole course of life in the seminary be so arranged that it may savor neither of excessive rigor nor indulge pernicious laxity. The vigilance of superiors should be so tempered and moderated in maintaining it that it will not pry too closely into minute details, nor so hamper the minds of youth, as it were with chains, as to impede the normal expansion of their energies." [1]

While the vigilance of superiors should be active in observing and prompt in correcting abuses, it should be entirely free from a spirit of espionage and distrust, which is calculated to make hypocrites, and to provoke the clandestine violation of rules. If the students are persuaded that they are habitually suspected and watched, they also will have their eye on their professors. They will take a morbid pleasure in eating the forbidden fruit, in drinking the "stolen waters, which are sweeter, and eating hidden bread, which is more pleasant." [2] Like those that try to avoid the *Octroi* in French towns, they will come to regard their offences as purely penal without any moral sanction attached to them.

I once heard of a professor who always presupposed that the students were untrustworthy until they gave proof of virtue. The opposite rule, which assumes that they are good until their vicious character is made manifest, is, certainly, to be preferred. A gentleman once informed me that the principal of the academy in Europe in which he had made his studies, had an observatory, from which he could view the boys in their respective rooms, and take note of any misdemeanor they might commit.

All right-minded men will agree that it is far better that youths should be religiously impressed with a sense

---

[1] III. Plen. Council, No. 158.   [2] Prov. ix. 17.

of God's presence, that their enlightened conscience should be their monitor, and that the Faculty should appeal to their moral rectitude and honor rather than to their sense of fear.

This generous confidence in the student's honor is calculated to develop a higher and nobler type of manhood, and to fit young men for the great world in which they will have no preceptors to admonish them, and in which their conscience will be their chief and often their only guide. And besides, wherever this method of government obtains, whatever chastisement may be inflicted on the transgressor in vindication of the law, will be sanctioned and applauded by the students themselves; for they feel that any grave violation of college discipline affects their personal honor and good name. I am happy to say that this system prevails in all the institutions of learning with which I am acquainted.

St. Augustine in his *Confessions*, complains of the excessive harshness and severity of some teachers of his time. They multiply, he says, the labors and sorrows through which the sons of Adam are obliged to pass. Youth are better governed by motives of love and filial reverence than by servile fear, and their tasks are more diligently learned when enjoined by principles of duty, than when enforced by threats of punishment; for "no one," he adds, "doth ever well what he doth against his will, even though what he doth, be well." [1]

The mode of punishment inflicted on refractory subjects has varied according to the popular sentiment prevailing at different times and in different countries. We are told in the *Life of Plutarch* that corporal chastisement

[1] Book I. Ch. XII.

was not tolerated in the school which he frequented in Greece. This authority was exercised only by parents. "The office of the teacher was to inform the mind. He had no power to extinguish the flame of freedom, or break down the noble independence of the soul by the degrading application of the rod." Plutarch informs us of a novel and ingenious method employed by his preceptor Ammonius in correcting his pupils : "Our master," he says, "having one day observed that we had indulged too freely at dinner, ordered his freedman, during his afternoon lecture, *to give his own son* the discipline of the whip in our presence. The philosopher all the while had his eye upon us, and we knew well for whom the example of punishment was intended." Our American youth would, I presume, submit with patient resignation to this vicarious sort of punishment, for it is easy to bear the misfortunes of others.

The experience of General Sheridan's school-days was not so agreeable. His teacher had less scruple than Ammonius about corporal punishment. He tells us in his *Personal Memoirs* that, when a youth, he attended a private school in Ohio. Whenever any one of the boys committed a serious breach of discipline, if the teacher was unable to detect the culprit, as was usually the case, "he would consistently apply the switch to the whole school without discrimination." It must be conceded that by this means he never failed to catch the real mischief-maker.

So great an authority as Dr. Johnson advocates moderate corporal punishment as an efficient means for curbing perverse and refractory spirits.

The ancient Lacedaemonian father was accustomed to inflict a second punishment on his son who complained of being chastised; for, he held, that "he who would take the trouble to correct the son, showed thereby his affection for the father." [1]

But the spirit of this country seems to be growing more and more averse to the application of the rod. I am persuaded that neither the authority of the sturdy Dr. Johnson nor the example of the Lacedaemonians will have any effect in supplanting the milder régime now in force in our educational institutions, especially in our Catholic colleges and seminaries; for while American fathers admit the wisdom of Solomon's maxim: "He that spareth the rod, hateth his son," [2] they are reluctant to delegate to others their paternal prerogative.

It will be generally admitted, in conclusion, that he is a model disciplinarian who combines the paternal and maternal attributes in his relations to his pupils. While he is always expected to maintain the authority of a father, he should exhibit in a more marked degree, the affection and tenderness of a mother; for he who gains our heart, easily commands the attention of our mind.

---

[1] Cornelius a Lapide in Prov. XIII.   [2] Prov. XIII. 24.

CHAPTER V.

IT was only after some hesitation and misgiving that I ventured, in the foregoing chapter, to make a few suggestions to teachers; for our honored superiors and professors have the grace of their vocation, and, in the exercise of their noble profession, they have an experience to which the writer can lay no claim.

The more grateful task now devolves on me of pointing out to our young students, and particularly to the aspirants to the sacred ministry, the duties which they owe to their superiors and teachers. These duties may be summed up in three words, gratitude, reverence, and obedience, which shall be treated in three separate chapters.

Next to the blessing that a youth enjoys of possessing virtuous parents, is the advantage of being trained by teachers conspicuous for enlightenment, rectitude of heart, and zeal in the discharge of their sublime office; for the education he receives, exerts a dominant influence in forming his character and in outlining his future career in life.

Plato was accustomed to give thanks to the Deity for two signal favors: first, that he was born and reared in a country so refined and civilized as Greece; secondly, that he had Socrates for his teacher. Our *alumni* should be still more grateful to God that their lines are cast in

America, that they are destined to announce the Gospel in a country in which they enjoy the blessing of civil and religious liberty, and that they are instructed by teachers who are the disciples of " *Christ, the power of God and the wisdom of God*," [1] whose doctrine surpasses that of Socrates in wisdom as much as the sun exceeds the moon in splendor.

The serenity of mind, the composure of countenance, the calm deliberation in all his movements that marked the character of Pericles, are gratefully ascribed by him to the lessons and influence of his teacher, Anaxagoras.

The greatest philosopher of antiquity was the chosen teacher of the greatest of ancient generals. Aristotle was selected by Philip, King of Macedon, as the preceptor of his son, the future Alexander the Great. Philip manifested in many ways his esteem for his son's teacher. He rebuilt the city of Stagira, in which Aristotle was born, and repeopled it with the inhabitants who had fled from it when it was destroyed. Alexander used to declare that his love for his tutor was equal to the affection that he bore his father, for he observed, " If I have received life from the one, the other has taught me how to live well." After his Persian conquest, he presented his master with eight hundred talents, amounting to almost a million of dollars.

The Emperor Marcus Aurelius in his *Meditations,* avows with gratitude his indebtedness to his parents and preceptors: " From the reputation and remembrance of my father," he says, " I learned modesty and a manly character ;

" From my mother, piety and beneficence and abstinence not only from evil deeds, but even from evil thoughts.

[1] I. Cor. I. 24.

"From my governors, I learned endurance of labor and to be content with little, to work with my own hands, not to meddle with other people's affairs, and not to be ready to listen to slander. I learned, also, freedom of will and undeviating steadiness of purpose, to look to nothing else except to reason, and to be always the same in sharp pains and in long illness."

Cicero manifests his gratitude for his preceptor, Aulus Licinius Archias, by the immortal oration which he pronounced in his defence in Rome. In his exordium he thus expresses his indebtedness to his teacher: "If, my lords, I am possessed of any ability, meagre as I am aware mine is; if I can boast of any practice in public speaking, an art to which I allow I have devoted no small degree of attention; if I can lay claim to any acquaintance with the theory of oratory, the result of education in the fine arts, a study to which at every period of my life I have been devoted, the defendant here to-day, Aulus Licinius, has the right to demand of me the fruit of all these acquirements. For as far as my recollection can recall the past and bring back the earliest memories of my boyhood days, I recognize that this gentleman has always had the chief share in urging me to enter upon this line of study and to persevere in it. If, then, I have been able to defend some and save others by this voice which his counsel and direction contributed to perfect, I certainly am obliged, as far as I can, to lend its aid to the one from whom I enjoy that power to defend and to save."

Alcuin, the preceptor of Charlemagne and of his royal sons, was tenderly loved by that illustrious prince, who mourned the death of the English scholar as that of a friend and master. He wrote his eulogy in some Latin verses which, if not distinguished for poetical merit, at least do justice to the honest affection that dictated them.[1]

These examples, taken with one exception from heathen sources, may suffice to show that gratitude is a characteristic trait of ingenuous souls. The absence of this virtue is a mark of an ignoble nature. Now, to whom after his parents is the youth more indebted than to the devoted teacher who has guided his steps through the paths of science and virtue, and whose divining rod has caused those hidden springs to gush forth that have been through life an unfailing refreshment to his spirit? By no amount of pecuniary compensation can he adequately requite his teachers for the pleasures of the intellect, the imagination, and the memory which he will enjoy in after years. Material food satiates once it is consumed; the intellectual banquet is a perennial joy to the soul.

"These studies give strength in youth and joy in old age. They adorn prosperity and are the support and consolation of adversity. At home they are delightful, and abroad they are easy. At night they are company to us. When we travel, they attend us, and in our rural retirement they do not forsake us."[2]

After students have drunk deep at the fountain of knowledge, and when their mind has been matured by age and intercourse with men, their admiration for their teacher's learning may become somewhat tempered. They may not fully share in the enthusiasm which the "gazing

[1] "Christian Schools and Scholars," Vol. I.

[2] Haec studia adolescentiam alunt, senectutem oblectant, secundas res ornant, adversis perfugium, ac solatium praebent, delectant domi, non impediunt foris, pernoctant nobiscum, peregrinantur, rusticantur." Cicero, pro Archia.

rustics" of Goldsmith's *Deserted Village* had for their pedagogue :

> " And still they gazed, and still the wonder grew,
>   That one small head could carry all he knew—"

but their gratitude for their teacher's self-sacrifice, forbearance, and kind indulgence grows with their growth and ripens with their years. Some of them may have forgotten or neglected the instructions imparted to them, but the image of their guide, philosopher, and friend is indelibly stamped on their heart and memory.

CHAPTER VI.

REVERENCE FOR TEACHERS.

FILIAL reverence for superiors and professors is another duty incumbent on students. It is a characteristic of manhood's noblest types. If the Scripture declares that the priests are deserving of double honor who worthily rule the flock,[1] surely, not less honor should be claimed for the professors who are the guides of the future shepherds themselves. This reverence will be all the more grateful to the Faculty, if, instead of savoring of diffidence or degenerating into servile fear, it springs from a genuine affection and confidence. One of the most acceptable ways in which the pupil can evince his respect for his teachers, is by a composed demeanor and close attention during lecture hours.

Plutarch gives a memorable instance of the courteous attention and graceful compliment paid him while lecturing in Rome. Among his hearers was Arulenus Rusticus, one of the most conspicuous citizens of Rome, distinguished as well by the lustre of his family as by an honorable ambition and glorious career, and honored with the friendship of the Emperor. "It once happened," says he, "that when I was speaking in public in Rome, Arulenus Rusticus was one of my hearers. When in the

---

[1] I. Tim. v. 17.

middle of my discourse, a soldier came in and handed him a letter from the Emperor. Upon this there was a general silence throughout the audience, and I paused to give him time to peruse the letter. But he would not suffer it, nor did he open the letter till I had finished my lecture and the audience was dispersed." [1]

If this eminent citizen of Pagan Rome showed courtesy so marked to Plutarch, surely, Christian students should not exhibit less respect for their teacher while addressing them. He prepares his lecture with scrupulous diligence. He covets no applause from the outside world. His words will not be heard beyond the walls of his class-room. His only ambition is to enlighten the disciples seated before him, and his greatest delight and reward are to command their undivided attention; while on the other hand, though he may repress his feelings, he cannot but be keenly and painfully sensitive to any levity or listlessness of manner betrayed by his audience.

This reverence, however, is perfectly compatible with the right and even with the duty which the student possesses of thinking for himself, of weighing the professor's arguments, of suspending his judgment till his doubt or difficulty is removed, and even of dissenting from them, if they do not accord with his conviction; for the Horatian dictum, " *Nullius addictus jurare in verba magistri*," applies to the students of young America, as well as to those of ancient Rome. The scholar that accepts every *ipse dixit* of his professor without subjecting it to the light of his own intelligence, will load his memory at the expense of his judgment. He may become a ready speaker, but he will hardly ever be a strong and clear

[1] Life of Plutarch, Preface.

thinker. The knowledge acquired by the pupil is proportioned to what he takes in, not to what the teacher gives out. It is only the quantity assimilated of intellectual, as well as material food, that imparts nourishment.

" A man," says Cardinal Newman, " may hear a thousand lectures and read a thousand volumes, and be at the end of the process very much where he was as regards knowledge. Something more than merely admitting it in a negative way into the mind, is necessary, if it is to remain there. It must not be passively received, but actually and actively entered into, embraced, mastered. The mind must go half-way to meet what comes into it from without." [1]

" Books," says Frederic Harrison, " are no more education, than laws are virtue." A student may be " deep-versed in books, and shallow in himself." [2]

The attendance at lectures will not make him a whit more learned, unless he appropriates and digests the mental food imparted, just as the best book in morals will not advance him a step in rectitude of conduct, unless his heart is in the work he reads.

If custom allows, the alumnus may submit his doubts or objections to the professor during class. Otherwise, he should not hesitate to do so when the lecture is over. So far from regarding his visit as an intrusion, the teacher will esteem it a mark of confidence to have difficulties presented to him, and he will take pleasure in endeavoring to solve them.

✓ The conduct of the Incarnate Wisdom in the Temple when a youth of twelve years, is the best reverential model

[1] Idea of a University.   [2] Choice of Books.

5

for an ingenuous pupil to follow. He sat among the doctors in a lower place, as became a disciple. He listened to them with respectful submission. He questioned them without being arrogant or disputatious, and he excited their admiration by the modesty and wisdom of his answers.

St. Thomas Aquinas, while pursuing his studies in Paris, gave an edifying proof of his humility and reverence for his superiors. One day, while reading in the refectory, he was corrected by the director regarding the pronunciation of a word. He bowed to the correction, though he knew that his own pronunciation was the true one, and that his master was at fault. When told by his companions that he should have publicly justified himself, he replied : "It matters not how a word is pronounced, but to practise on all occasions reverential submission is of the greatest importance."

A similar anecdote is related of Lanfranc, afterward Archbishop of Canterbury. Once, when reading in presence of the Community, the Prior corrected his Latin accent, and desired him to pronounce the *e* in *docere* short. Lanfranc complied without hesitation, and his docile acquiescence in the superior's erroneous correction was all the more worthy of admiration, as he had already acquired great reputation for learning. I am persuaded that these two superiors would not have taken it amiss, but would have been edified, had the Angel of the Schools and the future Archbishop of Canterbury privately called and represented themselves to be in the right.

CHAPTER VII.

Obedience to Teachers; Observance of Rules.

OBEDIENCE to superiors and the observance of college laws are indispensable to the discipline of the house. College and seminary rules serve a double purpose; they contribute to the good order of the community, and they indoctrinate the students in the virtue of obedience and in systematic habits, on which the fruit of their future ministry so much depends.

> "Order is heaven's first law; and, this confest,
> Some are and must be greater than the rest."

Now, there can be no order in the soul or in the family, in the State or in the Church, unless there exist a recognized authority on the one hand, to enforce the law, and on the other, subjects to obey it. In the kingdom of the soul, all the faculties and animal appetites must be under the dominion of reason. In the government of the family, the father commands; the children and the other members of the household obey. In the national Republic, the civil magistrates have the divinely-constituted right to maintain the laws which the citizens are bound to observe. In the Commonwealth of the Church, the spiritual rulers are invested with power, and the faithful are subject to them in matters appertaining to the kingdom of heaven. Even in the planetary system, are found marvellous order

67

and harmony, the result of the laws that govern the planets. They all move within their respective orbits, they do not deviate from their normal course, they do not clash nor collide with one another, and they are all controlled by one central sun.

In like manner, in the college community there must co-exist the three elements of government—law, authority, and obedience. Wherever the wise rules of a seminary are observed, there is found the reign of law ; while the flagrant and frequent violation of them would lead to anarchy and rebellion.

College discipline and the arrangement of hours for the various exercises of the day, are not capriciously made ; they are the result of observation and the experience of ages.

The pleasing variety of the daily duties, the judicious succession of prayer, study, and recreation, like the alternate succession of day and night and of the seasons, relieve the monotony and dispel the tedium of college life. They give a new zest to each recurring duty, so that the days and weeks glide away almost imperceptibly ; and the good order that prevails in the house is the reflection of the quiet and tranquillity that reign in every heart.

If, on the contrary, you desire to know the wretchedness and emptiness of a life without rule or obedience, you have only to consult a man who has no object to live for, who has no law to observe save his own whims and caprices, no superior to obey but his own will, no work to perform but what his own fancy may dictate. You will find that to such a man, life becomes an intolerable burden. His soul is a " land of misery and darkness, where the shadow of death, and no order, but everlasting horror dwelleth." [1] St. Bernard says that "he who is his own master, is the disciple of a fool."

While faithfully observing the seminary régime, the student enjoys not only the present blessing of interior peace, but also the prospective advantage of a well-ordered mind. Indeed, the spirit of discipline acquired during the course of studies, may be regarded as one of the most essential elements in ecclesiastical training. The habitual compliance with the rules of the institution, quickens his attention, strengthens his will, invigorates the energies of his soul, gives him decision of character, makes him prompt in responding to the call of duty, impels him by force of habit to sacrifice personal comfort to his legitimate obligations, endows him with docility and elasticity of mind, and renders him a well-equipped soldier of Christ.

The custom of rising promptly at the sound of the bell, of repairing to the prayer-hall and to the chapel, the refectory and the class-room, will afterward enable him with ease to be punctual at the altar, alert in attending sick-calls and in performing the other functions of the ministry. A cheerful and steadfast obedience to his superiors will fortify him to fulfil the solemn promise of reverence and obedience which he makes to the Pontiff at the foot of the altar, on the day of his ordination. He will realize the force of the prophet's words : " It is good for a man, when he hath borne the yoke from his youth."

I have seen that noblest of domestic animals, the horse, at the click of the electric alarm-bell, instantly rush from his half-devoured meal and submit to be harnessed and

[1] Job x. 22.

driven to the scene of a conflagration. Now man, like the lower animals, is in great measure the creature of habit. He responds without effort and almost instinctively in mature years to the calls of duty to which he was inured from his youth.

By making the daily rounds of the seminary exercises, the young levite is unconsciously preparing himself for the battle of ministerial life, just as the recruit is schooled for stern warfare by his peaceful military evolutions.

It cannot, indeed, be denied that during our late war, the volunteer officers, who had not received a regular military training, gave signal proofs of valor, skill, and efficiency. But at the same time, it is conceded that the regular officers, who had enjoyed the advantage of a military education at West Point or elsewhere, were better instructed in the art of war, were more relied on, and more successful in a critical campaign. Discipline told in their favor. And it has been well remarked that our raw volunteer soldiers rapidly became a splendid army *just because* of the large number of West Pointers commanding on both sides.

At the beginning of the war, in 1861, several volunteer colonels met near Quincy, Ill., to select a brigadier commander from their number. Col. U. S. Grant, who happened to be in the neighborhood with his regiment, was unanimously chosen because a West Pointer, although all the citizen-colonels outranked him—an evidence that the superiority of the regular officers was gracefully recognized by the volunteers themselves.[1]

The Grants, Shermans, Sheridans, and Thomases, on the Federal side; the Lees, Stonewall Jacksons, Long-

[1] "Ohio in the War," Whitelaw Reid.

streets, and Beauregards, on the Confederate side, shine forth as the most conspicuous figures and the most formidable generals of the war.

In like manner, heroic priests are found up and down the country, who, though deprived by circumstances of the benefit of an extended ecclesiastical discipline, are yet laboring fruitfully in the service of God. But it must be admitted that the great bulk of our most successful apostolic leaders, have, like the Apostles themselves, been qualified for their work by spending a series of years of rigid discipline in the school of Christ.

But you will say: Is it not a hard penance for one to submit to a strict rule of life, and to be subject to the will of another? Yes; and for this reason obedience is accounted among the most heroic and sublime virtues, being superior to voluntary poverty and to continence. By voluntary poverty, a man tramples on earthly goods; by continence, he controls the flesh; by obedience, he conquers his will.

Carlyle inveighs in his usual energetic style against the modern vice of lawless independence: "What is the universally arrogated virtue of these days? For some half century it has been the thing you name, '*Independence.*' Suspicion of '*servility*,' of *reverence* for superiors, the very dogleech is anxious to disavow. Fools! Were your superiors worthy to govern, and you worthy to obey, reverence for them were even your only possible freedom. Independence in all kinds, is rebellion, if unjust rebellion, why parade it, and every where prescribe?"[1]

But it is by this heroic self-sacrifice that he purchases freedom of soul. It is by passing through the novitiate

[1] Sartor Resartus.

of obedience and discipline, that the disciple of Christ is elevated to the glorious liberty of the son of God. He becomes master of his passions and inclinations, and makes them subservient to the law of reason. "An obedient man shall speak of victory." [1]

Every right-minded priest, now engaged in the ministry, will acknowledge that he possesses more freedom of soul and contentment of mind in the mission to which he was called by legitimate authority, than he would have enjoyed in a more desirable charge, had he compassed it by intrigue, influence, or importunity; for he has the testimony of his conscience that he is at the post assigned him by God.

It is related of the Duke of Wellington, that when a certain chaplain asked him whether he should preach the Gospel to the Hindoos, the disciplined soldier said to him : "What are your marching orders?" The chaplain replied : "Go ye unto all the world, and preach the Gospel to every creature." "Then follow your orders," said the Duke; "your duty is to obey."

The words of a great general may be appropriately quoted on this subject : "In positions of great responsibility, every one should do his duty, to the best of his ability, where assigned by competent authority, without application or the use of influence to change his position. I would cut my right arm off rather than make application to be removed to another command. If I had sought the place, or obtained it through personal or political influence, my belief is that I should have feared to undertake any plan of my own conception, and should

[1] Prov. xxi. 28.

probably have awaited direct orders from my distant superiors." [1]

Does not the history of mankind attest that all men who have been fired with the ambition of gaining conquests in the field of glory, or in that of literature, have voluntarily subjected themselves to a life of self-denial?

> " The youth who in the foot-race burns to win,
>   Must do and suffer much ere he begin,
>   Sweat himself down, bear cold and toil and pain,
>   And from the lures of love and wine abstain.
>   At Pythian games no piper ever played
>   But teacher had, and was of him afraid." [2]

St. Paul, referring to those who contended at the games which were celebrated at Corinth, says : " Every one that striveth for the mastery refraineth himself from all things : and they indeed that they may receive a perishable crown, but we an imperishable " [3]

I have before me the " Regulations for the United States Military Academy at West Point," and those for the United States Naval Academy at Annapolis, and I have, also, conferred with leading Army and Navy Commanders regarding the discipline in those two Institutions. The following table exhibits the daily routine in the Naval Academy :

[1] Personal Memoirs of Gen. Grant, Vol. i, pp. 459–60.

[2] " Qui studet optatam cursu contingere metam,
　　 Multa tulit fecitque puer, sudavit et alsit,
　　 Abstinuit venere et vino.　Qui Pythia cantat
　　 Tibicen, didicit prius, extimuitque magistrum."

　　　　　　　　　　　　　　　Horace, Ars Poetica.

[3] I. Cor. ix. 25.

Morning gun-fire and reveille...........................6 a. m.
Morning roll-call...6.50 a. m.
Breakfast immediately after roll-call..................7 a. m.
Prayers immediately after breakfast..................
Call to rooms and first forenoon recitation.. ....7.55 a. m.
Call to second forenoon recitation......................9 a. m.
Call to third forenoon recitation.......................10.20 a. m.
Call to fourth forenoon recitation.......................11.25 a. m.
Recall from recitations and release from rooms...12.35 p. m.
Dinner...1 p. m.
First afternoon recitation..................................1.50 p. m.
Second afternoon recitation...........................2.55 p. m.
Call to afternoon exercise and drills..................4.05 p. m.
Evening roll-call...6.30 p. m.
Supper immediately after roll-call......................
Call to rooms..7.25 p. m.
Evening gun-fire, tattoo, and release from rooms..9.30 p. m.
Warning-roll...9.55 p. m.
Taps...10 p. m.

The daily exercises at West Point are substantially the
same as those at Annapolis. After a careful comparison
of the rules observed at West Point with those of our
seminaries, it can be safely asserted that the discipline
is far more severe in the military academy than in our
ecclesiastical institutions.

The exercises at West Point are more numerous; the
orders are more minute, detailed, and searching; the
restraints on personal liberty more continuous and unrelenting; the strain on the mental and physical energies
is more trying; the sanctions appended to the law are
more solemn, and greater penalties are attached to its
violation; more publicity is given to personal faults, for
delinquencies are read in public; and there is a closer
inspection of rooms with a view to order and cleanliness.
Exemptions and dispensations from duty are rarer. There

is less familiarity between the officers and the cadets; more external marks of respect are required of the students toward their superiors and professors, the examinations are more rigorous, the recreations fewer. The vacation, also, is shorter at West Point than in ecclesiastical colleges, for only one vacation of two months and a half is allowed during the term of four years. All games of chance and the use of tobacco in any snape are forbidden.

Some years ago a venerable clergyman, who had served as chaplain in a Western fort, remarked to me: "If a man wants to know what absolute obedience is, let him serve for a week under a sergeant. He will issue the most peremptory and irritating orders without deigning an explanation. If you venture to ask for a reason, ne will say to you with Sir John Falstaff: "If reasons were as plenty as blackberries, I will give no man a reason upon compulsion."

Now, if our West Point and Annapolis cadets subject themselves to so rigid a discipline, in the hope of being enrolled among their country's defenders, surely the young soldier of Christ should not be less generous in cheerfully submitting to the salutary yoke of the seminary, especially as he is the disciple of Him whose watch-word is self-denial, and whose standard is the Cross.

They who are able to compare seminary life as found to-day in the United States, and as it existed forty years ago, cannot fail to observe that, while the discipline is maintained in healthy vigor, much more provision is now made for the comfort of the student than at that period. I do not know whether or how far this change has conduced to the physical strength and manhood of the alumni.

At all events, I am persuaded that they would be more than reconciled to their situation if they had a trial of some of the seminaries that I have visited in Continental Europe.

In February, 1887, His Eminence Cardinal Taschereau and myself dined together in one of the great seminaries of Paris. The floor of the refectory was paved with brick. There was neither fire nor fire-place. The day was intensely cold even for the season, and, though clothed in a heavy cassock and overcoat, we sat shivering. After dinner the seminarians took their recreation on the grounds without overcoats, several of them bare-headed. But this is the material out of which the Apostles of the Foreign Missions are made.

There is another circumstance that should stimulate the students to the observance of college rules, and that is, the personal example of the superiors and professors. They do not say to the young recruits: *"Go,"* but they say: *"Follow us."* They are always at the head of the column, leading on their little army. They do not shrink from the post of duty. They do not exempt themselves on the plea of age, nor of their sacred character, nor of their privilege as directors; but they attend the various exercises of the house, as far as practicable, from morning till night. They impose on themselves a double obligation, namely, the duty of guiding and directing as superiors, and that of obeying like the rank and file.

Let us not then, entertain for a moment the fallacious notion that there is anything degrading or slavish in obedience. It is, on the contrary, a most rational duty. No man nor aggregation of men has any inborn rights over another. Neither professor nor superior, neither bishop nor civil magistrate nor Pope has any inherent or self-constituted power to command another. In exercising authority they are the representatives of God by whom " Kings reign and law-givers decree just things." What our Saviour said to Pilate, is applicable to all temporal and spiritual rulers : " Thou shouldst not have any power, unless it were given thee from above." [1]

Hence, obedience is not an act of servility paid to man, but an act of homage paid to God. This circumstance ennobles the virtue of obedience and invests it with a dignity becoming the sons of God.

Our Saviour has added fresh lustre and nobility to those virtues which He practised on earth. Now, there is no virtue which shines more conspicuously in His life, than that of obedience : " I came down from heaven," He says, " not to do My own will, but the will of Him that sent Me." [2] " My food is to do the will of Him that sent Me, that I may perfect His work." [3] He subjected Himself to His own creatures, because He looked on them as His Father's representatives. Nay " He became obedient unto death, even the death of the cross," recognizing in Caiaphas, Pilate, and the Roman soldiery, the instruments of God in the humiliations He underwent : " the chalice which My Father hath given Me, shall I not drink it ? " [4]

The great Apostle of the Gentiles was ordered by Christ Himself to go to Ananias and to become his disciple, although the disciple was far more favored than his master both by natural acquirements and heavenly illumi-

[1] John xix. 11.
[2] Ibid. vi. 38.
[3] Ibid. iv. 34.
[4] Ibid. xviii. 11.

nations. Indeed the name of Ananias would never have come down to us, were it not for his relations with his illustrious pupil.

With how much more alacrity, then, should not the ingenuous scholar defer to his teachers, since he will have the candor to avow that they usually excel him in virtue as well as in knowledge?

St. Peter was placed over his apostolic brethren as their superior, though he had sinned more grievously than his colleagues. We never heard of the other Apostles reproaching him for his denial of his Master, still less of refusing to obey him on account of his transgression.

If any real or supposed maladministration should exist in the college; if there is any abuse of power, or excessive severity of discipline, or any grounds of complaint on account of a defect in the quantity or the quality of the food, there are two ways for redressing these and other such grievances.

The reprehensible method consists in cabals and secret complaints, in repinings and murmurings, which spread discontent, and cast an air of gloom over the community, and which sometimes break out in open rebellion against the authorities. This course, while subversive of discipline, checks no evil, and effects no reformation.

The rational, straightforward and honorable steps to take for the correction of any alleged abuse, are to make a respectful representation to the superior of the house, who will not fail to investigate the cause of dissatisfaction, and, if well grounded, to supply a remedy; for, no conscientious principal can feel happy while his students are discontented. He shares their sorrow as the head shares the pain of a suffering member in the human body, and his greatest source of joy is the sunshine reflected from the youthful hearts under his charge.

When Samuel J. Randall was Speaker of the House of Representatives, he was frequently annoyed and interrupted by a member who profited by every occasion to dissent from his rulings.   One day, in a full House, the Speaker withdrew, and requested the obnoxious congressman to occupy the chair in his absence.   Very soon the House was in an uproar, confusion reigned supreme, the temporary chairman lost his head, and it was only after the Speaker was sent for and resumed the chair, that order was restored.   The carping statesman was warned by his humiliating experience, to exercise afterward more discretion in questioning the decisions of the Speaker.

√The disposition to criticise the conduct and administration of superiors would be moderated in tone, and would be rendered less frequent by reflecting that to the Faculty, and not to the subordinates is given the grace of ruling well; that the removal of an occasion of complaint sometimes involves the sacrifice of a greater good; that in the human breast there lurks a perverse tendency to censure those who, by their official position, are exposed to public view; that we are all more prone to discover faults than to recognize points of excellence; and that submission to the yoke of discipline is not congenial to the natural man, but always demands a generous self-sacrifice.

CHAPTER VIII.

TRUTH AND SINCERITY OF CHARACTER.

THERE are certain natural virtues which our young men are habitually called upon to exercise in their relations with one another as students during their academic career, and afterward as citizens and priests in their intercourse with their fellow-beings in the world. Among these virtues, I shall single out three, because being leading and fundamental, they have a dominant influence on the others. These virtues are, *Truth, Self-respect*, and *Fraternal Charity*. They will be treated in the four following chapters.

The highest compliment that can be bestowed on a man is, to say of him that he is a man of his word; and the greatest reproach that can be cast on an individual is, to assert that he has no regard for the virtue of veracity. Truth is the golden coin with God's image stamped upon it, that circulates among men of all nations and tribes and peoples and tongues; its standard value never changes nor depreciates.

> "Truth has such a face and such a mien,
> As to be loved, needs only to be seen."

Like all valuable commodities, truth is often counterfeited. If it is a crime to counterfeit money, it is a greater crime to adulterate virtue. The more precious the genuine coin, the more criminal and dangerous is the spurious imitation; and as truth is more valuable than specie, its base resemblance is more iniquitous and detestable: *"Corruptio optimi pessima."*

As truth is the medium of social and commercial intercourse, so high is the value which civilized society sets upon it that, for its own protection, it metes out the severest punishment to any one who violates it in commercial transactions. Some time ago, a citizen, who had boasted of owning more property than any other person in the neighborhood of a large city, was afterward sent to the penitentiary for telling a lie on a scrap of paper, or for forging another man's name on a note.

If it is a sin to prevaricate in business transactions, how much more grievous is the offence to lie in religious matters! Ananias and Saphira were suddenly struck dead at the Apostle's feet, because they had made a false return of the price of their farm. Their transgression did not consist in giving the Apostle only a part of the price of the land they sold, for he declared that, as it was a free gift, they were at liberty to do what they pleased with it. But they sinned by telling a deliberate lie about it.[1]

The virtue of veracity is so indispensable an element in the composition of a Christian gentlemen, that neither splendid talents, nor engaging manners, nor benevolence of disposition, nor self-denial, nor all these qualities combined, nor even the practice of religious exercises, can atone for its absence. They all become vitiated, they lose their savor, if the salt of truth and sincerity is wanting.

[1] Acts v.

6

The vice of lying and hypocrisy is so odious and repulsive that it is obliged to hide its deformity, and clothe itself in the garment of truth.

While we feel at our ease and are disposed to be open and communicative in the presence of an upright and candid man, we are instinctively reserved and guarded before a deceitful person. He diffuses around him an atmosphere of distrust, and we shun him as we would a poisonous reptile. "There is no vice," says Bacon, "that so covereth a man with shame as to be false and perfidious."

So damaging and infamous in public estimation is the imputation of falsehood that, when we charge a man with unveracity, we rarely go so far as to call him a liar to his face; but we tell him in less offensive language that he has a vivid imagination, that his memory is defective, or that he has been betrayed into an error of judgment.

All men, Pagans and Jews, as well as Christians, pay homage to truth. They all profess to worship at her shrine. Pagan Rome supplies us with noble examples of fidelity to truth even at the sacrifice of life. When Regulus was sent from Carthage to Rome with ambassadors to sue for peace, it was under the condition, that he should return to his Carthaginian prison if peace was not proclaimed. When he arrived in Rome, he implored the Senate to continue the war, and not to agree to the exchange of prisoners. That implied his own return to captivity at Carthage. The Senators and the chief priest held that, as his oath had been extorted by force, he was not bound by it. "I am not ignorant," replied Regulus, "that tortures and death await me; but what are these to the shame of an infamous action or the wounds of a guilty mind? Slave as I am to Carthage, I have still the spirit of a Roman. I have sworn to return. It is my duty to go." Regulus returned to Carthage and, it is said, was tortured to death.

When Eleazar was threatened with death if he did not violate the law of God, he was urged by his friends to save his life by an act of dissimulation. But he replied: " It doth not become our age to dissemble : whereby many young persons might think that Eleazar, at the age of four score and ten years, was gone over to the life of the heathens. For though, for the present time, I should be delivered from the punishments of men, yet should I not escape the hand of the Almighty neither alive nor dead. Wherefore, by departing manfully out of this life, I shall shew myself worthy of my old age. And I shall leave an example of fortitude to young men if, with a ready mind and constancy, I suffer an honorable death for the most venerable and most holy laws. And having spoken thus, he was forthwith carried to execution." [1]

If there is one virtue reflected more clearly than another on the pages of the New Testament; if there is one virtue for which Christ and His disciples were eminently conspicuous in their public and private life, it is the virtue of truth, candor, ingenuousness, and simplicity of character; and if there is any vice more particularly detested by them, it is hypocrisy, cunning, and duplicity of conduct.

So great is our Saviour's reverence for truth, so great His aversion for falsehood, that He calls Himself "the way, the truth, and the life." His Holy Spirit, He names

[1] Machab. VI. 24–28.

" the Spirit of truth," while designating the devil " a liar, the father of lies and of liars." [1]

Even His enemies could not withhold their admiration for His truthfulness and sincerity : " Master," they said, " we know that Thou art true, and teachest the way of God in truth ; neither carest Thou for any one ; for Thou dost not regard the person of men." [2]

" Let your speech," says our Lord, " be yea, yea, nay, nay," [3] as if He would say : Let your conversation be always frank and direct, free from the tinsel of embellishment and exaggeration, divested of studied ambiguity with intent to deceive.

I can recall but two instances in which Christ pronounces the eulogy of any man outside of the apostolic circle. He extols John the Baptist for his constancy and austerity, and He praises Nathanael for his guilelessness and sincerity of character : " Behold an Israelite, indeed, in whom there is no guile." [4] When He was instructing His disciples for their future mission, He told them to be " wise as serpents and simple as doves." [5] While they were to be wary and reserved among a hostile and captious people, He never allowed them to prevaricate or deflect one iota or tittle from the truth even to save their lives. As the serpent is said to expose his whole body to protect his head, so the Apostles were admonished to surrender not only their goods and their body, but even to sacrifice their life, rather than betray the truth.

Christ is the martyr of truth as well as of charity. Caiaphas said to Him : " I adjure Thee by the living

[1] John VIII. 44.
[2] Matt. XXII. 16.
[3] Matt. v. 37.
[4] John I. 47.
[5] Matt. x. 16.

God that Thou tell us whether Thou be the Christ, the Son of God." How easily could Jesus have saved His life on this occasion by His silence or by an evasive answer! But by openly avowing that He was the Christ, He signed His own death-warrant.

It was not without a purpose that Christ gives us a little child as our model in our relations with our neighbor. "Unless ye become as little children, ye shall not enter into the kingdom of heaven."[1] Now, a child, until perverted by its vicious elders, is artless, open, and truthful. It speaks from the heart. It deals not in equivocations or mental reservations.

There was one class of persons toward whom our Lord was unsparing in His reprobation, and these were the scribes and Pharisees. He calls them a generation of vipers. "Wo to you, scribes and Pharisees, hypocrites," He says, "because ye make clean the outside of the cup and of the dish: but within you are full of rapine and uncleanness . . . Ye are like to whited sepulchres, which outwardly appear to men beautiful, but within are full of dead men's bones and of all filthiness. So you also outwardly indeed appear to men just, but inwardly you are full of hypocrisy and iniquity."[2] His language toward them is a scathing denunciation of their insincerity, selfishness, and perversion of the truth. We may judge how odious is deceit in His eyes when He says to the Pharisees: "Amen I say to you that the publicans and the harlots shall go into the kingdom of God before you."[3]

St. Paul says: "Putting away lying, speak ye the truth every man with his neighbor, for we are members one

[1] Matt. xviii. 3.   [2] Matt. xxiii. 25–28.   [3] Matt. xxi. 31.

of another."[1]   There is so absolute a trust and confidence between the members of the human body, that when the heart, or hand, or foot suffers pain, the head never suspects the afflicted member of practising deception. The same trustworthiness that subsists among our physical members should extend, also, to the domestic, collegiate, and social body. Without this mutual confidence, there could be no official nor friendly relations among men, and the wheels of social intercourse and commercial communication would suddenly stop. Nearly all the information that we acquire, is obtained from the testimony of others. Although we may at times be imposed upon, we have an instinctive faith in the veracity of our fellow-being.

So great is the esteem in which truth is held at West Point Academy that, if a cadet deliberately makes a misstatement to any of his superior officers, he is punished by expulsion. What a reproach would be the life of a Christian student who does not live up to the West Point standard! In Cornell, Harvard, Yale, and other universities, the same punishment is inflicted on students found guilty of presenting as their own essays, the compositions of another. If the virtue of truth is inviolably upheld in commercial life, in secular colleges, and military circles, it should, undoubtedly, be not less cherished by those that aspire to be the official heralds of the Gospel of truth, and the most honorable members of that mystical body of which Christ is the Head. If it is a shame, as St. Bernard declares, to be effeminate members under a Head crowned with thorns, surely it is not less revolting to be a lying mouthpiece under a Head that is the Oracle of truth.

[1] Eph. iv. 25.

St. Peter says : " Laying aside all malice and all guile and dissimulations and envies and all detractions, as new-born babes, desire the rational milk without guile that thereby you may grow unto salvation." [1] We are the spiritual children of a mother that never deceives us. So undoubting is our trust in her that we receive from her hands the bread of truth with as unquestioning a faith as the infant receives the milk at its mother's breast. The children should resemble the mother especially in her characteristic features of truth and sincerity.

St. Thomas à Becket was conspicuous from his youth for inflexible veracity. Even in his childhood he always chose to suffer any blame, disgrace, or punishment rather than to tell an untruth, and in his whole life he was never found guilty of a lie in the smallest matter.

St. Alphonsus, pleading a case before a court of justice, was accidentally betrayed into an error by interpreting the meaning of a document against the adverse party. When convinced of his mistake, so delicate was his sense of truth, so great his aversion for even the semblance of a lie, that he abruptly abandoned the legal profession and embraced the religious state.

There is no time nor place in which the soldier of Christ is permitted to lay aside the armor of truth. The breast of God's minister, like that of the priest of the Old Law, should be the depository of doctrine and truth.

The disciple of Christ should be the organ of truth not only when robed in the sacred vestments, but also in the secular garb ; not only in the sanctuary and pulpit, but

[1] I. Peter II. 1, 2.

in the public and private walks of life as well ; in gay and festive, as well as in serious moods :

" Ridentem dicere verum quid vetat ? "

Purchasers view with suspicion even genuine cloth offered for sale by those who are known to deal in shoddy merchandise.

Seneca says that the untruthful man must have a good memory, because the falsehoods that he has once uttered, must be kept in mind so as to be propped up with additional misstatements.[1]

One may be guilty of falsehood in many ways. He may lie by telling a half-truth, omitting a circumstance essential to the fidelity of the narrative. He may lie by a shrug of the shoulders, by a gesture, by a deceitful silence, or by palming off in class as his own production the fruit of another's brain ; for the essence of a falsehood consists in the intention to deceive. His life may be a colossal lie by being false to his profession or calling, appearing to be rich in grace and good works in the sight of men, but being poor and blind and miserable in the sight of God. There are others who have a habit of exaggerating from a morbid desire of imparting a relish to the conversation, and of attracting the attention of their hearers. The incidents they describe are usually of a startling and phenomenal nature, and their adventurous experiences have the flavor of a Gulliver or a Baron Munchausen.

The pernicious habit of retailing jocose lies and sensational stories, of making inaccurate statements, and of talking at random without weighing his words, will impair the offender's reputation for veraciousness in grave

[1] *"Oportet mendacem memorem esse."*

matters, and expose him to the penalty of not being believed even when he tells the truth. He will be an illustration of the boy in the fable, who had repeatedly given false alarms about the approach of the wolf; but when the wolf had actually invaded the fold his outcry remained unheeded.

The two chief causes that lead men to prevaricate, are prejudice against their neighbor, and inordinate self-love. Prejudice warps our judgment, and jaundices our mind, so that we view in an unfavorable light our neighbor's words and actions. Self-love and vanity prompt us to exaggerate our good deeds, and to underrate or palliate our own shortcomings.

Charity and humility are the guardians of truth. They are the two angels that defend the temple of the soul against the approach of the demon of falsehood. Charity counsels us not to judge our neighbor unjustly or to magnify his defects; and humility inspires us not to extenuate our own.

If we cannot be martyrs, let us be confessors of the truth. If we have not the courage, like our Master, to endure death for its sake, we should at least be prepared to suffer for it some passing humiliation or confusion.

Let it be the aim of your life to be always frank and open, candid, sincere and ingenuous in your relations with your fellow-man. Set your face against all deceit and duplicity, all guile, hypocrisy and dissimulation. You will thus be living up to the maxims of the Gospel, you will prove yourself a genuine disciple of the God of truth, you will commend yourself to all honest men. You will triumph over those that lie in wait to deceive, for the intriguer is usually caught in his own toils.

CHAPTER IX.

SELF-RESPECT AND HUMAN RESPECT.

SELF-RESPECT is another characteristic of an exemplary and honorable student. He is guided in his moral conduct by well-defined principles of rectitude, from which he never deviates, and by an enlightened conscience, which he reverences as the voice of God. He scorns to commit in secret any mean or dishonorable act that he would be afraid to do in public. He has the same standard of propriety during vacation, among strangers in a hotel, in a railroad car, or elsewhere, that he had in the college under the eye of his superiors. He has the courage of his convictions, and he will modestly but firmly adhere to an unpopular cause which his sense of duty dictates, rather than espouse the popular measure that would gain him applause. Like the Apostle of the Gentiles, he is not disquieted by the unfavorable judgment of men, provided his actions meet the approval of his conscience; nor is he deterred from the straight line of conduct by sneers, or ridicule, or by the imputation of unworthy motives. He will never stoop to obtain, by ignoble methods, the vantage-ground over an opponent; for he does not regulate his actions by the false maxim, that the end justifies the means.

The youth who is actuated by self-respect has, also, great respect for others. As his own conduct is regulated by upright intentions, he is slow to impute dishonest motives to others. He does not pry into the secret springs of action in his companions ; hence, he is tolerant of their opinions. His regard and affection for them is neither impaired nor diminished, but rather strengthened, by occasional discussions and disagreements with them ; for he knows that the bond of fellowship is not of so fragile a temper as to be easily broken by an animated and good-natured tilt of words and clash of opinion.

A clergyman once had a warm and prolonged discussion with the late Bishop Gilmour of Cleveland. Fearing that he might have offended the bishop by the freedom and earnestness with which he had upheld his views, the priest went that night to the bishop's room and said to him : " I beg to apologize for the boldness with which I argued with you to-day." " No apology is necessary," replied the sturdy bishop: " I would not give a straw for you if you had not the courage to express your convictions. I honor you all the more for speaking out like a man."

It is needless to say that the habit of self-respect presupposes in its possessor an unusual degree of force and strength of character. Many a man who fearlessly rushed to the cannon's mouth, on the field of battle, has quailed before the shafts of ridicule and derision. Young George Arthur, mentioned in *Tom Brown's School Days,* by going down on his knees and saying his prayers at Rugby School, in defiance of the jibes and jeers of his associates, and of the slippers aimed at him, exhibited a higher type of courage than his companions of riper years would have displayed by jumping into the river, to rescue a school-mate amid the plaudits of the spectators.

St. Gregory remarks that David, dancing with pious enthusiasm before the Ark of the Lord, heedless of the scoffings and reproaches of Michol, his wife, displayed a greater virility of soul than when he slew the lion and smote Goliath ; for in his feats of valor he conquered an enemy, while in his act of devout humility he conquered himself.

Daniel O'Connell showed less manhood and force of character in fighting a duel with D'Esterre than he evinced in after years by declining a challenge. In the former instance, he was swayed by a depraved public sentiment; in the latter, he obeyed the voice of conscience, regardless of popular clamor and the imputation of cowardice.

In 1811, Napoleon convoked an assembly of prelates, to obtain their views on the expediency of formulating a new code of relations between the Holy See and the Church of France. When the members of the commission appeared before the emperor, the judgment which they expressed, though very obsequious to the imperial will, was very prejudicial to the independence of the Pope. Rev. Mr. Emery, Superior-General of the Sulpicians, was the only member of the commission who dissented from the sentiments of the Council, and he fortified his opinion with sound arguments. The attending prelates were startled by his boldness. They manifested their disapproval by looks of defiance, and by withdrawing some distance from him. When the meeting was over, they apologized to his Majesty for the indiscretion of their colleague ; but to their surprise and discomfiture, the emperor applauded the frankness and apostolic courage of the priest. Mr. Emery displayed a grander heroism

on this occasion than even Archbishop Affre, of Paris,
exhibited when he risked his life on the barricades in
his efforts to stem the effusion of blood. The latter,
when throwing himself between the two contending
parties as a voluntary peace-offering, was cheered by
the approval of the spectators, as well as by that of
his own conscience; whereas the former was supported
solely by a stern sense of duty. He had nothing to
expect but the enmity of the prelates and the indignation and chastisement of the most formidable and
autocratic monarch of Europe.

The vice opposed to self-respect is human respect.
Human respect is a base condescension by which, from
the fear of offending others, or from the desire of
acquiring their esteem, a man says or does what his
conscience conceives to be unlawful. It is not easy
to exaggerate the baneful influence which this moral
cowardice exerts on mankind, especially on impressionable youth, under the alluring guise of friendship and
love of applause.

St. Augustine tells us in his *Confessions*, that in his
youth he was ashamed to be outdone in crime by his most
depraved companions and that, through fear of incurring
their contempt, he sometimes boasted of evil deeds which
he had not committed : "Among my equals," he says,
"I was ashamed of a less depravity when I heard them
boast of their flagitiousness, yea, and the more they were
degraded, the more they boasted ; and I took pleasure,
not only in the gratification, but also in the praise of the
deed. I made myself worse than I was, that I might
not be dispraised ; and when in any thing I had not
sinned as the abandoned ones, I would say that I had

done what I had not done, that I might not seem contemptible in proportion as I was innocent." [1]

God has established in your breast the sacred tribunal of conscience, by whose dictates you are bound to decide. But in yielding to human respect, you act the part of a temporizing judge like Pilate, who pronounced sentence, not in accordance with the evidence before him, but in obedience to the clamors of the multitude. You sacrifice principle to expediency, you subordinate the voice of God to the voice of man, you surrender your Christian liberty and manly independence, and you become the slave of a fellow-creature. You are guilty of treason to your conscience, and that is the basest kind of treason.

The slave of human respect is like the idol mentioned by the Psalmist. It "has a mouth and speaks not, eyes and sees not, ears and hears not." This animated statue sees through the eyes of others, hears through the ears of others. He is a mere puppet, a mouthpiece echoing the sentiments of others. He tries to please men, which is praiseworthy; but at the expense of his sense of duty, which is wrong. St. Paul does, indeed, tell you "to have peace with all men;" but he adds the proviso, "if it be possible, as much as is in you." [2] And elsewhere he declares: "If I yet pleased men" (in violation of my conscience) "I should not be the servant of Christ." [3] Whoever tries to please everyone, right or wrong, may end by pleasing no one, and, by his fruitless efforts, illustrate the fable of the old man and his beast. An old man was riding on his ass to town, his son following on foot. The first traveller that he met, called him a brute for

---

[1] *Confessions*, Bk. II.   [2] Rom. XII. 18.   [3] Gal. I. 10.

riding at his ease while his son was walking. In obedience to the remonstrance, the old man dismounted, and allowed his son to take his place. The second traveller that he met, suggested that donkeys were made to serve; whereupon the old man clambered up and rode behind the boy. And now a third appears on the scene. He, in turn, loudly reproached the riders for laying so weighty a burden upon the poor animal, and declared that they should be made to change places. The old man readily complied, and took the ass upon his shoulders; but, while crossing a bridge, the affrighted animal fell into the river and was drowned.

The slavish betrayer of his conscience has no fixed principles, or he is afraid to act up to them. His little bark is without a rudder in mid-ocean, drifting about, tossed to and fro by every gale of opinion. His judgment, like the cameleon's skin, is tinged by the prevailing color of popular sentiment:

> "As the cameleon, which is known
> To have no colors of his own,
> But borrows from his neighbor's hue
> His white or black, his green or blue."

"He holds with the hare, and runs with the hounds." He usually sits on the fence, ready to jump on the winning side.

During our late Civil War, I read of a man who was travelling from the South to a northern State. The political creed of the passengers was canvassed on the train, as was not unfrequent in those days. Being roused from sleep, the usual question was put to him: "Where am I?" he asked. When informed that he was in Penn-

sylvania, he promptly declared himself a Union man.
His patriotism was colored by the political complexion
of the State through which he was passing. He would
probably have avowed himself an ardent Confederate, had
he been questioned in Virginia.

When Tullus Hostilius, King of Rome, was about to
engage in battle with two neighboring tribes, Mettius
Fufetius, the Alban leader and the ostensible ally of
Rome, secretly informed the tribes that he would help
them as soon as the engagement began. Meantime, with
his forces at some distance from the field of battle, he
watched the issue of the conflict. When the Romans
had conquered, Mettius hastened to congratulate Tullus
Hostilius. But the king, aware of the double part that he
had played, ordered him to be bound to four horses, and
torn limb from limb. The perfidy and fearful punishment of Mettius exemplify the vacillation and mental
disquietude of the temporizer, who is torn and distracted
by conflicting doubts as to the side he should espouse.

Though sometimes unjust, overbearing, and tyrannical,
yet the master of the African slave was but one. But
the slave of human respect is subject to as many masters
as there are individuals whose censure he dreads or whose
friendship he desires to conciliate, though at the sacrifice
of his sense of duty. In order to pay homage to these
masters, he is obliged to study their particular humors
and dispositions, to ascertain their actual temper of mind,
and to regulate his obsequiousness according to their ever-
varying passions and caprices. How lamentable to find
men of intelligence and of keen moral sense afraid to
stand for the right in the presence of others, who are
often inferior to them in everything except boldness,

whom in their hearts they despise, but whose ridicule and sneers they are not brave enough to withstand !

The slave of human respect must, assuredly, be contemptible in his own eyes when he searches his heart and contemplates his dissimulation and cowardice; for he uses his speech as if it were given him to conceal, and not to express, his thoughts. He is despised by his companions, for what respect can they have for one who has not the courage to speak and act out his honest convictions? He is odious to God, whose inspirations he rejects, and whose cause he betrays out of a servile fear of man. "No man," says our Lord, "can serve two masters. For either he will hate the one and love the other ; or he will sustain the one and despise the other."[1] He who has never made an enemy in the discharge of his public or private duties, and who has never run counter to public opinion, will hardly succeed in leaving a record that will command the impartial admiration of posterity.

I cannot better close these remarks on human respect than by commending the following appropriate texts of Scripture to the earnest consideration of the reader :

"He that shall be ashamed of Me and of My words, the Son of man also shall be ashamed of him when He shall come in the glory of His Father with the holy angels."[2]

"It is not good to have respect to persons in judgment. They that say to the wicked man, thou art just, shall be cursed by the people, and the tribes shall abhor them."[3]

[1] Matt. vi. 24.　　　[2] Mark viii. 38.　　　[3] Prov. xxiv. 23, 24.

"Who art thou that thou shouldst be afraid of a mortal man and of the son of man who shall wither like grass?"[1]

"But to me it is a very small thing to be judged by you or by man's day."[2]

"Whosoever shall confess Me before men, I will also confess him before My Father who is in heaven."[3]

---

[1] Isaiah LI. 12.　　　[2] I. Cor. IV. 3.　　　[3] Matt. X. 32.

CHAPTER X.

CHARITY, POLITENESS AND CHEERFULNESS.

GENUINE benevolence toward our companions in the seminary, and afterward toward our brother priests in the ministry, as well as toward our fellow-beings generally, is not only the most indispensable of virtues, but without it all the other virtues become like Dead-Sea apples, insipid and worthless. If the virtue of fraternal charity is imperatively enjoined on all men, it should be especially cultivated by clergymen in their intercourse with one another.

Our Blessed Redeemer sets so high a price on this virtue that He makes it the subject of His last discourse and prayer before His crucifixion, and leaves it as a dying legacy to His disciples, the proto-preachers of the law of love: "A new commandment," He says, "I give unto you that ye love one another. By this shall all men know that ye are My disciples, if ye have love one for another."[1] "I pray (Father) that they all may be one as Thou, Father, in Me, and I in Thee, that they also may be one in Us: that the world may believe that Thou hast sent Me."[2] We may judge of the value which Christ sets upon fraternal charity among His disciples, since He here declares that it was to be the test of discipleship, and the most luminous evidence of His own divine mission.

[1] John XIII. 34, 35.   [2] Ibid. XVII. 21.

St. Paul commends this queenly virtue with his usual force and condensation. If his words are always deserving of our respectful attention, they specially command our reverential consideration in the following exhortation which he delivers from his prison in Rome: "I, the prisoner of the Lord, beseech you that you walk worthy of the vocation in which you are called, with all humility and mildness, with patience, supporting one another in charity, careful to keep the unity of the Spirit in the bond of peace. *One body* and *one spirit* as ye are called in *one hope* of your calling. *One Lord, one faith,* one baptism. *One God and Father* of all who is above all, and through all, and in us all."[1]

You should love one another, says the Apostle, because you belong to the same collegiate body as students, or to the same clerical body as priests, or to the same mystical body as Christians; and you should manifest toward one another the same tender feeling and active sympathy that the organs of the human body exhibit toward one of its suffering members.

You should be united in the bonds of fellowship, because you are animated by the same divine *Spirit.* No matter what may be your grade or rank in the hierarchy of the Church, you are all illumined and sanctified by the same Holy Ghost, just as the members of your body are quickened by the same soul. "There are diversities of graces, but the same Spirit. There are diversities of ministries, but the same Lord. And there are diversities of operations, but the same God who worketh all in all."[2] As the members of the body move in harmony under the guidance of the soul, so should the members of Christ,

[1] Eph. IV. 1-6.   [2] I. Cor. XII. 4-6.

especially those of His teaching body, act in concert under the sweet influence of the Spirit of love and peace, for the Holy Ghost "is not the God of dissensions, but of peace."

You should be attached to one another, because *you have the same faith.* Your mission is to offer the same Sacrifice, to administer the same Sacraments, and to preach the same Gospel. You are the chosen leaders in the army of the Lord. There is usually an *esprit de corps,* a bond of fellowship among the members of the same profession or guild. You have often heard of the untiring efforts which a member of the Masonic Fraternity will make to protect a fellow-mason. Why should the bond of secrecy exert more influence on him than the hallowed bond of faith on you?

What will it avail you to have the light of faith without the fire of charity? "The devils believe and tremble." "If I speak," says the Apostle, "with the tongues of men and of angels, and have not charity, I am become as sounding brass, or a tinkling cymbal. And if I have prophecy, and should know all mysteries and all knowledge, and if I have all faith so as to remove mountains, and have not charity, I am nothing."[1] In vain are the roots of faith sound and healthy, if the fruits of the tree are inwardly eaten by the worm of rancor and jealousy. With what embarrassment and confusion must a minister of the Gospel address his congregation on the subject of fraternal concord, when he nourishes in his own breast a spirit of resentment toward a brother priest or one of his neighbors ! What fruit can be produced by a tree so poisoned? Will not his hearers, if conscious of

[1] I. Cor. XIII. 1, 2.

his enmity, say in their hearts what they may be deterred by a feeling of reverence from declaring with their lips : " Physician, heal thyself? "

You should exercise a spirit of benevolence toward one another, because "you are all called in the *one hope of* your vocation." You are all in the same bark of Peter, guided by the celestial chart which our great Captain has left us. You share the storms and sunshine of life. You are buffeted alike by the waves of adversity. You are impelled by the same winds. You are steering for the same eternal shores, aspiring to the same glorious heritage. As you hope to be loving fellow-citizens in the heavenly Jerusalem, why not cultivate those friendly relations in the land of your probation? Our dislikes and animosities will be irrevocably excluded from the kingdom of God. We must part with them here, or not enter there at all.

You should live as brothers, because you are brethren of the same *Lord* and Saviour Jesus Christ. The orthodox Crucifix represents Him with arms wide-stretched on the cross, to remind us that His love is all-embracing, and that He died for all. The Apostles had all abandoned their Master before the crucifixion. One of them had denied Him, another had betrayed Him. When He arose from the grave, He made no allusion to their infidelity, but He sent them this message of love: "Go and tell My disciples that I ascend to their Father and to My Father, to their God and to My God." The very first Apostle to whom He appeared, was the one that had denied Him. With such an example before us, how can we steel our heart against an offending brother? How can we refuse to speak to him for whom Christ did not disdain to die?

Lastly, you should cherish a mutual brotherly affection, because you are children of "one God and Father of all who is above all, and through all, and in us all."

These considerations are but a running commentary on the words of St. Paul. The same Apostle will now point out to us the salient features of charity, and the manner of exercising that royal virtue: "Charity is patient, is kind. Charity envieth not, dealeth not perversely, is not puffed up, is not ambitious, seeketh not her own, is not provoked to anger, thinketh no evil, rejoiceth not in iniquity, but rejoiceth with the truth: beareth all things, hopeth all things, endureth all things." [1]

Let me briefly refer to one characteristic form of charity, which is most frequently demanded of us in the daily walks of life. I refer to Christian politeness. Politeness, or courtesy, is not governed by artificial rules. It is the spontaneous expression by word and act of genuine kindness of heart. As St. Francis de Sales observes, it resembles water "which is best when clearest, most simple, and without taste." It has been well remarked that a beautiful form is more attractive than a beautiful face, and beautiful behaviour is more attractive than a beautiful form. Affability and good breeding are indispensable for a clergyman in his intercourse with the world; and the want of them is apt to impair, if it does not neutralize, his usefulness. "Civility," says Lady Montague, "costs nothing and buys everything."

I give it as my solemn conviction, that one of the best means that a priest can adopt for preserving peace and concord among the members of his household and his colleagues, is to observe the canons of politeness and the

[1] I. Cor. XIII. 4–7.

rules of exterior decorum, though without permitting them to degenerate into cold and rigid formality. I am equally persuaded that the studied reserve and misunderstanding sometimes existing among clergymen of the same household and neighborhood, may often be traced to the neglect of these exterior acts of courtesy toward one another.

"Wisdom and virtue," observes Samuel Johnson, "are by no means sufficient, without the supplemental laws of good-breeding, to secure freedom from degenerating into rudeness, or self-esteem from swelling into insolence; a thousand incivilities may be committed, and a thousand offices neglected, without any remorse of conscience or reproach from reason."[1]

But, perhaps, you will say: I admit, indeed, the propriety of exhibiting marks of decorum to strangers and to friends whom we meet only occasionally, but what is the use of observing polite behaviour toward the members of one's own household with whom we habitually come in contact? I answer: It is just because you meet them so frequently that you should extend to them marks of civility. Is not politeness a social and domestic virtue? And who has a greater claim to its exercise than your fellow-laborers and the other members of your family? The most influential of virtues are those that are most in request for daily use, just as water, air, fire and light are the most essential elements of life and health. The precious gems of domestic charity hang like pearls on slender threads, and these threads are common civility and gentle manners. As religion cannot long subsist in the heart without the external forms of ceremony, so charity cannot long abide in the household without polite behaviour and good-breeding.

[1] The Rambler.

Cheerfulness is the daughter of innocence and charity; and therefore the soul that is the seat of guilelessness and pure affection, is habitually joyous. "The voice of rejoicing and of salvation is in the tabernacles of the just."[1] "The kingdom of God is not meat and drink; but justice, and peace, and joy in the Holy Ghost."[2] Cheerfulness does not consist in a fitful, gushing and boisterous mirthfulness which soon evaporates, but it is a steady stream of the milk of human kindness flowing from a serene heart at peace with God and man. A person of a happy frame of mind is not affected by the clouds and sunshine of daily life: "Rich or poor, if his heart is good, his countenance shall be cheerful at all times."[3]

✓ A cheerful disposition contributes much to the rational enjoyment of life. So attractive is a man of a sunny nature, that we are instinctively drawn toward him, while we are involuntarily repelled by an individual of a sour disposition.

Cheerfulness imparts a certain elasticity to our spirits, and a spring to our movements. The man of a fretful humor often sinks under his burden; while the buoyant man is borne on the wings of hope and love. "I have run," says the Prophet, "in the way of Thy Commandments, when Thou didst enlarge my heart."[4]

Some are endowed by nature with a gladsome disposition; a melancholy temperament is inborn in others. Cheerfulness, however, like every other habit, can be trained and developed.

✓ Cultivate, therefore, a joyous spirit, and let its rays be diffused throughout every home which you will enter to dispense the Bread of life, and to administer the consolations of religion; for "God loveth a cheerful giver."

[1] Ps. CXVII. 15. [2] Rom. XIV. 17. [3] Ecclus. XXVI. 4. [4] Ps. CXVIII.

Above all, let them radiate among the members of your own household.

Our diocesan clergy residing in the same presbytery, have few occasions to meet and converse together during the day, except at meals. Hence they should profit by the time devoted to bodily refection, by consecrating those moments also to wholesome relaxation of mind, like the primitive Christians who " took their meat with gladness and simplicity of heart."[1]

As a bright and airy dining room is conducive to physical health, so a warm and genial disposition helps digestion, and is profitable to the soul; while a gloomy, morose, and uncongenial temper is hurtful to mind and body. " Drive away sadness far from thee, for sadness hath killed many, and there is no profit in it."[2]

We may apply to the cheerful man what the Scripture says of Wisdom : " Her conversation hath no bitterness, nor her company any tediousness, but joy and gladness."[3]

By cordiality of manner during the meal, by striving to be agreeable to the company, by avoiding subjects calculated to wound or irritate those around you, or that may be injurious to the good name of others; by seasoning the food with the salt of entertaining and edifying conversation, you will unbend the bow strained by mental or physical exertion; you will lighten the labors, and sweeten the cares of the ministry; you will interchange with your colleagues useful points of information; you will foster a more hearty co-operation in the work of the parish; you will strengthen the bonds of fraternal fellowship and good will among your companions, and will realize the truth of the Prophet's words: " Behold how good and how pleasant it is for brethren to dwell together in unity."[4]

[1]Acts II. 46.   [2]Ecclus. xxx. 24, 25.   [3]Wis. viii. 16.   [4]Ps. cxxxii. 1.

CHAPTER XI.

Hindrances to Charity.

THE bonds of fraternal charity are usually weakened or dissolved among clergymen by one of the four following causes:

First: Discords and contentions may be fomented among students and priests by uncongeniality and incompatibility of temper; for there are diversities of character and temperament in collegiate and clerical circles, as well as in the world at large. Some are constitutionally warm-hearted and affectionate; others are cold and reserved. Some are naturally quick and hot-tempered; others are cool and self-possessed. One is of a suspicious and quarrelsome disposition; another is of a peaceful and benevolent nature. One is rude and undisciplined; another has affable and refined manners. "It is no great thing," says Kempis, "to associate with the good and gentle; for this is naturally pleasing to all, and every one preferreth peace, and loveth best those that have like sentiments. But to be able to live peaceably with the hard and the perverse, or with the undisciplined, and those that contradict us, is a great grace, and a highly commendable and manly thing."[1]

[1] Bk. II. Ch. III.

107

The man that has the habit of wandering abroad and contemplating the defects of his neighbor, has little time for introspection and for correcting his own moral delinquencies. We shall, therefore, preserve peace in our own heart and promote that of others by overlooking or condoning their faults, and by studying to get rid of our own. It is not improbable that, while we are observing the mote in our brother's eye, he is looking at the beam in ours. If he sometimes taxes our patience, we may often be a source of disquietude to him.

Secondly : Another cause of dissensions are <u>envy and jealousy</u>. A student may happen to be more talented and diligent than some of his companions. He makes greater progress in his studies, he receives more attention and more expressions of approval from his professor, and he is especially popular among his fellow-students. Some of his less favored associates are stung by the green-eyed monster jealousy. They feel slighted, and imagine that they are unfairly dealt with. They suspect their superiors of undue partiality. They detect imaginary faults in their gifted companion, and regard him as a personal enemy. They speak disparagingly of him, or kill him with faint praise. Like the envious brothers of the patriarch Joseph, they put a sinister construction on his most harmless words, and they accuse him of over-weening ambition.

We should guard against jealousy, which is a source of injury to others and of misery to ourselves. St. Paul tells us "to rejoice with those that rejoice, to weep with those that weep." We manifest greater magnanimity in rejoicing than in weeping, because in sympathizing with others, we are following the impulse of nature, we are tacitly indulging self, we are exercising unconscious superiority and a patronizing spirit over those with whom we condole. But in rejoicing with them that rejoice, we are performing an act of unselfish generosity. Moreover, as faith is inferior to charity, so is compassion inferior to rejoicing. In commiserating the sorrowful, we are practising a virtue necessarily confined to the present life; whereas, the charity that rejoiceth with the happy, is a virtue that will be perfected in heaven.

Nay, must we not fear that the demon of jealousy may sometimes find access to the hearts of clergymen of the same household? One may be envious of another, because he is more popular with the congregation; he has more engaging manners, more winning ways. His sermons are more attractive, his confessional more frequented; he makes more converts, and he is otherwise more sought after.

Again, a pastor observes that the rector of a neighboring parish is making large accessions to his congregation (without, however, any violation of the diocesan statutes, or of the rules of justice and charity). Although the success of this rector is due to his unction and force in the pulpit, to his zeal in the confessional, to his devotedness to the sick and the afflicted, he becomes the object of his brother's enmity and the victim of his unfavorable comments.

If we are actuated by a genuine zeal for God's honor and the extension of His kingdom, we shall rejoice in the successful labors of our brother priest as in our own. The merchant views a lucrative business transaction of his partner with as keen a sense of satisfaction as if he had accomplished it himself, because he has an equal share in the profits. And do we not participate in the merits of our colleague's prosperous ministry by rejoicing in it? When Josue heard that some men were sharing in the prophetic office of Moses, he said to the Lawgiver: "My lord, forbid them." But Moses answered: "Why hast thou emulation for me? O that all the people might prophesy, and that the Lord would give them His Spirit!"[1]

When John told his Master that he had forbidden a man to cast out devils, because he was not a follower of the apostolic band, our Lord said to him: "Do not forbid him. For he that is not against you, is for you."[2] How much more forcibly do the words of Christ apply to your brother priest who is associated with you in the apostolic ministry!

St. Paul thus writes of certain preachers who were envious of his honor and success: "But what then? So that by all means, whether by occasion, or in truth, Christ be preached; in this also I rejoice, yea, and I will rejoice."[3]

Our Saviour reproved the Apostles, when they were contending among themselves as to which of them seemed to be the greater, and He gave them this lesson of humility: "But he that is the greater among you, let him become as the younger; and he that is the leader as he that serveth."[4] Pride is the root of envy. We are emulous, indeed, of God's glory, but we would have some of its rays descend on ourselves. The words of Christ are intended not only as an instruction to His disciples, but also as a warning and an example to us.

[1] Num. XI. 28, 29.　　　　[3] Phil. 1. 18.
[2] Mark IX. 38, 39.　　　　[4] Luke XXII. 26.

Thirdly. Animosities are engendered, also, by religious discussions; and the *odium theologicum*, though more rare than other causes of enmity, is proverbially intense and implacable. The contestants in the controversy confine themselves for awhile to the subjects under consideration. After hotly arguing the question for a time, they gradually glide into personalities, and impugn each other's motives. While both were probably within the line of orthodoxy, one took a conservative, the other a liberal view of the subject. The one leaned to the side of authority, the other contended for freedom. The conservative begins to call his liberal opponent a radical; the liberal stamps the conservative a reactionary. The conservative goes a step further, and throws out thinly veiled hints about his antagonist's heterodoxy—a method of controversy which is aptly styled "poisoning the wells." The liberal retaliates by calling his opponent a fossil. The respective allies of the two combatants take up the dispute and fan the flame. The arena of this war of words is still more widened when the newspapers plunge into the debate and sometimes, without caring to ascertain the original basis of the discussion, decide the dispute with oracular dogmatism according to their individual prejudices. Once the subject of discussion has drifted away into the open sea of promiscuous controversy, it is as hard to lead it back to its first moorings as to gather up feathers scattered by the winds.

St. Paul thus describes the contentious man: "He is proud, knowing nothing, but sick about questions and strifes of words, from which arise envies, contentions, blasphemies, evil suspicions, conflicts of men." [1] Later,

¹ I. Tim. vi. 4, 5.

he exhorts Timothy to "avoid foolish and unlearned questions, knowing that they beget strifes. But the servant of the Lord must not wrangle, but be mild toward all men, apt to teach, patient, with modesty admonishing them that resist the truth."[1]

✓ Religious discussions are not an evil in themselves. On the contrary, they are an evidence of a healthy mental activity, a proof of zeal for the cause of truth. But in order that they may be useful and edifying, the parties engaged in them should be actuated solely by a love for truth. They should present their views with calmness and moderation; they should adhere with conscientious fidelity to the question under consideration, without encumbering it with side issues or irrelevant matter; they should invariably treat their opponent with courtesy and benevolence, never ascribing to him base or sinister motives; and they should abandon the controversy if they discover that charity is likely to be offended by it. In a word, the motto of St. Vincent Lerins should be studiously adhered to: " *In necessariis unitas, in dubiis libertas, in omnibus caritas.*"

"Differences always have been, always will be in the Church," writes Cardinal Newman; "and Christians would have ceased to have spiritual and intellectual life, if such differences did not exist. It is part of their militant state. No human power can hinder it; nor, if it attempted it, could do more than make a solitude and call it peace. And thus thinking that man cannot hinder it, however much he try, I have no great anxiety or trouble. Man cannot, and God will not. He means such differences to be an exercise of charity. Of course I wish as

[1] II. Tim. II. 23, 25.

much as possible to agree with all my friends; but if, in spite of my utmost efforts, they go beyond me or come short of me, I can't help it and take it easy." [1]

Lawyers and statesmen usually exhibit toward one another, even in the heat of discussion, a courtesy and forbearance worthy of our praise and imitation. They rarely permit the clash of professional strife to cause any breach in their friendly relations. William Wirt, the celebrated Maryland lawyer, and Daniel Webster were once pitted against each other in an important suit in Boston. Notwithstanding their divergence on national and State politics, and their impassioned efforts for their respective clients, Mr. Wirt writes home from Boston that he received from Mr. Webster cordiality of attention and warmth of hospitality that could not be exceeded. [2]

I once listened in the Senate to a speech of Mr. Blaine, in which he vehemently assailed the policy of the Democratic party. After concluding his remarks, he crossed to the other side of the chamber, and held a familiar conversation with a leading Democratic Senator. The same evening, on meeting the latter statesman, I expressed my surprise that he should be on terms so intimate with a political antagonist. "O," he replied, "we don't allow our official utterances to mar our personal friendship."

Fourthly. Nationalism is another occasion of the breach of charity among students and priests. To scorn and despise a fellow-clergyman because he happens to be of a different nationality from ourselves, is a sentiment as senseless as it is criminal.

[1] Letter to W. G. Ward.
[2] Memoirs of William Wirt (Kennedy).

Was not the Divine Head of the Church a foreigner?
And yet we have never heard of Christians of any country
being ashamed of the Founder of the Christian religion
because he was an alien. Did the Roman Empire reject
the teachings of the Apostles, because they were not " to
the manor born?" Did the Corinthians and the Athenians refuse to listen to Paul, because he was a native of
Tarsus? Was Peter less honored in Antioch, because he
was born in Galilee? Was John less beloved in Ephesus,
because he was a Jew? England cherished her apostle
Augustine none the less, although he was sent to her from
across the Channel. Ireland's veneration for Patrick is
as strong as it would have been had he claimed the Green
Isle for his birth-place. Germany reveres her apostle
Boniface, though he was an Englishman; and France has
erected one of her grandest churches to St. Owen, an
Irishman. St. Francis Xavier, the apostle of India, was
a Spaniard. The name of the Belgian, Father De Smet,
is held in benediction among the Indian tribes of North
America.

Christianity is not indigenous to any soil. Its growth
throughout the world would have been absolutely impossible, if its seed had not been planted originally by alien
missionaries.

The Church of Christ is essentially Catholic, or world-
wide, and the bond of fellowship between her consecrated
sons is not restricted by State lines or national boundaries.
I am associated with all Americans by the ties of citizenship and patriotism. I am associated with all Catholics
by the ties of faith, hope, and charity. I am associated
with all priests by the closer ties of apostolic brotherhood

whereby we are made the fellow-"ministers of Christ and the dispensers of the mysteries of God." [1]

Could our Lord have more strikingly contrasted the sectionalism of the Jewish priest with the all-embracing scope of the Christian minister than He has done in the parable of the Good Samaritan? The intercourse and beneficence of the Hebrew priest were confined to his own nation. The good fellowship and friendly relations of the Christian priest are to extend to his brethren of all nations. I do not see how any Catholic clergyman can seriously read this parable, and not blush for shame at the narrow spirit of provincialism by which he excludes from his benevolence a brother priest, because he happened to be born in another country, or has a mother-tongue different from his own.

If a provincial or sectional spirit would be reprehensible among the clergy of Europe, which for centuries has been enjoying the blessings of Christian faith, a like prejudice would exhibit base ingratitude on the part of our native clergy, since our country is not only exclusively indebted to immigrant missionaries for the first seeds of faith sown here, but is also largely beholden to them for the continuous cultivation of this portion of the Lord's vineyard to the present day.

But if our American clergy would sin against charity in discriminating against their brethren of foreign birth, how shall we characterize the latter if they manifest a clannish disposition with respect to priests of American birth? It is sweet, indeed, and honorable in them to love and cherish the land of their origin; but it is their solemn and sacred duty to identify themselves with the

[1] I. Cor. iv. 1.

country of their adoption, where they intend to live and die, and where they enjoy the blessings of civil and religious liberty.

To the honor of our Catholic clergy, it must be said, that they have betrayed this sectional animosity much less frequently than the ministers of Protestant denominations. While the leading sects became hopelessly divided during our Civil War on the subject of slavery and State rights, the bond of fraternity was never broken nor even strained among the Catholic clergy south and north of Mason and Dixon's line.

Nothing contributes better to efface race prejudices than the cohabitation under the same roof of students of diverse races.

The alumni of St. Mary's Seminary in Baltimore represent a great variety of nations, and yet I have never heard that this circumstance had engendered any feeling of antipathy or discord among them. On the contrary, this very diversity of origin broadens and deepens their sympathies, and tends to divest them of the narrowness and provincialism characteristic of those who have spent their lives among their own kindred, within the confines of their native homes.

I sat at dinner some time ago with a body of clergy, who represented fourteen different nationalities, and to whom the words of the Psalmist could be applied : " Behold how good and how pleasant a thing it is for brethren to dwell together in unity !"

"When peers thus knit, a kingdom ever stands." [1]

I shall conclude this chapter with a brief portrayal of the exemplary Christian scholar :

[1] Pericles, Act II.

The model student is always a welcome visitor to the circle of his companions. Unconsciously he sheds sunshine around him. He is frank and ingenuous without being oracular and dogmatic. He is neither a silent nor a garrulous bore. He is an attentive listener, as well as an agreeable talker. He is earnest in argument, though not disputatious. He discusses questions with spirit, but without loss of temper. He meets his opponent's arguments without being betrayed into the common fault of becoming personal by assailing his opponent himself or impugning his motives.

He can be humorous and entertaining without ever descending to grossness, buffoonery, or indecency. He has the gift of amusing, without wounding, his companions. His shafts of wit leave no sting after them. He never intentionally, and rarely unintentionally, hurts the feelings of others. He does not bristle nor lose his temper at a repartee. He takes it with good grace, and he even joins in the merriment at his expense. He is free from the childish sensitiveness that is apt to detect a vicious motive in a bantering word. He knows that "Charity is not provoked to anger, thinketh no evil, is not suspicious." He never repeats a story that would be hurtful or injurious to another. He is a non-conductor of the electric current of calumny; it is buried in his own breast.

In the field of college games and amusements, or in that of intellectual strife, he is not elated by success nor depressed by defeat. He rejoices with the victor, he sympathizes with the vanquished, and he encourages the weak and timid. He knows how to praise a friend without flattering him, and to correct him without giving

offence.   As true fellowship is based on virtue, the
Christian disciple will never sacrifice truth and honor
to friendship.   He follows the maxim of Aristotle:
"*Amicus Plato, amicus Socrates, sed magis amica veri-
tas.*" [1]   He is punctual in his engagements, faithful to
his promises, and prompt in the payment of his debts.

He is opposed to party or factious spirit as a student in
college, or as a priest in the ministry, where all should
live as brethren. While he cherishes a few special friends,
he has a heart full of benevolence for all.   He is never
for Paul or Apollo, but always for Christ.

---

[1] Plato is my friend, Socrates is my friend, but truth is a friend that
I value above both.

CHAPTER XII.

THE SPIRIT OF POVERTY.

IF wealth could contribute to the peace and happiness, as well as to the real glory of the priesthood and the salvation of souls, Christ would certainly have chosen for Himself and have recommended to His Apostles, a life of affluence and luxury.

But the experience of nineteen centuries has amply proved that the Christian ministers who have set their heart on the accumulation of money, to the neglect of higher and holier interests, have never been happy, nor has their honor been augmented in public estimation by their temporal possessions. "They have forsaken the Fountain of living waters, and have digged to themselves cisterns, broken cisterns, which can hold no water."[1]

We know that Christ was born in the most abject poverty From His childhood to His crucifixion, He was destitute of all the luxury, and even of many of the comforts of life. He could say of Himself what few vagrants and tramps can affirm of themselves: "The foxes have holes, and the birds of the air nests; but the Son of Man hath not where to lay His head."[2] He had neither house nor garden, vineyard nor farm. He had barely enough to supply Himself and His disciples with

---

[1] Jer. II. 13.   [2] Luke IX. 58.

the necessaries of life. We know that, on one occasion, He and Peter did not possess between them as much as a didrachma to pay the tax.[1] St. Paul says that Jesus Christ "being rich, He became poor for your sake that, through His poverty, you might be rich."[2]

The first sentence that He utters to His disciples in His Sermon on the Mount, is a declaration of the blessedness of voluntary poverty : "Blessed are the poor in spirit, for theirs is the kingdom of heaven."[3]

The great prophets of old, Elias and Eliseus, Isaiah and Jeremias, led a life of great austerity and privation. Their food was simple and precarious; their clothing coarse and scanty; and they had no fixed abode. In the words of the Apostle, "They wandered about in sheep-skins, in goat-skins, being in want, distressed, afflicted, of whom the world was not worthy, wandering in deserts, in mountains, and in dens, and in caves of the earth."[4]

St. John the Baptist, the Precursor of our Saviour, had neither an extensive wardrobe nor sumptuous fare. His dress consisted of camels' hair, and his food of locusts and wild honey.

We are told in the Gospel that, on a certain occasion, "Jesus went through the corn on the Sabbath, and His disciples *being hungry*, began to pluck the ears and to eat."[5] How eloquently does this simple incident unfold to us the privations endured by the Apostles, who relieved their hunger by eating a few ears of corn in their hasty passage through a field ! How rarely are our most destitute missionaries reduced to such straits as to be obliged to make their daily round on an empty stomach !

[1] Matt. xvii. 23.   [3] Matt. v. 3.   [5] Matt. xii. 1.
[2] II. Cor. viii. 9.   [4] Heb. xi. 37, 38.

✓ When Peter and John were asked for alms by the lame
man at the gate of the Temple, Peter said : "Silver and
gold I have none ; but what I have, I give thee : in the
name of Jesus Christ of Nazareth, arise and walk."[1]
How sublime is apostolic poverty when allied with apostolic power ! St. Thomas Aquinas once paid a visit to
Pope Innocent IV., while a heap of gold coins happened
to be lying on his table. The Pontiff, pointing to the
gold, playfully remarked to the saint : " You see, Brother
Thomas, that I cannot say with Peter : 'Silver and gold
I have not.'" "True," modestly replied the Angelic
Doctor, " neither can your Holiness say with Peter : 'In
the name of Jesus Christ of Nazareth, arise and walk.'"
The Pontiff humbly felt that Peter possessed the richer
treasure.[2]

St. Paul, speaking of himself and his fellow-Apostles,
says : " Even unto this hour we both hunger and thirst,
and are naked, and are buffeted, and have no fixed abode,
and we labor working with our own hands."[3] Again he
says : We are " as sorrowful yet always rejoicing, as
needy, yet enriching many, as having nothing, and possessing all things."[4] Writing to the Thessalonians, he
says : " You remember, brethren, our labor and toil :
working night and day, lest we should be chargeable to
any of you, we preached among you the Gospel of God."[5]

Is it probable that the religious revolution of the sixteenth century would have caused so terrible an upheaval
in England had not the king and his courtiers been allured
by the enormous wealth and temporal possessions of some

[1] Acts iii. 6.
[2] Saint Jure, L' Homme Religieux.
[3] I. Cor. iv. 11, 12.
[4] II. Cor. vi. 10.
[5] I. Thess. ii. 9.

of the churchmen and ecclesiastical institutions of the realm?

The privations and labors endured by many of the pioneer bishops and missionary priests of the United States, were a counterpart of the lives of the Apostles themselves.

The Rev. Gabriel Bruté (afterward Bishop of Vincennes) when stationed as a priest at Emmittsburg, was accustomed to walk from that place to Baltimore, a distance of sixty miles. A crust of bread, which he carried with him, and a glass of water formed his only refection on the way.

I have known missionaries in the Carolinas who were obliged to carry on their backs the *chapelle*, or case containing the sacred vestments, as they traversed the mountains, visiting the scattered members of their flock, not knowing where they would obtain a scanty meal, nor where lay their head at night. Their physical sufferings, moreover, were in no small measure aggravated by the suspicion, and even hostility, with which they were regarded by the Protestant community, who were then intensely prejudiced against the Catholic religion.

A clergyman in North Carolina used playfully to remark that he could not afford to commit a mortal sin, as he had not sufficient means to resort for confession to the nearest priest, who resided over one hundred miles from him.

The Rev. Jacob A. Walter, who died in Washington, in 1894, was forty years a priest, and as poor on the day of his death as on that of his ordination. Whilst he was Rector of St. Patrick's Church, large sums of money fell into his hands; but none of it clung to them. It was distributed among the orphans, or secretly dispensed to the poor, and especially to genteel, but indigent applicants for office in the Departments, who daily called on him. Profuse in his hospitality to visiting clergy, his own private apartment was more destitute of ornaments and comforts than that of a seminarian.

I have visited some of the Indian Missions of New Mexico, and have conversed with missionaries from Alaska. These self-denying men renounce the attractions of civilized life. They share in the poverty and in the homely, even repulsive, fare of the tribes to whom they are sent to preach the Gospel.

The acquisition of immense revenues and the display of courtly pomp on the part of many churchmen in some of the old monarchies of Europe, are easily explained, if not excused. In ages of military sway, especially when ministers of the Gospel were associated with the civil functionaries in upholding the authority of the government, public sentiment was not shocked or surprised at seeing the spiritual rulers sharing in some of the temporal possessions and earthly grandeur with which the civil power was surrounded.

But no such plea can be advanced in our country where union of Church and State does not exist, where republican simplicity obtains, and where the dignity of Christ's representative is estimated not by his elevated rank or the extent of his wealth, but by the splendor of his virtues.

✓ 1°. The first fruit, or practical application of poverty of spirit, consists in the exercise of judicious economy. We are to regard ourselves as the stewards rather than as the absolute owners of what we possess. What a beautiful double lesson of plain-living and frugality is found in the Gospel recording the multiplication of loaves in the desert! Five barley loaves and two fishes are miraculously multiplied to such an extent as to supply the wants of five thousand men, besides women and children. First, they were barley loaves, the usual food of the common people, in contradistinction from wheaten bread, the food of the rich in those days. We may also assume that this was the ordinary food of Christ's disciples, as it was the only bread they carried with them. Secondly, God, our Saviour, infinite in creative power, who gives fecundity to the earth, who for forty years fed the Israelites in the wilderness, commands that the fragments of the bread be gathered up, "lest they be wasted." It is not improbable that Christ Himself, as well as His disciples, were afterward sustained by these fragments.

But God forbid that we should permit our habits of economy to degenerate into avarice, to savor of penuriousness, or to exempt us from the sacred duties of hospitality so strongly recommended in Sacred Scripture! Parsimony is not economy. A priest may be actually poor, and yet like Judas devoured by the passion of covetousness. Another may abound in wealth, and yet possess a lofty spirit of detachment like St. Charles Borromeo. Genuine poverty of spirit consists in abstemiousness toward ourselves and generosity in responding to the calls of charity. "A man's poverty before God," says St. Augustine, "is judged by the disposition of his heart, and not by his coffers. God regards not the wealth, but the attachment to it."

St. Francis de Sales had a large house in Annecy. But he habitually occupied a poor, dingy room, which he called *Francis' room*. He had another, spacious and well-furnished, for the accommodation of his guests, and this he called the *Bishop's room*.

When a priest is known to be a man of frugal and abstemious habits, his exhortations to his people to be patient in privation, will have immeasureably more weight than they would possess if he had the reputation of accumulating money and indulging in sumptuous fare.

2°. We should submit with patience, and even with cheerfulness, to the privations and discomforts which may be incident to the exercise of the ministry. Happy is he who can maintain the same composure of mind that the Apostle exhibited amid the vicissitudes of his laborious life: "I have learned in whatever state I am, to be content therewith. I know both how to be brought low, and I know how to abound: (everywhere and in all things I am instructed) both to be full and to be hungry; both to abound and to suffer need." [1] Would to God that every priest would, likewise, be content with his mission whether rich or poor, sparsely or densely populated, in the city or in the country !

I have known young lawyers and doctors, after they had graduated and entered on their professional career, to spend some years in very straitened circumstances, the former having few clients, the latter few patients to patronize them. If these young men endure without murmuring months and years of indigence; if they heroically confront a cold and unsympathizing world, without a friend to cheer them or a patron to commend them to public favor, surely, young clergymen, who serve a mortified Master, ought not to yield to discontent and com-

[1] Phil. iv. 11, 12.

plaints when they are met by hardships in the work of the ministry.

A commander selects for a post of danger and privation the bravest and most intrepid of his captains. In like manner, the bishop not unfrequently singles out for the poorest and most trying field the most devoted and self-denying missionary who is ready to endure the poverty and inconveniences of life; for he knows how hurtful it would be to a mission to have assigned to it a priest who is wedded to the comforts of life, and who shrinks from hard labor and physical suffering. What a consolation are such generous souls to their chief pastor! How precious are they in his sight! They complain not that they do not receive the full salary commonly allowed to clergymen. Like the Apostle, they rejoice in their tribulation, and ever make merry over their discomforts. They are generally the happiest and most light-hearted of men, because they have the affection of their flock and the testimony of a good conscience, which is infinitely more valuable than gold and silver.

When did such servants of God ever want the necessaries of life, and when were they reduced to the straits to which many young lawyers, physicians, and literary men are sometimes subjected? The faithful, as a rule, are willing to share their last dollar with a devoted priest. Must not the poorest laborer in the Lord's vineyard be compelled to answer as the Apostles did when they were thus questioned by their Master: "When I sent you without purse and scrip and shoes, did you want any thing? But they said, nothing." [1]

[1] Luke xxii. 35, 36.

3°. It is a mark of great self-denial, as well as of Christian politeness, to cultivate a spirit of indifference regarding the food that is set before us, and to accommodate ourselves to the circumstances in which we are placed, conformably with this injunction of our Lord: " In the same house remain, eating and drinking *such things as they have.*" [1] Let us not make an unsavory and uninviting meal more unpalatable by pouring on it the vinegar of discontent, but rather season it with the sauce of good humor and gentle breeding, never complaining of the meat that is served, nor making it the subject of conversation.

Christ manifested an absolute indifference about faring sumptuously or meagrely. To-day, He is entertained by Zaccheus with the choicest viands set before Him; another day, He is living on barley bread and fishes with His disciples. He always deports Himself as a *gentleman* in the highest sense of the word. He never discusses the food, unless to make it the text of a nobler subject.

It is true, indeed, that the diocesan priest makes no special vow of poverty. But it is equally true, that, at his ordination, he takes the Lord as the portion of his inheritance. To him may be truly applied the words addressed to the priests of the Old Law: " They shall have no inheritance, I am their inheritance; neither shall you give them any possession in Israel, for I am their possession." [2] " He who has God for the portion of his heritage," says St. Ambrose, " becomes the possessor of all nature, for with his Master he has become the master of the universe." He should be the master, not the slave,

[1] Luke x. 7.   [2] Ezec. xliv. 28.

of wealth ; and he should not set his heart on the accumulation of money.

Again, though it is difficult, and even impracticable,
to carry out literally this injunction of our Lord, " Take
neither staff, nor scrip, nor bread, nor money;"[1] nevertheless, the principle of self-denial implied in these words
always remains.   They should serve, at least, to remind
us that He is the Staff on which we are to lean, the
Bread that is to sustain us, and the Treasure we are to
prize above all earthly riches.

Every priest would do well to ponder the words of
Paul to his disciple Timothy : " Godliness with contentment is great gain.   For we brought nothing into this
world, and certainly we can carry nothing out.   But
having food and wherewith to be covered, with these we
are content.   For they that will become rich, fall into
temptation and into the snare of the devil, and into many
unprofitable and hurtful desires which drown men into
destruction and perdition.   For the desire of money is
the root of all evils ; which some coveting have erred
from the faith, and have entangled themselves in many
sorrows.   But thou, O man of God, fly these things ;
and pursue justice, godliness, faith, charity, patience, mildness."[2]   " Blessed is the rich man," and thrice blessed is
the priest, " that is found without blemish, and that hath
not gone after gold, nor put his trust in money nor in
treasures.   Who is he, and we will praise him ? for he
hath done wonderful things in his life.   He shall have
glory everlasting."[3]   So rare and sublime is this virtue
of detachment that its possessor is said by the Sacred

[1] Luke ix. 3.   [2] I. Tim. vi. 6–11.   [3] Ecclus. xxxi. 8–10.

Writer to have accomplished wonders, yea, miracles of grace. Happy is the priest who can say from his heart with the Wise Man : O Lord, " give me neither beggary nor riches. Give me only the necessaries of life." [1]

The Third Plenary Council of Baltimore,[2] as well as the Third Provincial Council of New York, earnestly recommends that clergymen should not die intestate, but should make their will while they are in the full possession of their faculties. By this prudent foresight, they can conscientiously and freely dispose of the means of which they may die possessed ; they will take precautions against expensive and scandalous litigations, and they will enable their executor to avoid the danger of confounding the revenues of the Church with their personal property.

If, at the close of his life, the servant of God is possessed of means, he will merit the benediction of Heaven, the praise of his flock, and the admiration of all good men, by leaving them to religious and charitable purposes, bequeathing to his family his blessing with some modest tokens of filial or fraternal affection. I have known several pious clergymen to have made this disposition of their personal fortune. The memory of their good deeds is a more precious legacy than earthly possessions.

No spectacle, on the other hand, is more disedifying than that of a priest dying rich, and leaving his inheritance to his family. He may violate no law of justice, but does he not do violence to the Catholic conscience? Does he not grieve his own spiritual children and compel them to the silence of charity when they would sound

[1] Prov. xxx. 8.   [2] III. Plen. Council, No. 277.

9

his praise? Does he not arouse the unfavorable criticism of the public at large?

I may conclude in the words of Cardinal Manning: "It is the part of honor in a good priest to die without sins, without debts, and without wealth acquired in the work of the ministry."

CHAPTER XIII.

SACERDOTAL CHASTITY.

CHASTITY is the most glorious, the most distinctive, and the most indispensable ornament of a priest. He might possess the faith of Abraham, the wisdom of Solomon, the piety of David, the zeal of Elias, the patience of Job, the apostolic heroism of John the Baptist, and the eloquence of Paul, and yet his spiritual armor would be incomplete, if it were not crowned with the helmet of sacerdotal chastity. The other gifts and graces enumerated above, acquire additional lustre from the aureola of a stainless life.

The minister of God should be pure in body: "I beseech you, therefore, brethren, by the mercy of God," says St. Paul, "that you present your bodies a living sacrifice, holy, pleasing unto God." [1]

He ought to be chaste in speech and conversation: "But fornication and all uncleanness, or covetousness, let it not so much as be named among you, as becometh saints; or obscenity, or foolish talking, or scurrility." [2] "But now, lay you also all away . . . filthy speech out of your mouth." [3] He should never, under pretence of entertaining and enlivening the company, indulge in conversation or anecdotes that savor of immodesty; because

[1] Rom. XII. 1.   [2] Eph. v. 3, 4.   [3] Col. III. 8.

though his remarks may seem harmless to himself, they may be hurtful to others. The lips that are the consecrated organs of Christ's Gospel and that are daily purpled with the Blood of the Lamb, should never be defiled by indecorous language. Surely, the range of cheerful and diverting colloquy covers a field sufficiently large without trenching on forbidden ground.

The priest should be pure in heart and mind : " Blessed are the clean of heart, for they shall see God." [1] Purity of heart illumines the mind in the contemplation of God and in the investigation of heavenly truths; while sensuality obscures the intellect, for " the animal man perceiveth not those things that are of the Spirit of God." St. Thomas says : " The perfection of intellectual operation in man, consists in a certain abstraction from the phantasms of sensible things; and therefore, the more the intellect of man is free from these phantasms, the better it is able to consider intellectual subjects. Darkness of mind arises from carnal pleasures. Chastity, on the contrary, singularly disposes a man for the perfection of mental pursuits." [2] Cleanness of heart not only enlightens the understanding, but it is a source of interior joy and tranquillity to the heart, by appeasing its passions; while the opposite vice is the parent of melancholy. Not only an overt act, but even an unhallowed thought, or a complacent contemplation of a sinful deed, is condemned by the more searching law of the Gospel. Our Saviour declares that whosoever looketh on a woman with an evil desire, " hath already committed adultery with her in his heart." [3] " Evil thoughts are an abomination to the

[1] Matt. v. 8.   [2] 2ª, 2ᵃᵉ, Quæst. xv. Art. iii.   [3] Matt. v. 28.

Lord : and pure words most beautiful shall be confirmed by Him." [1] Our speech is the echo of our thoughts. If our heart is undefiled, our language will be edifying; for "from the fulness of the heart the mouth speaketh." "Know you not," says the Apostle, "that you are the temple of God, and that the Spirit of God dwelleth in you? But if any man violate the temple of God, him shall God destroy. For the temple of God is holy, which you are." [2] If the Christian laity, to whom these words were addressed, should be pure of heart, since they are the *temple* of God, how unsullied should be the soul of a priest who is the *sanctuary* of God !

"What a happiness," says St. Francis de Sales, "voluntarily to observe chastity even in this life as the angels and blessed spirits observe it in heaven ! This virtue is so noble that it renders souls as fair as lilies and as pure as the sun. It consecrates the body and procures it the inestimable advantage of being entirely dedicated to the Divine Majesty, so as to be able to say, 'My heart and my flesh have rejoiced in the living God.'"

✓ The strongest incentive to a chaste life is furnished by the example and precepts of our Lord. He was born of a virgin Mother. He led a life of perpetual continence. He chose a virgin precursor in the person of the Baptist. He showed a special predilection for the virgin disciple John, and He selected Joseph to be the chaste consort of His Mother.

It is a significant fact, that while Jesus permitted Himself to be accused of being a blasphemer, a Sabbath-breaker, a seditious man, a wine-bibber, a liar, and an

[1] Prov. xv. 26.　　　　　[2] I. Cor. iii. 16, 17.

impostor, He never allowed the imputation of immorality to rest upon Him.

In like manner, though He permitted His disciples to yield to sins of ambition, avarice, moral cowardice, disloyalty, and treachery, He shielded them from the suspicion of impurity.

Not only did He select continent men to be His disciples and followers during His mission on earth, but He singled them out to be His cherished companions, and the assistants at His throne in His heavenly kingdom: "And I beheld : and lo a Lamb stood upon Mount Sion, and with Him an hundred forty-four thousand, . . . and they sung, as it were, a new canticle, before the throne, . . . and no man could say the canticle but those hundred forty-four thousand. . . . These are they who were not defiled with women ; for they are virgins. These follow the Lamb whithersoever He goeth." [1]

In embracing a life of continence, we are anticipating the glorious and eternal state in the celestial Paradise, in which the saints "shall neither marry nor be married ; but shall be as the angels of God in heaven." [2]

The sacred calling of a priest demands of him a life of chastity : "This is the will of God, your sanctification, that you should abstain from fornication, that every one of you should know how to possess his vessel in sanctification and honor, not in the passion of lust. . . . For God hath not called us unto uncleanness, but unto sanctification." [3] If the Apostle thus inculcates continence on the Christian laity, how much more imperatively is this virtue enjoined on the anointed minister, who conse-

---

[1] Apoc. XIV. 1, 3, 4.　　[2] Matt. XXII. 30.　　[3] I. Thess. IV. 3, 4, 5, 7.

crates himself to perpetual chastity by a solemn vow at
his ordination, who is in daily contact with sacred things,
and who ought to be a living exemplar of a pure life to
others?

"Be ye clean, you that carry the vessels of the Lord."[1]
If this commandment was given to the priests of the Old
Law, how much more strictly are those of the New Law
bound to be clean of heart, who daily offer up the spotless Victim, and hold with uplifted hands the chalice of
salvation, containing the immaculate Blood of Christ!

The hand of God fell with swift and terrible retribution on the king of Babylon for touching with polluted
lips the sacred vessels of Jerusalem's Temple. How
much more grievous is the sacrilege of God's anointed
who profanes the living vessel of his body, which was
once irrevocably consecrated to the Lord!

"For know ye this and understand that no fornicator,
or unclean, or covetous person (which is a serving of
idols) hath inheritance in the kingdom of Christ and of
God. Let no man deceive you with vain words: for
because of these things cometh the anger of God upon
the children of unbelief."[2] If unchastity draws down
vengeance so dire on the unbelieving world, how shall
God's chosen minister escape who sins against the light?

Chastity of life is precious not only in the sight of God,
but also in the sight of men: "O how beautiful is the
chaste generation with glory! for the memory thereof is
immortal, because it is known both with God and with
men. It triumpheth crowned forever, winning the reward of undefiled conflicts."[3] The man of God who is

---

[1] Isaiah LII. 11. [2] Eph. v. 5, 6. [3] Wisd. IV. 1, 2.

proof against the allurements of the flesh, is regarded by the community as a superior being; for the greatest evidence of moral strength is self-control, and the highest manifestation of self-control is in the victory over the carnal appetite.

He enjoys the esteem and admiration of the faithful. With what confidence the frail and erring members have recourse to him as to their spiritual physician, to obtain an antidote against the sins of the flesh from which he is happily exempt!

It is a well-known fact, that the priests of the Oriental Church, who, under certain circumstances, are permitted to marry, do not possess among the laity the same degree of influence or authority that the unmarried clergy enjoy.

The priest's victory over the senses secures for him the glorious liberty of the sons of God, and his detachment from family cares enables him to devote himself with entire freedom to the service of his Master and of the people committed to his charge. "I would have you," says the Apostle, "to be without solicitude. He that is without a wife, is solicitous for the things that belong to the Lord, how he may please God."[1]

On the other hand, there is no vice which people more abhor, which they are less disposed to condone than clerical incontinence. The world, which is so indulgent to its own votaries, is unrelenting toward the ambassador of Christ who is unfaithful to his vows. A sin which it would easily pardon as an indiscretion if committed by a layman, it condemns as a sacrilege if perpetrated by a priest. O how hard it is for him to repair his reputation once it is sullied by a single stain!

[1] I. Cor. VII. 32.

All transgressions, indeed, have a peculiar malice in a priest; but incontinence is a moral leprosy that not only renders him loathsome in the eyes of God and man, but dulls the sense of decency and self-respect in himself. He has little regard for his reputation, for a healthy public opinion, or for the scandal he brings to the Church and her members. All these considerations he sacrifices on the altar of passion.

Sensuality is the most seductive of all vices. It fascinates and blinds us, while aiming at accomplishing our ruin. Its pleasures are portrayed to the imagination as incomparably more delightful than they really are. It weakens and enslaves the will, and diminishes or takes away our power of resistance. It makes us insensible to the danger, which is realized only after the fall.

How precious, then, is the boon of chastity which delivers us from this degrading bondage of the flesh! "But we have this treasure in earthen vessels, that the excellency may be of the power of God, and not of us."[1] Though the treasure is above all price, the vase which contains it is most frail and brittle; though the virtue is the most indispensable, it is the most easily lost. It is a mirror which a breath may tarnish. It is a lily. Touch it, and "it withers on its stalk with languished head." It is like the snow of heaven which a little dust may stain.—But who will blanch the sullied snow of innocence?

The first step toward preserving and fostering this angelic virtue, is to value it at an inestimable price, and to have an earnest desire to cherish it. Our efforts are the measure of our desires, and our success is measured

[1] II. Cor. IV. 7.

by our exertions. You should have the same esteem for
it that Solomon had for wisdom, and say from your
heart: "I wished, *and the spirit of chastity* was given
me. . . . And I preferred her before kingdoms and
thrones, and esteemed riches nothing in comparison with
her. . . . I loved her above health and beauty, and
chose to have her instead of light. . . . Now all good
things came to me together with her, and innumerable
riches through her hands;"[1] yea, the riches of an upright
conscience and joy of spirit.

To this desire should be joined vigilance and prayer:
"Watch ye and pray, that ye enter not into temptation."[2]
If our Lord says, "without Me ye can do nothing," He
also declares, "My grace is sufficient for you." And if
the Apostle asserts that we are unable of ourselves even
to conceive a good thought, he also adds, "I can do all
things in Him who strengtheneth me."[3] Assuredly, since
we cannot entertain a pious thought without divine grace,
we cannot hope without God's aid to cultivate the virtue
which transcends human strength.

To prayer should be united the mortification of the
flesh, "always bearing about in our body the mortification of Jesus, that the life also of Jesus may be made
manifest in our bodies."[4] Chastity is a fragrant flower
that blooms among the thorns of self-denial. When our
Lord had expelled the demon from the body of the possessed man, His disciples asked Him why they could not
exercise that power. He answered: "This kind is not
cast out but by prayer and fasting."[5] As we cannot
exorcise the demon of impurity from other men but by

---

[1] Wisd. vii. 7, 8, 10, 11.   [3] Phil. iv. 13.   [5] Matt. xvii. 20.
[2] Matt. xxvi. 41.   [4] II. Cor. iv. 10.

mortification coupled with prayer, neither can we secure ourselves against his assaults except by self-abnegation combined with pious supplication. The Pontiff thus addresses the candidates on the day of ordination : "As you expel demons from the bodies of others, so will you endeavor to ward off all uncleanness and iniquity from your mind and body, lest you succumb to those whom you put to flight by your ministry." [1]

Gluttony and intemperance are great incentives to impurity. "Take heed to yourselves," says our Lord, "that perhaps your hearts be overcharged with surfeiting and drunkenness." [2] St. Paul associates satiety in meat and strong drinks with licentious habits : "Let us walk," he says, "honestly, as in the day, not in rioting and drunkenness, not in chambering and impurities." [3]

"Be not drunk with wine, wherein is luxury, but be ye filled with the Holy Spirit." [4] "I will never regard the drunkard as a chaste man," says St. Jerome. "This is my conscientious conviction ; I care not who says the contrary." He also observes that Lot, who had been proof against the abominations of Sodom, yielded to the lecherous influence of wine, so far as to commit an incestuous crime.

Be habitually engaged in some useful and healthful occupation ; "for idleness hath taught much evil." [5] "Adam, while living in idleness," says St. Chrysostom, "fell from the earthly paradise; Paul, in labor and hardships, was lifted up to the third heaven." There is no crime recorded of David while he was actually engaged

---

[1] In Ordin. Exorcist.   [3] Rom. XIII. 13.   [5] Ecclus. XXXIII. 29.
[2] Luke XXI. 34.   [4] Eph. v. 18.

in the field; he was betrayed into the sin of adultery while living at home in indolent luxury. Our imagination is constantly receiving impressions from the outer world. Our soul is vitiated and defiled, or it is purified and ennobled, according as these impressions are degrading or elevating in their character.

The mind is an active principle, a restless faculty. If it is not engrossed by righteous and wholesome considerations, it is apt to descend to thoughts of a vain, frivolous, and even criminal nature. The soul, like the body, is affected by the food it consumes and by the atmosphere that it breathes.

Avoid the occasions of sin. "He that loveth danger shall perish in it."[1] Keep custody over your senses, which are the avenues leading to the citadel of the soul. If the avenues are left unguarded, the enemy can easily enter and take possession of the spiritual fortress. A wanton glance was the occasion of David's fall. His bitter experience prompted him afterward to exclaim: "Turn away my eyes, that they may not behold vanity."[2]

Lastly, if you would preserve the angelic virtue of virginal integrity, be vigilant and circumspect on all occasions. Be ever animated by a salutary fear of the Lord. There should be no truce to this vigilance and fear. It should abide with you during your whole life, for neither length of years, nor robust virtue, nor acquired merits, nor exalted reputation for sanctity affords an absolute guarantee against a fall. We are neither stronger than Samson, nor holier than David, nor wiser than Solomon, and yet all these three yielded to this slippery

[1] Ecclus. III. 27.   [2] Ps. CXVIII. 37.

vice. It was in his old age that the heart of Solomon became depraved.[1]

"Believe me," says St. Augustine, "I speak the truth in Christ, I lie not, I have seen the cedars of Libanus, and the leaders of the flock fall, whose ruin I no more expected than I would that of Gregory Nazianzen or of Ambrose."

But let this fear be tempered with confidence in God. He will be your friend and protector; for "he that loveth cleanness of heart shall have . . . . the King for his friend."[2] Be encouraged by the words of our Lord: "My grace is sufficient for thee; for power is made perfect in infirmity."

Your ministerial life will, indeed, bring you daily face to face with moral evil in the confessional, on sick calls, and in your necessary intercourse with persons of a dissolute life. But God, who calls you to be the soul's physician, to cleanse the leprosy of sin, to be a light to them that are in darkness, to purify the poisonous atmosphere, will make you proof against its infection. While engaged in the faithful discharge of your duty, you may rely with confidence on your Master. "There shall no evil come to thee, nor shall the scourge come near thy dwelling. For He hath given His angels charge over thee, to keep thee in all thy ways. Thou shalt walk upon the asp and the basilisk, and thou shalt trample under foot the lion and the dragon."[3] Though in response to the call of duty you walk through haunts reeking with vice, God will protect you even as He protected Daniel in the lions' den, and the three children

---

[1] III. Kings XI. [2] Prov. XXII. 11. [3] Ps. XC. 10, 11, 13.

in the fiery furnace, so that your garments of innocence will not be scorched by the flames of wantonness that encircle you.

Milton pays the following beautiful tribute to the majestic power of this angelic virtue:

> "She that has chastity is clad in complete steel,
> And like a quivered nymph with arrows keen,
> May trace huge forests and unharbored heaths,
> Infamous hills, and sandy perilous wilds;
> Where through the sacred rays of chastity,
> No savage fierce, bandit, or mountaineer,
> Will dare to soil her virgin purity.
> Yea, there where very desolation dwells,
> By grots and caverns shagged with horrid shades,
> She may pass on with unblenched majesty,
> Be it not done in pride or in presumption.
> So dear to heaven is saintly chastity
> That, when a soul is found sincerely so,
> A thousand liveried angels lackey her,
> Driving far off each thing of sin and guilt,
> And in clear dream and solemn vision
> Tell her of things that no gross ear can hear;
> Till oft converse with heavenly habitants
> Begin to cast a beam on the outward shape,
> The unpolluted temple of the mind,
> And turns it by degrees to the soul's essence,
> Till all be made immortal." [1]

Blessed are you in having been specially chosen by your Lord to walk from your youth in the paths of righteousness; in being privileged like John to lean on your Master's breast; in being freed from the tumult of domestic passions and the rebellion of the senses. Happy are you that your flesh is subject to the law of

[1] Milton's *Comus.*

reason and of the Spirit of God, and that the kingdom of Christ, the kingdom of peace and Christian liberty, is within you.

More glorious is our triumph in conquering self than if we had taken cities. "Thanks be to God, who hath given us the victory through our Lord Jesus Christ." [1]

----

[1] I. Cor. xv. 57.

CHAPTER XIV.

HUMILITY.

GENUINE humility consists not in disclaiming any good in ourselves, but in ascribing all our gifts of nature and grace to the Author of our being. This idea is admirably expressed by the Apostle when he says: "Such confidence we have, through Christ towards God. Not that we are sufficient to think anything of ourselves, as of ourselves; but our sufficiency is from God."[1] "For if any man think himself to be something, whereas he is nothing, he deceiveth himself."[2] "But he that glorieth let him glory in the Lord. For not he who commendeth himself, is approved, but he whom God commendeth."[3]

Christ has taught us this great virtue by His life and examples, as well as by His precepts. "Learn of Me," He says, "because I am meek and humble of heart."[4] As St. Augustine remarks, He does not say: "Learn of Me to construct the world, to create all things visible and invisible, to work miracles, and to raise the dead, but that I am meek and humble of heart." He is born in a stable; He is circumcised as a sinner. When the people desire to exalt Him and crown Him King, He withdraws from them and hides Himself. When they resolve to

[1] II. Cor. III. 4, 5.
[2] Gal. VI. 3.
[3] II. Cor. X. 17, 18.
[4] Matt. XI. 29.

144

degrade and vilify Him, He confronts them and bows to the humiliation. Only three men behold Him in His glorious transfiguration, and even they are commanded by Him to be silent on the subject till after His resurrection; the populous and crowded city of Jerusalem was a witness of His degradation. He performs the menial task of washing His disciples' feet after the Last Supper, and then He delivers to them this beautiful instruction: "Know you what I have done to you? You call Me Master and Lord; and you say well, for so I am. If then I, being *your* Lord and Master, have washed your feet; you also ought to wash one another's feet. For I have given you an example, that as I have done to you, so you do also." [1]

But what humiliation can be compared with the Incarnation of our Saviour and His shameful death on the cross? "Let nothing," says the Apostle, "be done through contention, neither by vain-glory: but in humility, let each esteem others better than themselves: each one not considering the things that are his own, but those that are other men's. For let this mind be in you, which was also in Christ Jesus; who being in the form of God, thought it not robbery, to be equal with God; but emptied Himself, taking the form of a servant, being made in the likeness of men, and in habit found as a man. He humbled Himself, becoming obedient unto death, even to the death of the cross. For which cause God also hath exalted Him, and hath given Him a name which is above all names; that in the name of Jesus every knee should bow of those that are in heaven, on earth, and under the earth; and that every tongue should confess that the Lord

[1] John XIII. 12–15.

10

Jesus Christ is in the glory of God the Father." [1]   What
stronger incentive can we have to self-abasement than the
reflection that the more we are humbled for justice' sake,
the more conformable we become to Christ, the most perfect type of manhood !

Our Lord says of Himself: "I seek not My own glory;
there is one that seeketh and judgeth . . . . If I glorify
Myself, My glory is nothing. It is My Father that glorifieth Me." [2]   As our Saviour was content to have His
glory vindicated by His eternal Father, so our honor and
good name are secure in the hands of God.

We find our Redeemer repeatedly condemning the pride
of the Pharisees, rebuking the ambition of His disciples,
and profiting by every occasion to guard them against
vain-glory and to insinuate lessons of humility. He tells
the Jews that their desire for human applause is the greatest obstacle to their acceptance of the Gospel message:
"How can you believe, who receive glory one from another, and the glory which is from God alone you do not
seek?" [3]   He says on the other hand, that child-like simplicity and lowliness of mind are the best dispositions for
illumining the intellect and enabling it to apprehend the
truths of divine revelation: "I confess to Thee, O Father,
Lord of heaven and earth, because Thou hast hidden these
things from the wise and prudent, and hast revealed them
to little ones. Yea, Father, for so it hath seemed good in
Thy sight." [4]

The two sons of Zebedee besought our Lord, through
the mediation of their mother, to obtain for them the
highest places in His earthly kingdom, which, they im-

---

[1] Phil. II. 3–11.   [3] Ibid. v. 44.
[2] John VIII. 50, 54.   [4] Luke x. 21.

agined, was to be surrounded by all the pomp of regal splendor : "Say," she asked, "that these my two sons may sit, the one on Thy right hand, and the other on Thy left, in Thy kingdom." Turning to them, He replied : "You know not what you ask."[1] "My kingdom is not of this world." "The kingdom of heaven suffereth violence, and the violent bear it away." And as an evidence that jealousy and contention pursue the ambitious man, as the shadow follows the substance, "the ten hearing it, were moved with indignation against the two brothers."

Alas ! is not the intercession of friends and relatives still sought for the promotion of churchmen? And is not our ambition less excusable than was that of the Apostles? —for the enlightening and purifying day of Pentecost, which had not yet dawned upon them, has shone upon us with meridian splendor.

When the first priests of the New Law had "a dispute among themselves which of them seemed to be the greatest," our Lord administered to them the following lesson of humility, fortified by His own example : "The kings of the Gentiles lord it over them : and they that have power over them, are called beneficent. But you, not so : but he that is the greater among you, let him become as the younger ; and he that is the leader, as he that serveth. For which is the greater, he that sitteth at table, or he that serveth? Is not he that sitteth at table? But I am in the midst of you as he that serveth."[2] The emptiness of vain-glory is insinuated in the text. The Apostles contend among themselves, not as to which of them

[1] Matt. xx. 21, 22.   [2] Luke xxii. 25–27.

was, in reality, the greatest in virtue, zeal, and good works, but which of them should *seem* to be so in public estimation.

We may judge how selfish and insatiable is the spirit of ambition, and how painful to the sensitive nature of Christ was the contention of the Apostles, from the circumstance that their strife for preëminence occurred at the time He had washed their feet, and a few hours before His shameful death. Are not some priests actuated by the same unholy emulation by contending for a vacant post of honor, or by even setting their heart upon it, while its incumbent is yet lingering between life and death?

On another occasion, when the Apostles abruptly ask our Lord, "Who is the greatest in the kingdom of heaven?"— He holds up a child as a model of humility, because infancy is usually exempt from the fever of ambition, vainglory, envy, and jealousy, which agitates the breasts of the proud and overbearing. "And Jesus calling unto Him a little child, set him in the midst of them, and said: Amen I say to you, unless you be converted, and become as little children, you shall not enter into the kingdom of heaven. Whosoever therefore shall humble himself as this little child, he is the greater in the kingdom of heaven." [1]

And what are the grounds of our self-complacency? "What hast thou," says the Apostle, "that thou hast not received? And if thou hast received, why dost thou glory, as if thou hadst not received *it*?" [2] Surely, we cannot claim an absolute ownership nor glory in the possession of those gifts of which we have only an uncertain tenure,

---

[1] Matt. xviii. 2–4.   [2] I. Cor. iv. 7.

and which may be wrested from us at any moment. The beast of burden is not ennobled nor puffed up by the precious wares it may carry. And that we have been chosen as vessels of honor, should be to us a subject not of vain-glory, but of humble gratitude.

Let us briefly enumerate the principal gifts of nature and of grace we have received from God, and we can easily conclude from the uncertainty of the ownership, how vain it is for us to exult in their possession.

How can we boast of health and physical beauty, which can be impaired and disfigured by a brief illness? It is folly to take complacency in our talents and mental accomplishments; for the brightest intellect is clouded by sickness, darkened by old age, and extinguished by death. Neither can we flatter ourselves on being the objects of public esteem and adulation; for we all know from observation and the light of history, if not from personal experience, how subtle and evanescent is the breath of popular favor, and how ephemeral and capricious is human applause. A great prelate " that once trod the ways of glory, and sounded all the depths and shoals of honor," that basked in the sunshine of royal smiles and courtly homage, exclaimed when his sun was suddenly set :

> "Cromwell, I charge thee, fling away ambition ;
> By that sin fell the angels, how can man then,
> The image of his Maker, hope to win by 't?"

It would be great presumption for any man to glory in his spiritual gifts, when he recalls the fate of a Solomon or a Judas. " Let not the wise man glory in his wisdom, and let not the strong man glory in his strength, and let not the rich man glory in his riches. But let him that glorieth glory in this, that he understandeth and knoweth Me."[1]

As "pride is hateful before God and men,"[2] so is humility loved and cherished in heaven and on earth. So great is the value attached to this virtue, so amiable and attractive is it in public estimation, that we all desire to pass for humble men, we shrink from the imputation of haughtiness, and the proudest man is anxious to hide his vain-glory under the veil of a modest deportment.

Humility is the foundation of peace and tranquillity. "Learn of Me," says our Saviour, "because I am meek and humble of heart, and you will find rest to your souls."[3] It was only when Wolsey lost the favor of the King and the Court, and when all hopes of worldly ambition were blasted, that he turned to God, in Whom he enjoyed solid peace and repose:

> "*Cromwell.* How does your Grace?
> *Wolsey.* Why, well;
> Never so truly happy, my good Cromwell.
> I know myself now; and I feel within me
> A peace above all earthly dignities,
> A still and quiet conscience. The King has cured me;
> I humbly thank his grace; and from these shoulders,
> These ruin'd pillars, out of pity taken
> A load that would sink a navy, too much honor:
> O 't is a burden, Cromwell, 't is a burden,
> Too heavy for a man that hopes for heaven."[4]

If we examine the sources of our troubles and agitations, we find that they almost invariably spring from a desire of appreciation or a fear of contempt. A man that

[1] Jer. IX. 23, 24.
[2] Ecclus. X. 7.
[3] Matt. XI. 29.
[4] Shakspeare, Henry VIII.

has a clear insight into his own heart, and that is free from restless ambition, is not much disquieted by injurious words, or by the withdrawal of esteem, because he is not over-pained that others should see him as he sees himself, and he is not unduly troubled by the loss of honor to which he was not inordinately attached.

Meekness is the sister of humility, and our Lord says: "Blessed are the meek, for they shall possess the land"[1] of their own heart.

All men have, indeed, an unquenchable thirst for honor; and as this desire is universal, it must have been implanted in our breast by Almighty God. It cannot, therefore, be unlawful. Our fault lies in seeking human instead of divine glory. Now, the road of humility is the path to true glory.

Under the parable of a marriage-feast, our Lord insinuates the preëminent distinction which the humble-minded will enjoy in the celestial banquet of the great King: "When thou art invited to a wedding, go, sit down in the lowest place, that when he who invited thee cometh, he may say to thee: Friend, go up higher. Then shalt thou have glory before them that sit at table with thee. Because every one that exalteth himself, shall be humbled: and he that humbleth himself, shall be exalted."[2] "He hath regarded the humility of His handmaid; for behold from henceforth all generations shall call me blessed. . . . He hath put down the mighty from their seat, and hath exalted the humble."[3] "God resisteth the proud, but to the humble He giveth grace. Be you humbled therefore

[1] Matt. v. 4.   [2] Luke xiv. 10, 11.   [3] Ibid. i. 48, 52.

under the mighty hand of God, that He may exalt you in the time of visitation." [1]

St. Paul expressly declares that the sublime exaltation in heaven of the Man-God over angels and archangels, principalities and powers, and all that is not God, is the reward of the unparalleled depths of humiliation to which He descended when on earth : " He humbled Himself, becoming obedient unto death, even to the death of the cross. For which cause God also hath exalted Him, and hath given Him a name which is above all names : that in the name of Jesus every knee should bow, of those that are in heaven, on earth, and under the earth, and that every tongue should confess that the Lord Jesus Christ is in the glory of God the Father." [2]

Our Blessed Redeemer in His sermon on the Mount, bids us avoid ostentation in our works of religion and charity. He declares that they who perform such acts with the view of courting popular admiration, cannot hope for an eternal recompense : " Take heed that you do not your justice before men to be seen by them : otherwise you shall not have a reward of your Father who is in heaven. Therefore when thou dost an alms-deed, sound not a trumpet before thee, as the hypocrites do in the synagogues and in the streets, that they may be honored by men. Amen I say to you, they have received their reward. But when thou dost alms, let not thy left hand know what thy right hand doth, that thy alms may be in secret, and thy Father who seeth in secret, will repay thee. And when ye pray, you shall not be as the hypocrites, that love to stand and pray in the synagogues

[1] I. Pet. v. 5, 6. [2] Phil. ii. 8-11.

and corners of the streets, that they may be seen by men. Amen I say to you, they have received their reward. But thou when thou shalt pray, enter into thy chamber, and having shut the door, pray to thy Father in secret, and thy Father who seeth in secret will repay thee." [1]

[1] Matt. vi. 1–6.

CHAPTER XV.

HUMILITY SPECIALLY INCUMBENT ON PRIESTS.—
ENTIRELY COMPATIBLE WITH MAGNANIMITY.—
THE PRACTICE OF HUMILITY.

MANY of the arguments in the foregoing chapter in favor of Christian humility apply to priest and layman alike. But there are special reasons which make it incumbent on the ministers of God to exercise this fundamental virtue.

The priest occupies a conspicuous place in the community. He is set upon a pinnacle where he is revered by his own flock, and is usually respected and admired even by those who are not of the household of the faith. He is addressed by many endearing and honorable titles. He is called Reverend Father, the Shepherd of Souls, the Judge of Faith and Morals, Spiritual Physician, the Minister of Christ, and the Dispenser of the Mysteries of God. Not only does he preside in the church, but the place of honor is generally accorded to him in assemblies and banquets. His sermons, even though they should not rise above mediocrity, are often extolled as eloquent productions. Many are disposed to flatter him, while few are bold enough to remind him of his faults.

Raised to such lofty heights, is he not in danger of growing dizzy, and of exaggerating his own merits? Need we be surprised at the frequent admonitions to

humbleness of heart he receives from our Lord and the
Holy Ghost in the Sacred Volume? "He that is the
greater among you," says Christ to His Apostles, "let
him become as the younger; and he that is the leader, as
he that serveth." [1] "Have they made thee ruler (or
rector)? be not lifted up. Be among them as one of
them." [2] "The greater thou art, the more humble thyself in all things, and thou shalt find grace before God;
for great is the power of God alone, and He is honored
by the humble." [3] When the seventy-two disciples, on
returning from their missionary labors, said to Jesus:
"Lord, even the devils are subject to us in Thy name;"
though their language seemed to be a tribute only to our
Saviour's power, and the outpouring of grateful hearts,
yet He cautions them against vain-glory by saying to
them: "I saw Satan like lightning falling from heaven.
Behold, I have given you power. . . . But yet rejoice
not in this, that spirits are subject unto you; but rejoice
in this, that your names are written in heaven." [4] He
tells them in another place, that even after they have
performed their duty to the best of their ability, far from
being elated by success, they should have an eye on their
shortcomings, and regard themselves as unworthy ministers: "When you shall have done all these things that are
commanded you, say: We are unprofitable servants." [5]

I desire here to meet an objection that may have
occurred to your mind while reading the preceding lines.
May you not be entertaining a lurking suspicion that
humility is a servile and ignoble virtue, degrading to a

[1] Luke XXII. 26.   [2] "Rectorem te fecerunt."   Ecclus. XXXII. 1.
[3] Ibid. III. 20, 21.   [4] Luke X. 18–20.   [5] Ibid. XVII. 1€

freeman and destructive of noble aims? But this prejudice rests on no solid foundation. Genuine humility is
stamped with the nobility of truth. It is not only perfectly compatible with magnanimity, but is even inseparable from it. It has high and noble aspirations; it is
not discouraged by failures, nor put to flight by obstacles
and persecutions, nor dismayed and crushed by humiliations. It displays a moral heroism under the most formidable adversity. It is equal to every emergency,
because its trust is in God and in the righteousness of its
cause.

St. Thomas points out the intimate connection between
humility and magnanimity. The former, he says, checks
and curbs the mind, that it run not to excess after high
things; the latter strengthens the mind against despair,
and urges it on to the prosecution of great enterprises.[1]

St. Paul is an admirable model of humility combined
with greatness of soul. No man had a clearer insight
into his own frailties; yet no man had a loftier ambition
to accomplish great undertakings. In one breath, he says
of himself: "I am as one born out of due time. For I
am the least of the Apostles, who am not worthy to be
called an Apostle, because I persecuted the Church of
God." In the next breath he adds: "But by the grace
of God, I am what I am, and His grace in me hath not
been void, but I have labored more abundantly than all
they: yet not I, but the grace of God with me."[2] Again
he says: "To me, the least of all the saints, is given this
grace, to preach among the gentiles the unsearchable
riches of Christ."[3]

[1] 2a, 2æ, Quæstio LXI. Art. I.   [2] I. Cor. xv. 10.   [3] Eph. III. 8.

Neither contempt and ridicule, nor scourging and stoning, nor prison and shackles can break his spirit or make him lose heart. On the other hand, neither visions nor revelations, nor the admiration of his disciples, nor the marvellous success of his ministry can elate him or disturb the equanimity of his soul. He takes things as they come with a single eye to God: "I know," he says, "both how to be brought low, and I know how to abound. I can do *all things* in Him who strengtheneth me."[1]

In fact, a profound self-abasement resulting from a consciousness of his own weakness, joined to nobility of soul springing from his trust in God, is the key-note of the Apostle's life. This twin sentiment confronts us in many passages of his Epistles. It is the secret of his strength. The Lord said to him: "My grace is sufficient for thee; for power is made perfect in weakness." "Gladly, therefore," adds the Apostle, "will I glory in my infirmities, that the power of Christ may dwell in me. For which cause I please myself in my infirmities, in reproaches, in necessities, in persecutions, in distresses for Christ; for when I am weak, then am I powerful."[2]

He seems to have himself in view, when he speaks thus of the Apostles: "The weakness of God is stronger than men. . . . The foolish things of the world hath God chosen, that He may confound the wise; and the weak things of the world hath God chosen, that he may confound the strong; and the base things of the world, and the things that are contemptible, hath God chosen, and things that are not, that no flesh should glory in His sight."[3]

---

[1] Phil. IV. 12, 13.   [2] II. Cor. XII. 9, 10.   [3] I. Cor. I. 25-29.

Writing to Timothy, he says: "*I was* before a blasphemer and a persecutor and contumelious. But I obtained the mercy of God. . . . A faithful saying, and worthy of all acceptation, that Christ Jesus came into the world to save sinners, of whom I am the chief. But for this cause have I obtained mercy, that in me first Christ Jesus might show forth all patience, for the information of them that shall believe in Him unto life everlasting."[1]

The founders of Religious Orders had to pass through the rough sea of humiliations and contradictions before they established their communities on a solid basis. No one can read the lives of St. Francis of Assisi, St. Bernard, St. Ignatius, St. Vincent de Paul, or St. Alphonsus, without being convinced that, had they not been clothed with the triple armor of humility, magnanimity, and confidence in God, they would have abandoned their work in despair.

But if you are content with possessing diffidence in yourself by the mere consideration of your frailties and shortcomings, without acquiring a strong trust in God, you will be easily discouraged by the least opposition; you will be a moral coward; you will be morbidly sensitive to criticism; you will hesitate to launch out into the deep, from the fear of encountering the winds of envy and jealousy, and will be satisfied with hugging the shore; you will pursue the beaten path of mediocrity, and will not dare to open up and explore new fields of labor. In a word, the priest that combines self-knowledge with trust in God, is like a rock that stands unshaken amid the raging billows; while he that has humility without divine confidence, is like a log that drifts about with the tide.

[1] I. Tim. i. 13–16.

A few words in conclusion on the practice of humility and the means of acquiring it. It is a good rule to speak rarely of self, either approvingly or even disparagingly; for self-condemnation is too often only a bait thrown out to catch a word of praise. The most odious form of pride is the "pride that apes humility." Those that are habitually underrating their own merits and confessing their imperfections, would not be pleased if they were taken at their word. A lady who had invited a clergyman to tea offered him some biscuits, saying apologetically that she feared they were not fit to eat as she had made them herself. Her guest, with more frankness than discretion, and without the fear of an angry woman before his eyes, said on tasting them that they might, indeed, be better. "They are good enough for you, sir," was the quick retort of the lady.

If you are commended for a good deed, reflect how imperfectly you may have performed it, and dread the sentence of Christ: "Amen, they have received their reward." If you are unjustly accused, be silent or defend yourself with moderation, remembering that the false imputation is more than counterbalanced by the fulsome eulogies you have often received. I may add that a minister of the Gospel may, without prejudice to humility, earnestly assert and vindicate his patriotism and his civil and political rights when they are unjustly assailed, as Paul did when he protested against the indignity of being scourged, because he was a Roman citizen. It is, I think, likewise an imperative duty of a clergyman to defend himself from false and injurious aspersions on his character, whenever his humiliation and disgrace affect not only his own good name, but also the interests of religion, of which he is an acknowledged minister. Peter promptly repudiated the charge of intoxication brought against the Apostles by some of their hearers in Jerusalem.

We may, also, become more humble-minded by observing the good points in our neighbor's character. I have never spent a considerable time in the company of any priest or layman, without forming comparisons to his advantage, and to my own disparagement.

In the exercise of this virtue, we should consider our triple relation,—to our superiors, to our brethren in the ministry, and to the people. We should be reverential to superiors, deferential to equals, and condescending to our inferiors in rank or in station of life.

Our Saviour in the midst of the doctors in the Temple, is a Pattern of the respect and submission that we owe our superiors and elders in the ministry. He modestly listens to the doctors; He proposes and answers questions as becomes a junior; but though He is Wisdom incarnate, He does not dogmatize or assume the rôle of a teacher.

The demeanor of the clergy toward one another should be marked by sincere courtesy and civility, "in honor preferring one another." Such respectful homage contributes very much to foster mutual charity and good fellowship. While slow to take umbrage at a bantering word which may cause you some momentary confusion, you should be careful not to retaliate by putting the humble forbearance of your brother to a similar test. While Socrates was dining on one occasion with Plato and a number of friends, he happened to rebuke publicly one of the guests. "Would it not have been better," said Plato, "to have administered this censure in secret?" "Yes," replied

Socrates, " but would not you, also, have done much better to have reminded me of my fault in private? "

St. Peter, in his first Epistle, gives a striking illustration of loving condescension to subordinates: " The presbyters, therefore, that are among you, I beseech, who am myself also a presbyter, ... feed the flock of God which is among you, ... neither as lording it over the clergy, but being made a pattern of the flock from the heart." [1] How modest and respectful is the language in which the Apostle addresses the clergy! The Prince of the Apostles, the Leader of the whole Church of God, calls the priests not by a title inferior to his own; but he entreats them as his associates and fellow-laborers in the vineyard of the Lord. How well calculated is such condescension to win the hearts and command the adhesion of his subordinates, and what added force is given to the injunction by his own example! The words of the Apostle contain a beautiful lesson to pastors to avoid imperiousness of manner in their relations with the junior clergy and the people.

Meditation on the life of Christ and on the words of Holy Scripture inculcating humility, is an excellent means for acquiring that virtue; but hard knocks of humiliation are better still. The one instructs in the theory, the other in the practice of humility. As patience is acquired by suffering, and science by study, so is humility learned by humiliations.

There are three kinds of humiliations. The first comprises those which we voluntarily impose on ourselves; and they are good. But these self-inflicted strokes are usually few and far between. They are light and tender, and we seldom wince or smart under such *discipline*.

[1] I. Pet. v. 1-3.

11

The second embraces those humiliations administered by our lawful superior; and they are better, because confusion is more keenly felt when our delinquencies are denounced by one in authority over us, than when secretly deplored and punished by ourselves. But this medicine is generally dispensed by superiors in homœopathic doses, and the pills are sugar-coated out of a delicate regard for the patient's sensibilities, and a fear of irritating his bile.

The third kind includes those that we encounter in the daily discharge of our duties. Such humiliations are the best, because they are not of our own selection. They are rarely foreseen, and they are inflicted on us without any regard to our personal feelings. They are a drastic medicine which goes to the root of the disease. They are sent by a direct visitation of God, or they come to us, by divine permission, from the malice of men whom God uses as His instruments to subdue our rebellious spirit, to draw us to Himself, and to make us more "conformable to the image of His Son."

It has been truly said that one ounce of humiliation and correction from the hand of another, is more profitable than a hundredweight that is self-imposed.

To this abasement was David subjected when he was rebuked by the Prophet Nathan and cursed by Semei. He bent his back like a man to the chastening rod. To the denunciation of the prophet, he humbly replies without any extenuation of his crimes: "I have sinned against the Lord." When Semei curses him, and throws stones at him in his flight from his son Absalom, he says to his servants who sought to kill his tormentor: "Let him alone and let him curse: for the Lord hath bid him curse David. Perhaps the Lord may look upon my affliction, and the Lord may render me good for the cursing of this day." [1]

Like the Royal Prophet, we have all offended Thee, O Lord, more or less grievously. With him, therefore, we shall say when words of reproach and contumely arise against us: "Before I was humbled, I offended; therefore have I kept Thy word. It is good for me that Thou hast humbled me, that I may learn Thy justifications." [2]

———————

[1] II. Kings XVI. 10–12.   [2] Ps. CXVIII. 67, 71.

CHAPTER XVI.

THE AMBASSADOR OF CHRIST SHOULD BE A LEARNED MAN.—SOLITUDE AND SILENCE THE HANDMAIDS OF STUDY.

WHEN Almighty God established the ancient priesthood, the first commandment He gave to the priests was, that they should be thoroughly instructed in the divine law: "It is an everlasting precept through your generations, that you may have knowledge to discern between holy and unholy, between unclean and clean, and may teach the children of Israel all My ordinances which the Lord hath spoken to them by the hand of Moses."[1] As the Hebrew priests were enjoined to enlighten the people on the moral and ceremonial law, so are the priests of the New Dispensation required to have adequate knowledge for instructing their flocks in the precepts of the Gospel, and to solve their doubts on all questions of faith and morals and ecclesiastical discipline.

"The lips of the priest shall *keep* knowledge, and they shall seek the law at his mouth, because he is the angel of the Lord of hosts."[2] The word *keep* in the text is significant. The priest must be not merely the organ or mouthpiece, but also the custodian and depository of the law. He should not content himself with cramming for

[1] Levit. x. 9–11.   [2] Mal. II. 7.

the occasion, but his mind should be abundantly stored with knowledge, so that he may be able to impart it in season to the searchers after truth. "Drink water out of thine own cistern," says the Book of Proverbs, "and the streams of thine own well. Let thy fountains be conveyed abroad, and in the streets divide thy waters."[1]

The priests of the New Law should excel those of the Old Law as much in knowledge, as they surpass them in dignity and power. Hence, our Saviour says to His Apostles: "To you it is given to know the mystery of the kingdom of God, but to the rest in parables."[2] It is your sacred duty and particular privilege to be intimately acquainted with the hidden truths of the Gospel. Now, we know that the knowledge of God's law is not communicated to His ministers by a special revelation, but that it is acquired only by arduous labor. We are not lifted up to the heights of heaven, as was St. Paul, to learn there the divine mysteries; but we must, by daily exertion, ascend step by step the rugged path of science.

The Apostle of the Gentiles enumerates the titles of pastor and teacher among those of a priest. He joins together these two qualifications in order to point out the intimate and inseparable union between the office of pastor and that of teacher, and to remind us that the shepherd of souls must, also, be a man of learning. In the history of his own life, he tells us that he was "brought up at the feet of Gamaliel, taught according to the truth of the law of the fathers."[3]

And how intent he was on the study of the Scriptures, even to the hour of his death, may be inferred from the

[1] Prov. v. 15, 16.   [2] Luke VIII. 10.   [3] Acts XXII. 3.

instructions he gave to Timothy during the last days of his life, to have his books and parchments brought to him in prison, that he might be nourished and sustained by them in his solitude.[1]

In one of his Epistles, the same Apostle commends Timothy for his diligent application to the study of the Sacred Scriptures from his early youth;[2] and in another Epistle, he exhorts his disciple to persevere in perusing and announcing them, that he may save himself and the flock committed to his care.[3]

St. Peter, also, includes knowledge among the essential qualifications of a minister of God.[4]

But does not St. Paul say that "Knowledge puffeth up, but charity edifieth?"[5] Yes, but what the Apostle condemns, is the knowledge that inflates, not the knowledge that is counterpoised by charity and humility; and this is the knowledge that I am contending for. The most learned churchmen I ever met, were as conspicuous for profound humility as for depth of learning. Science, indeed, like every other gift, may be abused; but this possible perversion can never be reasonably urged as a plea for ignorance.

I may be told that the Apostles were the most fruitful ministers of Christ; and yet, with the exception of St. Paul, they were illiterate men. I answer that, apart from the special inspirations they received, they were far from being deficient in theological knowledge. They exhibited a marked familiarity with the ancient prophecies; and did they not study divinity for three years at

[1] II. Tim. IV. 13.   [3] I. Tim. IV. 16.   [5] I. Cor. VIII. 1.
[2] II. Tim. III. 15.   [4] II. Pet. I.

its very Source? Did they not listen daily to the words of wisdom that came from the lips of their Master? And did they not profit by His instructions? Were they not always prepared to confront the errors, and to meet the popular objections of their times?

Now, it cannot be denied, that since their day, knowledge has become more generally diffused throughout the world, new fields of science have been explored, and new errors have multiplied. How can the apostle of our generation fulfil his duty, if he does not keep pace with the trend of modern thought, demonstrate the harmony of religion with every department of science, and present fresh and substantial refutations to every new form of error that lifts its head?

The Sacred Scriptures are as vehement in their denunciations of sacerdotal ignorance and supineness, as they are earnest in stimulating priests to the pursuit of knowledge.

Isaias compares the uninstructed and slothful priests of his time to dumb dogs: "His watchmen are all blind, they are all ignorant: dumb dogs not able to bark, seeing vain things, sleeping and loving dreams. The shepherds themselves knew no understanding; all have turned aside into their own way, every one after his own gain from the first even to the last." [1]

The Prophet Osee ascribes the culpable ignorance, the enormous transgressions, and the national calamities of the Hebrew people to the intellectual stagnation of the priests: "There is no knowledge of God in the land. Cursing, and lying, and killing, and theft, and adultery have overflowed, and blood hath touched blood. Therefore, shall the land mourn, and every one that dwelleth

[1] Isaias LVI, 10, 11.

in it, shall languish with the beasts of the field, and with the fowls of the air. . . . My people have been silent, because they had no knowledge: because thou hast rejected knowledge, I will reject thee, that thou shalt not do the office of priesthood to Me; and thou hast forgotten the law of thy God, I also will forget thy children." [1]

The Prophet Malachi declares that God made the priests objects of scorn and contempt before all men, because of their neglect to study and proclaim His law: "You have departed out of the way, and have caused many to stumble at the law; you have made void the covenant of Levi, saith the Lord of hosts. Therefore, have I also made you contemptible and base before all people." [2]

Our Saviour Himself pronounces a malediction on the scribes and Pharisees, not indeed on account of their ignorance, but of the perverted use they made of their knowledge, which is still more reprehensible. They smothered the life-giving word amid the rubbish of vain traditions; they bewildered the people by their pernicious interpretations of the law; and they insidiously distorted the Sacred Text, to gratify their selfish ends, and to practise extortions on the public: "Woe to you, lawyers, for you have taken away the key of knowledge: you yourselves have not entered in, and those that were entering in you have hindered." [3] "Woe to you that say: whosoever shall swear by the altar, it is nothing: but whosoever shall swear by the gift that is upon it, is a debtor. Ye blind, for whether is greater, the gift or the altar that sanctifieth the gift?" [4] "They are blind, and leaders of the

[1] Osee IV. 1–6.   [3] Luke XI. 52.
[2] Mal. II. 8, 9.   [4] Matt. XXIII. 18, 19.

blind. And if the blind lead the blind, both fall into the pit." [1]

But even if the Scriptures were silent on the subject, sober reflection would demonstrate the excellence, the importance, the necessity, and the paramount advantages to religion and society of a learned clergy.

We cannot pay a higher homage to religion than in consecrating to the God of truth our intellect, the noblest faculty of the soul, and in making it more worthy of the uncreated Wisdom by developing it to the full extent of our ab'/ities.

The priesthood is pre-eminently one of the learned professions. If the well-being of society demands that the physician should be thoroughly acquainted with the causes and the remedies of diseases; that the judge be well-versed in jurisprudence; that the legal practitioner should master the principles and facts bearing on his client's cause; that the merchant should study the fluctuations of the market; that the general be instructed in the science of military tactics; that the statesman be familiar with statecraft, and the constitution of his country; that the journalist be conversant with the topics of the day;—surely the interests of the Christian Commonwealth require that the Minister of Christ should be thoroughly grounded in the divine law which is the art of arts.

And if the members of every craft and profession take a natural pride in their calling, certainly the clergyman should glory in his sacred ministry, which is the most sublime of all avocations, and in the knowledge of divinity, which is the queen of sciences.

[1] Matt. xv. 14.

But how can he be said to have his heart in his work, unless he is ambitious to cultivate his mind, and to expound the truths of religion with force and dignity?

In fact, the priest embodies in his own person the three-fold profession of judge, of advocate, and of physician. As judge, he is called upon to decide doctrinal and moral questions—which requires a knowledge of the divine and ecclesiastical law; as advocate, he must plead the cause of God before the people—which demands a well-furnished and disciplined mind; as physician, he has to prescribe the remedies for spiritual maladies—which presupposes a deep insight into the human heart, and a study of its complex distempers.

"Knowledge is power" not only in the scientific and mechanical, but also in the social and religious world. Knowledge is a recognized Leader. Men admire it, pay homage to it, and are swayed by it, especially when it is combined with rectitude of character.

The respect of mankind for Christianity and its influence on human thought, have always been proportioned to the intellectual and moral standard of the clergy.

It cannot be doubted that Cardinal Newman, for instance, exerted a far more wide-spread power for good in his day and generation, than he could have commanded, if his life of exalted piety and ministerial labor had not been adorned by vast and varied erudition.

Contemplate the Church of the fourth and fifth centuries, the golden age of patristic learning, the age of Ambrose, Augustine, Leo, Jerome, and Hilary, of Athanasius, Chrysostom, Basil, Ephrem, Epiphanius, and of Gregory of Nazianzen, who enriched not only their own times, but all succeeding generations with the treasures of their learning. What lustre they shed on the Christian name, and what influence they exerted in extending the kingdom of God! What virility of faith and of character they exhibited and infused into others! It was, indeed, a period of religious storms, but of storms that purified the moral atmosphere. While their uncompromising adherence to truth often exposed these champions to the tyranny of princes, their literary fame, intrepid conduct, and evangelical lives won the admiration of their enemies. Under leaders so accomplished, the Church may often be assailed, but despised never.

On the other hand, there is no spectacle more deplorable and humiliating to the Church, than that of an ignorant and torpid clergy. While no man is more respected and honored in the community than the ambassador of Christ who is conspicuous for erudition combined with a blameless life, no man is held in greater contempt than the slothful minister who is destitute of the scholarly acquirements demanded by his sacred calling.

Piety in a priest, though indispensable, can never be an adequate substitute for learning. He may have zeal, but not the "zeal according to knowledge"[1] which the Apostle commends. Knowledge without piety may, indeed, make a churchman vain and arrogant; but piety without knowledge, renders him an unprofitable servant. The absence of piety makes him hurtful to himself, but the absence of knowledge makes him a stumbling-block to others.

"I would prefer," says St. Teresa, "to consult a learned confessor who did not practise prayer, rather

[1] Rom. x. 2.

than a man of prayer who was not learned ; for the latter could not guide me in the truth." [1]

An ill-instructed priesthood is the scourge of the Church. The great religious upheaval of the sixteenth century may be justly ascribed to the intellectual darkness, as well as to the moral depravity of the clergy. "If in the sixteenth century," says Cardinal De La Luzerne, "heresy made such rapid progress, infected a great part of Europe, and wrested from the faith of Jesus Christ a great number of churches, it was to the ignorance in which the clergy stagnated that it owed its success. The embankment which should have kept it within bounds, proving feeble and impotent, the terrible inundation spread its ravages in all directions. It swept away in its destructive course, even many of the consecrated Piers that had been erected to arrest it, and which yielded without resistance to its incursions." [2]

Silence, solitude, and study are the three great prerequisites for knowledge. Silence and solitude are the hand-maids of study. The most learned books ever written, the most sublime works of artistic and scientific genius ever conceived, the most eloquent discourses ever pronounced, had their inspirations in solitude. Without interior recollection and intense thought, no great work was ever achieved. "Conversation," says Gibbon, "enriches the understanding, but solitude is the school of genius."

"The common sense of mankind has associated the search after truth with seclusion and quiet. The greatest thinkers have been too intent on their subject to admit

[1] Autobiography, Chap. XIII.   [2] De L'Etat Ecclesiastique.

of interruption. Pythagoras, the light of Magna Graecia, lived for a time in a cave. Thales, the light of Ionia, lived unmarried and in private, and refused the invitations of princes. Plato withdrew from Athens to the groves of Academus; Aristotle gave twenty years to a studious discipleship under him. Friar Bacon lived in a tower upon the Isis." [1]

I do not hesitate to say that the priest who aims at being thoroughly equipped for the ministry, must be a habitual student from the period of his ordination. No matter how successful he may have been during his theological course, a little reflection and observation will convince him of the imperfect and insufficient fund of knowledge he had then acquired. He had simply learned how to learn. The foundation was laid; the superstructure is the work of his whole life. No conscientious lawyer or judge is content with the legal lore gained before his graduation. Why then should a priest be an exception?

I once met a justice of the Supreme Court of the United States, tired and exhausted, after his day's work. He informed me that the duties of his office involved about twelve hours of labor each day, and that even a portion of his vacation was spent in the preparation of his decisions.

To make no progress, is to go backward, because we easily forget what we have learned unless our mind is replenished by renewed application. The most fertile field will yield only weeds and briars, if not diligently cultivated. An indolent and unstudious priest may abound in speech, but it will be superficial and unin-

[1] Cardinal Newman.—*Idea of a University.*

structive. A teacher who fails to keep up his studies, is on the high road to mental bankruptcy. His notes will go to protest, or to speak more plainly, the people will silently protest against the reproduction of his old stock in trade.

I may be told that apostolic men, like the Curé d'Ars, are found in every country, who, though deficient in acquired learning and natural talent, are eminently successful in converting souls. Would to God that the number of such shepherds were multiplied; for they are the glory of Jerusalem, they are the joy of Israel, and the honor of the people of God! What these priests lack in book-learning, is more than compensated by infused knowledge in meditation; for books are not the only instruments of science. They study like St. Thomas Aquinas at the foot of the cross. With the Psalmist they can say: "The Lord is my light." They gain an intuitive perception of the truth which is vouchsafed to others only by arduous study. Far from being slothful, they make the best possible use of the faculties that God has given them. They certainly afford no justification to those who presume, without any intellectual qualifications, to be heralds of the Word.

A young levite once remarked to his Professor: "God can dispense with my learning." "Yes," was the reply, "but He has still less need of your ignorance." A gentleman said to an untutored minister: "Why do you preach, since you haven't studied?" "The Lord," he answered, "hath opened my mouth." "Such an event," was the rejoinder, "happened before in the days of Balaam, but these divine favors are very rare in our days."

It is evident, also, that a priest's studies should have a direct or an indirect reference to his sacred profession. They should proximately or remotely bear upon his ministry, and tend to the cultivation, the development, and the enriching of his natural faculties. If the time that ought to be allotted to serious mental labor is wasted on newspapers and novels, or in the perusal of literature which acts like an opiate on the intellect, he will become "a sounding brass, or a tinkling cymbal," in the pulpit, and will be "as one beating the air." The intellectual mill is sure to grind out whatever it receives. If supplied with wheat, it will give forth nutritious food; if supplied with sand, it will yield but dust. The law of reproduction applies to the mind as well as to the land. "What a man soweth, that shall he reap also."

And if in every age learning was demanded of a minister of religion, it is especially imperative in our country that he should be clothed with the panoply of Christian science. Americans are a reading and an inquisitive people. They explore all regions of thought "in the heaven above, in the earth beneath, and in the waters under the earth." They investigate subjects of Scripture and theology, history and biography, astronomy and geology, and every other branch of human knowledge. The priest of God must be prepared to answer all inquiries in the domain of science, as well as of religion. He should apply to himself the words of the Poet:

"Homo sum: humani nil a me alienum puto."

While the missionary, engrossed as he is by a multitude of ministerial duties, can hardly be expected to make very deep researches into these departments of secular study, he should have a sufficient acquaintance with them to prove that no historical fact or scientific discovery can shake the impregnable foundations of Christianity, and that there is perfect harmony between the God of science and the God of revelation.

The more profound investigation of scientific questions will naturally devolve on those favored levites who will have enjoyed the special privilege of a university course.

CHAPTER XVII.

PERSONAL ADVANTAGES AND PLEASURES OF A STUDIOUS LIFE.

WE must not overlook the personal advantages which the anointed minister of Christ derives from studious habits. Study is not only a source of knowledge, but it is also a handmaid of virtue, and a perennial fountain of intellectual enjoyment. Some hours of a priest's daily life are usually spent apart from the society of living men. In his library he is surrounded by the concentrated wisdom of ages; and he is never less alone than when alone with such company. "They are never alone," says Sir Philip Sidney, "that are accompanied by noble thoughts." In perusing the writings of saints and sages, we are unconsciously moved to imitate their lives: "*Abeunt studia in mores.*" We are drawn nearer to great and good men, and we know them better in reading their thoughts than in viewing their portraits. Their portraits are the work of another; their thoughts are the photograph of their own mind. The portrait fades with time; but the words of the author are as fresh as when first spoken. Homer still lives in his writings, though Troy has been in ashes for ages. Cicero still speaks to us, though the Roman Senate which echoed his voice is in ruins.

12   177

The glory of Jerusalem has departed ; but the sacred songs of David are ascending to heaven in sweet harmony, from thousands of temples throughout the globe. They are the inspiration and joy, the hope and consolation of Christian millions.

The reader will find in his books delightful companions to enrich his mind with the treasures of knowledge, to entertain and cheer him in his solitude, to console him in adversity, to counsel him in doubt, to support and strengthen him in temptation, to caution him against impending dangers, to rebuke him in his transgressions. If our companion is the Bible, it will, like Beatrice guiding Dante through the abodes of the blessed, conduct us into the most sacred and memorable scenes that have ever been presented to the gaze of mankind. It will lead us to Mount Sinai, where we may contemplate God Himself speaking to Moses and delivering to him the tables of the Law. It will accompany us to the mountains of Judea, where we can hear the prophets denouncing the iniquities of the Jewish people. We can follow the children of God in their devious wanderings through the wilderness before they enter the Promised Land. With the multitude we can sit down on the grass, and be attentive listeners to our Lord, while He is preaching His sermon on the Mount. We can reverently stand beside Him while He is conversing with the Samaritan woman at the well of Jacob, or reclining at table with Zaccheus, or consoling Mary and Martha at the tomb of their brother Lazarus, or delivering His last discourse to His disciples.

The remembrance of some phrase spoken by our Saviour, is a powerful antidote against temptation. It is a spiritual bouquet, diffusing around us a healthful and delicious odor; it is a moral disinfectant in an atmosphere of vice; it is a ready weapon against a sudden attack. "What things soever were written," says the Apostle, "were written for our learning;"[1] and hence the conduct of Christ, when tempted in the desert, was manifestly intended as a pattern for our guidance under similar circumstances. When tempted to gluttony by the evil spirit, He answered: "*It is written:* Not by bread alone doth man live, but by every word that proceedeth from the mouth of God." When tempted to presumption, He said: "*It is written:* Thou shalt not tempt the Lord thy God." When tempted to vain glory, He replied: "*It is written:* The Lord thy God shalt thou adore, and Him only shalt thou serve."[2]

Or if sacred and secular eloquence has special attractions for us, what is more captivating and inspiring than this highest manifestation of human intelligence? We can listen to Demosthenes pouring forth his matchless philippics against the King of Macedon. We can mingle with the crowd in the Roman Senate and in the Forum, while Cicero in thundering tones is inveighing against the treason of Cataline and the official corruptions of Verres.

We can hear the Apostle of the Gentiles in the Areopagus, proclaiming the one, true God to the refined, but idolatrous, Athenians. We can, in spirit, contemplate John Chrysostom denouncing the lasciviousness of the Court of Constantinople. We can be spectators during that almost unrivalled speech of Edmund Burke, delivered in the British House of Commons in presence of England's representative nobility and gentry, on the

---

[1] Rom. xv. 4.   [2] Matt. iv. 10.

occasion of the impeachment of Warren Hastings. We can fancy ourselves sitting in the Senate chamber, while Webster is delivering his historic speech in reply to Hayne, surrounded by such illustrious colleagues as Clay, Calhoun, Benton, and Silas Wright. We miss, indeed, the sonorous tones of the living voice; we miss the sensible emotions and the applause of the audience, but we hear the identical words that were spoken, and our imagination can fill the chamber with an eager and animated assemblage.

We rise from the perusal of these discourses, impressed with the charms of human eloquence and its power to sway the minds of men. The pleasure we derive from the silent reproduction of such scenes, is second only to the delight of being spectators of them. The distance of time and space that divides us from the living speakers, is in some measure compensated for by the advantage we enjoy of pausing to admire at our ease every fresh gem of thought that fell from their lips.

If we take up History for our companion, we can note the rise, the progress, and the fall of ancient empires marked out as distinctly as we can trace a river from its source to its mouth. In studying the causes of a Commonwealth's decay, we realize the truth of Scripture, that nations, as well as individuals, are subject to God;[1] that "justice exalteth a nation; but sin maketh nations miserable;"[2] that God has used even heathen princes, like Pharaoh, Cyrus, and Titus, as the instruments for the providential deliverance of His people, and as the unconscious agents of the fulfilment of His prophecies.

[1] Wisd. viii. 14.   [2] Prov. xiv. 34.

But the most entertaining and instructive of all companions is Biography. It is the portraiture of character that has made *Plutarch's Lives* so popular and attractive to all classes of readers. The biographical feature of the Scriptures, apart from their inspiration, always lends to the Sacred Volume a special charm; and the same observation applies to *The Lives of the Saints*. How absorbing and inspiriting is the record of those men in particular who have been martyrs to truth and justice! What enthusiasm and admiration they enkindle in our breast! With what feelings of righteous indignation, we see the Baptist beheaded in prison, out of zeal for conjugal purity!

We gaze with loving wonder on the Apostle of the Gentiles wielding his pen, as he can no longer wield "the sword of the Spirit," in his Roman dungeon, confronting death with composure, and exhorting his disciple to the practice of apostolic virtues.

We contemplate the emaciated, but intrepid, Basil standing before the tribunal of Modestus, refusing to surrender his Catholic faith, though threatened with confiscation, imprisonment, and death.

What more thrilling and touching picture can be presented to our view than that of Chrysostom, the fearless champion of Christian morality, dying in exile, worn out by fatigue and brutal treatment!

What a spectacle to the world is Athanasius of Alexandria! During the six and forty years of his Episcopate, he continues to be the victim of unrelenting imperial persecutions. Five times he is driven from his See, and hunted like a wild beast.

The genial and accomplished Sir Thomas More voluntarily surrenders the great Seal as Lord High-Chancellor of England, is immured in the London Tower, and executed for the sake of conscience and righteousness.

But when we look on the King of martyrs towering above them all, and dying amid humiliations unexampled, we realize more than ever the nobility of that suffering which rises superior to strength and power, to grace and beauty, to learning and eloquence; and in the privations inseparable from our own ministry, we are incomparably more consoled by the trials of Christ and His heroic followers, than by the sublimity of their words. The splendor of their natural acquirements so admired during their life, pales before the glory of their ignominy which then excited only pity or contempt. With what complacency we smile at the breath of opposition or calumny that we may encounter in the exercise of our official duties, when we witness the fierce blasts of persecution that beat against those sturdy oaks!

After exhibiting to us models of apostolic firmness, our library companion will hold mirrored before us the portraits of men conspicuous for their private virtues. Their exemplary lives will stimulate us to follow in their footsteps, while the career of others who had fallen from grace will serve as cautionary signals, warning us to shun the snares which occasioned their ruin. When we read of the patience of a Job amid the accumulation of temporal calamities, and the pious submission of Tobias, we learn to bow with resignation to the visitations of Providence. When we contemplate the chastity of Joseph and Susanna, who preferred to be deprived of liberty, reputation and even life itself rather than sully their souls, we conceive a fresh admiration for that angelic virtue.

On the contrary, when we read of men once distinguished for their sanctity, but who had suddenly fallen from their lofty pinnacle, when we behold a Samson, a David, and a Solomon,—those towering oaks, overthrown by a single shock of temptation, we are admonished to be wary and circumspect, and not to confide in virtues already acquired.

There is this distinguishing characteristic of our library celebrities, that they are always readily approached. Even if we had been the contemporaries of the great, the good, and the learned who shed a lustre on their age, how hard it would be to have access to them, and hear their living voice! Mountains and seas might be a barrier between them and us; and though they lived close to us, it might be difficult or impossible to converse with them. What an insignificant fraction of the human family have cast their eyes on our Saviour and his Apostles, on Demosthenes and Cicero, on Chrysostom and Augustine! What a small percentage of the Christian world have beheld the reigning Pope!

But there is no barrier to prevent us from drawing nigh to those who speak to us through the pages of their books. We need no letter of introduction to them; they are never preoccupied; they are always willing to open their mouth, and communicate their thoughts to us, whenever we choose to listen to them.

The mute companions of our solitude possess another distinguishing characteristic rarely found among living men;—they are fearless preachers. Our most intimate friend, from a sense of delicacy, or from the fear of being regarded as censorious and hypercritical, and as adopting the rôle of a superior, will hesitate to remind

us of our faults; or he will touch the sore point of our
character with extreme tenderness. Even Socrates took
it amiss to be gently rebuked by his friend Plato, especially in the company of others.

Though our conscience may accuse us, we shrink from
the reproof of a living voice: "I hate the Prophet
Micheas," said king Achab, "for he doth not prophesy
good to me, but evil." [1]

There are, moreover, few professing Christians that
more rarely have the living word addressed to them than
our clergymen. They preach and hear the Gospel announced to others; but there are seldom any sermons
directed to themselves, except, perhaps, on the occasion
of an annual retreat.

We have, therefore, to rely on our silent associates for
exhortation. They will not pander to our vanity, nor
connive at our faults. They will probe our moral ulcers.
Like true friends, they will proclaim the truth without
the fear of offending us; for we never quarrel with our
books or question their sincerity, how severely soever
they may rebuke us.

These moralists of ours never bore us, or thrust themselves upon us. As soon as we desire to close the conference, their lips are sealed, and they resume their narrow
cell. When tired of one monitor, we can listen to
another. By way of relaxation, we can pass with ease
from a grave to a gay and jovial companion. The bow
must be sometimes relaxed:

> "A little humor now and then,
>   Is relished by the best of men."

Many a sage maxim is clothed in a festive garment.

[1] III. Kings XXII. 8

Numerous examples might be furnished of the signal conversions and other blessings wrought by the reading of a good book. Many a Christian luminary has found in a single page or sentence the germ of his moral reformation. The great Patriarch, St. Antony, was inspired to lead an austere evangelical life by a passage of the Gospel. St. Augustine ascribes his conversion to a sentence of St. Paul. Seduced in his youth from the religion of his pious mother into the Manichean heresy, he became not only shipwrecked in faith, but dissolute in morals. One day, while in company with his friends Alypius and Pontitianus, the latter recounts the extraordinary life and sanctity of St. Antony. After listening to the narrative, Augustine remarks with emotion: "These ignorant men take heaven by violence, and we with all our learning remain wallowing in the mire of sin." Withdrawing afterward from his companions, he sits under a fig-tree, and gives vent to his tears. While struggling with conflicting feelings, he hears the voice of a child uttering these words: "Take up and read; take up and read." As no child was in view, he accepts the call as a heavenly admonition, and returning to the house, he finds the Epistles of St. Paul open before him.

The rest of the incident may be best told in his own touching words: "I seized, opened, and in silence read that section on which my eyes first fell: '*Not in rioting and drunkenness, not in chambering and impurities, not in contention and envy: but put ye on the Lord Jesus Christ, and make not provision for the flesh, in its concupiscences.*' [1] No further would I read; nor needed I: for instantly at the end of this sentence, by a light as

[1] Rom. XIII. 13, 14.

it were of serenity infused into my heart, all the darkness of doubt vanished away." [1]

St. Ignatius, when a soldier, disabled by a wound received at the siege of Pampeluna, asked for a book of romances to divert his mind. No such work being at hand, a volume of *The Lives of the Saints* was brought to him, and its contents so inflamed his soul that he resolved henceforth to be a soldier of the Cross.

Dr. Wolff, a celebrated clergyman of the church of England, was moved to enter on his missionary career by the perusal of the *Life of St. Francis Xavier*. If such a biography exercised so great a sway on a Protestant reader, well may we suppose that it has quickened the zeal of many a minister of Christ, and inspired many an ingenuous Catholic youth to consecrate himself to a life of apostolic labors.

"A natural turn for intellectual pursuits," says Thomas Hood, "probably preserved me from moral shipwreck so apt to befall those who are deprived in early life of their parental pilotage. My book kept me from the ring, the tavern, the saloon."

The surprise is sometimes expressed that clergymen can be content with their solitary mode of life. I am far from being averse to society in its proper time and place; and yet I am firmly persuaded that a priest who is attached to his books, experiences a delight more exquisite, more healthful, and more enduring than the pleasure derived from social reunions. It is, moreover, a delight that is never marred by those displays of ill-temper and disputes, of stinging jests and sharp repartees into which the best of friends are sometimes betrayed.

Confessions, *Book VIII.*

But if a shepherd of souls has no taste for seclusion and study, how will he occupy his leisure hours, especially in a country mission where wholesome, intellectual diversions are commonly so rare? Not in secular pursuits, for he is debarred from them by his sacred profession. He will spend them in devouring novels which will soon pall on him; in wading through literary garbage whose exhalations will poison his soul; in morbid reflections, vain imaginations; in a spirit of ennui and discontent. Or, perhaps, unable to endure the irksomeness of a solitary life, he will seek comfort in the circle of boon companions, or in some other unhealthy excitement; he will indulge in convivial habits, and may, at last, yield to the seductive charms of sensuality.

How true are the words of the Wise Man: "Idleness hath taught much evil!"[1] "Be engaged," says St. Jerome, "in some work, that the demon may always find you occupied." "On account of idleness," says St. Bernard, "King Solomon became involved in many fornications, and lustful desires led him to worship idols."

The minister of God, while exhorted to cultivate habits of retirement and study, is by no means expected to be a recluse. The Prince of pastors was not an anchoret. He was found in the family circle, as well as in the Synagogue, and His light shone as luminously in the banqueting hall as in the Temple.

The sphere of the missionary priest is a dual one; he has a field of religion to cultivate in social and public, as as well as in domestic and private life. He sanctifies the hearth as well as the cloister. His mission is to regenerate his age, as well as to save his own soul. The words

[1] Ecclus. xxxiii. 29.

predicated of the Church, may be appropriately applied to the priest: "The Church knows of the double life divinely prescribed and commended to her; the one in labor, the other in rest; the one in work of action, the other in the reward of contemplation." [1]

This variety of pursuits exerts a wholesome and bracing influence on soul and body. The hours spent in retirement and in the work of the sanctuary, far from incapacitating him for company, are the best school to fit him for social intercourse. "No man," says Kempis, "can safely appear in public, but he who loves seclusion. No man can safely speak, but he who loves silence." [2] The talkative and superficial man is always saying something; the discreet and learned man has always something to say. Hence, no man is more sought after in familiar and friendly relations than the genial and scholarly clergyman. No man's conversation is more profitable and entertaining. With his store of knowledge, he is ever prepared to illustrate any subject that comes up, by a historical allusion, or an anecdote, or a personal reminiscence that enlivens the conference, and relieves it of dull monotony. His well-timed remarks on religious topics, which may naturally be suggested by the flow of conversation, often make a more salutary impression than when they are stamped with the official seal of the pulpit. In a word, the pastor that is revered in the sanctuary, is sure to be admired and loved in the homes of the people.

---

[1] St. Augustine, Tract. cxxiv. *in Joannem.*   [2] B. 1. ch. xx.

CHAPTER XVIII.

PERSEVERING LABOR, THE KEY TO KNOWLEDGE.

IT HAS long been a mooted question whether men are more indebted to genius or to laborious industry for their intellectual achievements.

> "The charms of verse,—the question is not new—
> Are they to art or inborn genius due?
> In all fine work, methinks each plays a part—
> Art linked with genius, genius linked with art;
> Each doth the other's helping hand require,
> And to one end they both like friends conspire." [1]

I believe, however, that the majority of eminent scholars attribute their success in the field of literature, science, and art more to persevering study than to native talent. They have not hesitated to say that everything can be accomplished by labor, and that no excellence is attainable without it.

Genius has well been defined "an infinite capacity for taking pains." Every man who has left the imprint of his genius on literature, philosophy, and art, has been an indefatigable worker.

[1] "Natura fieret laudabile carmen, an arte,
Quæsitum est: Ego nec studium sine divite vena,
Nec rude quid possit video ingenium: alterius sic
Altera, poscit opem res, et conjurat amice."

Horace, *Ars Poetica.*

189

Buffon, the great naturalist, has remarked that patience is genius. The power of great men, in his judgment, consists chiefly in their faculty of continuous working and waiting. "Invention," he says, "depends on patience. Contemplate your subject long. It will gradually unfold itself till a sort of electric spark convulses for a moment the brain and spreads down to the very heart a glow of irritation. Then come the luxuries of genius, the true honors for production and composition;—hours so delightful that I have spent twelve and fourteen successively at my writing-desk, and still been in a state of pleasure."

It is related that a rival playwright, named Alcestis, once made this jeering remark to Euripides: "It has taken you three days to compose three verses, while I have dashed off one hundred in the same time." "Yes," retorted Euripides, "but your one hundred verses in three days will be dead and forgotten, whilst my three will live forever."

When Apelles was reproached with the paucity of his productions and the minute care with which he retouched his paintings, he replied that he painted for perpetuity.

We know what herculean efforts were made by Demosthenes, the greatest of orators, before he mastered his profession and became the pride and glory of Athens as a public speaker. He had a small chamber built underground, in which he used to occupy himself for two or three successive months in study. He shaved one side of his head that the confusion of appearing in public in this condition, might compel him to remain in his retreat. Here he composed those admirable orations of which his

envious rival⋯ ⋯ the lamp." " Yours,"
he replied t⋯ ⋯st you so much labor."
He copied ⋯ ⋯es, to form his style after
the great h⋯

Cicero's ⋯ ⋯he first order.   He was dis-
tinguishe⋯ ⋯ty of talent rather than for
any pr⋯ ⋯s.   We may trace to his un-
wearie⋯ ⋯gular position which he holds
in th⋯ ⋯f letters.   He devoted his chief
atte⋯ ⋯claiming daily in Greek and Latin
wi⋯ ⋯lemen who were his competitors in
t⋯ ⋯honors.   Nor was he satisfied with
attend⋯ ⋯the lectures of the best teachers in the
Capital.   H⋯ ⋯an assiduous listener to the pleadings
in the Forum.   On returning home, he would spend
many hours of the night reproducing the speeches he had
heard, and repeating them for practice to private tutors.

The industry that he displayed in early life was but an
earnest of that which he evinced in maturer years.   " He
suffered no part of his leisure to be idle," says Middleton,
" or the least interval of it to be lost : but what other
people gave to the public shows, to pleasure, to feasts, nay
even to sleep, and the ordinary refreshments of nature,
he generally gave to his books and the enlargement of
his knowledge.   On days of business, when he had any
thing particular to compose, he had no other time for
meditating but when he was taking a few turns in his
walks where he used to dictate his thoughts to his scribes
who attended him.   We find many of his letters dated
before daylight ; some from the Senate ; others from his
meals and the crowd of his morning levee."   Thus he
found time without apparent inconvenience for the busi-

ness of the State, for the turmoil of the courts, and for philosophical studies.[1]

Bossuet, the Eagle of Meaux, has perhaps been unrivalled in sacred eloquence. His sermons combine in a marvellous degree strength and grace, sublimity of thought and simplicity of language, and display an erudition that always delights while it instructs. Gibbon, the historian, says of him: "The English translations of two famous works of Bossuet, Bishop of Meaux, achieved my conversion, and I surely fell by a noble hand."[2] So close and unremitting was his application to study that his college companions, by a playful allusion to his name, spoke of him as "*Bos-suetus aratro*," the ox inured to the plough.

Fenelon wrote eighteen copies of his Telemachus, each covered with erasures, before he gave the work to the press.

Henry Clay, in an address to young men, revealed to them the secret of his triumphs in the field of oratory. "I owe my success," he said, "chiefly to one circumstance, that, at the age of twenty-seven, I commenced and continued for years the process of daily reading and speaking upon the contents of some historical or scientific book. These off-hand efforts were made sometimes in a cornfield; at others, in the forest; and not unfrequently, in some distant barn with the horse and the ox for my auditors. It is to this early practice of the art of all arts that I am indebted for the primary and leading impulses that stimulated me onward, and have shaped and moulded my whole subsequent destiny."

---

[1] See Newman's *Sketch of Cicero*.   [2] Gibbon's *Memoirs*, Vol. I.

Daniel Webster was a laborious student, and took the utmost care in revising all his speeches and addresses which were published under his authority. His famous Plymouth discourse was not officially printed in pamphlet form until one year after its delivery. He spent his leisure moments in the intermediate time pruning and correcting it, thus rendering it one of the finest oratorical compositions that now exist in the English language. He himself said on one occasion, that he would as soon think of appearing before an audience half clothed, as half prepared; and at another time, he told one of his friends that he would as soon stand up and tell his audience that he had garments enough at home, but did not think it worth while to put them on, as to tell them that he could have made a satisfactory speech, perhaps, if he had taken the requisite pains.[1]

Virgil spent three years on his *Bucolics*, or *Pastoral Poems*. He devoted seven to the composition of his *Georgics*, and for ten years he was engaged on the *Æneid*. And yet so deeply was he impressed with the imperfections of this immortal epic, and so far did it fall short of his ideal, that, when he felt his death approaching, he ordered his friends, Varius and Plotius Tucca, to burn the manuscript. Happily, however, for the literary world, the Emperor Augustus intervened, and prevented the destruction of a work which has been the delight and admiration of posterity.

According to Bentley and other commentators, Horace consumed about fifteen years in writing his poems, from the time that he began his *Satires* till he had finished *The Art of Poetry*.

[1] *A History of Oratory and Orators*, by Henry Hardwicke.

13

Alexander Pope says of himself:

> "As yet a child and all unknown to fame,
> I lisped in numbers, for the numbers came."

But this precocious aptitude for versification never weakened his industry. Dr. Johnson says: "His intelligence was perpetually on the wing, excursive, vigorous, and diligent, eager to pursue knowledge and attentive to retain it. His natural gifts he improved by incessant and unwearied diligence. He had recourse to every source of intelligence, and lost no opportunity of information. He was never content with mediocrity when excellence could be attained. If conversation offered anything that could be improved, he committed it to paper. If a thought or perhaps an expression more happy than was common rose to his mind, he was careful to write it. He was one of those few whose labor is their pleasure. He was never elevated to negligence nor wearied to impatience. He examined lines and words with minute and punctilious observation, and retouched every part with indefatigable diligence till he left nothing to be forgiven." [1]

For this reason, he kept his pieces very long in hand while he considered and reconsidered them. His manuscripts were usually written four times over before they were committed to the press.

Addison's *Spectator* is justly regarded as the best model of English classical literature. Its author was a most painstaking writer. The reader of the *Spectator* might be led to believe that each paper was written at the date assigned to it; but we are informed that he had compiled

[1] Johnson's *Life of Pope*.

three folio volumes of manuscript before he began the *Spectator*. It is also reported of him that, when he occupied a position under the government, he was, on a certain occasion, too late in furnishing an important State paper, on account of the careful revision to which it was subjected.

Milton consumed five years of solitude in reading the ancient writers before he composed his *Paradise Lost*.

Dante began the *Divina Commedia* nearly thirty years before he completed it.

It is said that seven years elapsed from the day that Gray began his *Elegy* until he had finished it. But if he consumed so much time in creating that charming poem, he was amply rewarded by the eagerness with which it was read and the admiration in which it is still held. If easy writing is usually hard reading, the inverse proposition is generally true, namely, that painstaking writing affords pleasant and instructive reading.

Moore considered ten lines a day good work, and he would keep the little poem by him for weeks waiting for a single word.

In the quarto edition of Lord Byron's Poetical Works, is given a fac-simile of a few verses of *Childe Harold* as they came from the hands of the poet. The corrections and erasures are countless. In some instances there are several alterations of one word. The specimen given is a fair type of the whole manuscript copy. He spent the leisure hours of nearly four years in composing the first two cantos.

A friend, after reading a short stanza of Tennyson's, remarked to the author: "Surely, Mr. Tennyson, this verse did not cost you much study. The words flow so smoothly and fit in so naturally that they must have come spontaneously to your mind." The poet quietly replied: "I have smoked a box of cigars over these four lines." After his first publication, he buried himself for ten years among his books, and was heard of no more by the public during all that time. He became a laborious student, a painstaking thinker, with the great view of fitting himself for the career that his talents and ambition impelled him to pursue.

Cardinal Newman wrote in 1869 to Rev. John Hayes: "I have been obliged to take great pains with everything I have written; and I often wrote whole chapters over and over again, besides innumerable corrections and inter-linear additions. I don't get any better for practice. I am as much obliged to correct and rewrite as I was thirty years ago." He informs us, also, that he was engaged for over a year on a brief essay treating of the inspiration of the Scriptures before he was satisfied with it, though the subject had occupied his life thoughts. Who would have believed all this if the Cardinal himself had not told us? There is no apparent effort in his style, his language flows in a clear and limpid stream, he seems never to be at a loss for a word, and he always uses the right expression in the right place.

Dickens was popularly regarded as a facile writer. But he himself tells us that his works cost him infinite pains. "The one, serviceable, safe, certain, remunerative, attainable quality in every study and every pursuit is the quality of attention. My own invention, or imagination, such as it is, I can most truthfully assure you," he says, "would never have served me as it has, but for the habit of commonplace, humble, patient, daily, toiling, drudging attention." When I heard Mr. Dickens give a public recitation in Baltimore, in 1865, I fancied that he read extracts from his own writings without any previous preparation. But it is said that, on being requested to read at such a recitation a new selection from his works, he excused himself on the ground that he had not time to prepare himself, as he was in the habit of *reading a piece once a day for six months before reciting it in public.*

Edmund Burke revised the proof-sheets of his *Reflections on the French Revolution* a dozen times before they were finally committed to the press.

While we deplore the skepticism of Gibbon, the historian, we cannot but admire his indefatigable industry, his vast erudition, as well as the measured grandeur of his sentences. With the view of forming his Latin style, he adopted the laborious, though efficacious, method of translating the *Epistles* of Cicero into French. He after ward re-translated his French into Latin, and then compared his own version with the original text of the Roman orator. He adopted the same method in his efforts to master the French language, translating the historian Vertot into Latin, and then turning his Latin into French. To perfect himself in Latin, he carefully perused Terence, Virgil, Horace, Tacitus, and other authors three times, and never suffered a difficult passage to escape till he had viewed it in every light of which it was susceptible. He conceived the idea of writing *The Decline and Fall of the Roman Empire* in October, 1764, and of the conclusion of that work, he says: "It was on the night of the 27th of June, 1787, that I wrote the last lines of the last page." We see by this statement that twenty-three years elapsed from the day that he formed the idea of writing the history till its completion. He wrote out his *Memoirs* nine times before he was satisfied with them.[1]

Hume labored assiduously for thirteen hours a day in compiling his *History of England*. He was fifteen years engaged on the work.

Dr. Lingard consecrated about twelve years of earnest labor to his admirable work, *The History of England*. The first volume appeared in 1819, and his task was not completed till 1830.

It is said that twenty-four years elapsed from the time that Allison commenced his *History of Europe* till he put to it the finishing touch.

Macaulay spent eight years on his *History of England*.

Matthew Hale, the great jurist, devoted himself to legal subjects during sixteen hours a day for many years; and when fatigued with the study of the law, he would divert himself by that of philosophy and other departments of science.

Montesquieu, referring to one of his works, said to a friend : " You will read it in a few hours ; but, I assure you, it cost me so much labor that it has whitened my hair."

Pliny, the Younger, tells us that the elder Pliny, his uncle, the naturalist, had himself carried in a litter to the Senate House that, reading and writing by the way, he might not lose an instant. He was so economical of time that he read at his daily meals. After devoting the whole day to business affairs, he was in the habit of spending several hours of the night at his favorite investigations. During his course of studies, he kept by

[1] Gibbon's *Memoirs*, Vol. 1.

him his tablets and copyist, for he took notes of every thing he read.

Sir Isaac Newton is said to have written his *Chronology* fifteen times before it entirely pleased him. His great work on *Optics* was not published till 1704, though it was begun as early as 1675. When questioned as to how he had made his wonderful discoveries, he replied : " By always thinking unto them." On another occasion, he said : " I keep the subject continually before me, and wait till the first dawnings open slowly by little and little into a full and clear light." He remarked to Dr. Bentley : " If I have done the public any service, it is due to nothing but industry and patient thought."

Adam Clarke, in his preface to his *Commentary on the New Testament,* says : " In this arduous labor, I have had no assistants, not even a single week's help from an amanuensis; no person to look for common places, or refer to an ancient author, to find out the place and tran scribe a passage of Greek, Latin, or any other language, which my memory had generally recalled, or to verify a quotation. I have labored alone for nearly *twenty-five years* previously to the work being sent to press; and *fifteen years* have been employed in bringing it through the press to the public; and thus about *forty years* of my life have been consumed."

We shall hardly find among the Fathers of the Church a more indefatigable laborer in the department of sacred science than St. Jerome. He chose for his sphere one of the most arduous portions of the field of theology,— biblical studies in general, besides the translation of the Bible, and what we would now call biblical criticism in particular. The difficult task of comparing texts and collating manuscripts was one of the numerous occupations that divided his time in the grotto of Bethlehem. Nor did he limit himself to the Sacred Writings, for the great theological questions of the day called forth all his energies. He devoted himself to biography, and yet he found time for those numerous epistles, in which the character of the man is so well portrayed.

When we reflect on the extent of his biblical studies, his revision of the Vulgate according to the text of the Septuagint, his numerous commentaries and, above all, his translation of the Old Testament from the Hebrew, we are almost at a loss to know how so much work could be crowded into one life. And yet this was only a portion of St. Jerome's labors. He found time to translate the *Chronicles* of Eusebius into Latin, he interpreted the *Homilies* of Origen, and he composed treatises on various subjects, besides taking an active part in the great controversies of his day, and being engaged in very extensive correspondence.

What was the secret of his success? I think I can safely answer that it was his constant application. Talents of a high order he, indeed, possessed; but his talents would have availed him little without an indomitable will. At the age of thirty, he began the study of Hebrew, knowing how useful and even necessary this language would be to him in his scriptural researches. "How much labor," he says, "it cost me, what difficulties I encountered, how often I despaired, how frequently I gave up, and again striving to learn, began anew, I, the sufferer, can testify, as well as those who lived with me, and I thank the Lord that I now reap the sweet fruit of that bitter pathway of study."

In Bethlehem, St. Jerome slept little, prayed much, and spent the rest of his time in teaching others, in receiving strangers who came to him from all parts of the Christian world, and in answering their questions. His nights he reserved for his own studies, and the works he has bequeathed to us are the fruit of many a silent night-watch.

The leaders in the field of art not less than in the world of letters, have attributed their success to diligent labor and patient industry. Sir Joshua Reynolds, writing to Barry, says: "Whoever is resolved to excel in painting, or indeed in any other art, must bring all his mind to bear upon that one object from the moment that he rises till he goes to bed."

Michael Angelo's sublime conceptions would have faded like a dream, had his industry not perpetuated them in marble or on canvas. He was a most indefatigable worker. He sustained himself with a little bread and wine during his daily working hours, and very frequently he arose at night to resume his labors. One day, he was explaining to a visitor (perhaps impatient of the artist's delay) what progress he had made on a statue since his previous visit: "I have," he said, "retouched this part, polished that, softened this feature, brought out that muscle, given some expression to this lip, and more energy to that limb." "But they are trifles," observed the visitor. "It may be so," rejoined the artist, "but recollect that trifles go to make perfection, and perfection is no trifle."

Titian was eight years engaged on his great painting, "The Martyrdom of St. Peter," and seven on his "Last Supper." Writing to Charles V., he said: "I send your Majesty 'The Last Supper,' after working at it almost daily for seven years." At the age of eighty-one, he executed "The Martyrdom of St. Lawrence," now in a church of Venice, and he continued to work till he had attained his ninety-ninth year.

Leonardo da Vinci is said to have walked the length of the city of Milan, to give a tint to his "Last Supper."

Turner, the celebrated English painter, of whom Mr. Ruskin speaks in terms of the highest praise, was once asked by a lady what was the secret of his success. He answered : "Work, Madam, work."

"You have no idea," said Mr. Ruskin, the eminent art critic, "of the labor and pain it is to me to write these books of mine that seem to you so easy." Putting into his visitor's hand the manuscript of his most recent publication, he added : "Look at that. You will scarcely find one sentence as it was first written." And such was the case. Words were crossed out, and others substituted in their place, sometimes whole sentences rearranged, and this throughout the whole manuscript.

From these examples, we see that they who have attained to eminence or distinction in the field of oratory, literature, art, or science, have been hard and indefatigable workers. They have concentrated their mind on the goal of knowledge to which they aspired. They have made even their discursive reading subservient to that end, just as the bee converts into honey the nourishment it snatches from every flower on which it alights. The more the mind is centred on one particular subject, the more tenacious is its grasp of it, just as the heat of the sun's rays is more intense when brought to a focus.

If our attention is divided among many objects, its force is proportionately weakened :

" Pluribus intentus minor est ad singula sensus."

So much, indeed, have profound thinkers been absorbed by their studies, that they have often been beguiled into a state of abstraction and absent-mindedness, which rendered them unconscious of what was transpiring around them.   It is related in the Life of St. Thomas Aquinas that, being invited to dine with Louis IX., King of France, he sat at table rapt in his own thoughts, entirely oblivious of the presence of his royal host and the guests.   All of a sudden, he vehemently struck the table, exclaiming : " The argument is conclusive against the Manichees." His Prior, who sat next to him, pulled his mantle, and bade him remember where he was.   The Angelic Doctor apologized to the King for his forgetfulness ; but Louis, fearing lest St. Thomas should lose sight of his train of thought, ordered his secretary to write it down on the spot.

The biographer of Dante relates that the poet went one day to a great public procession, and entered the shop of a bookseller to be a spectator of the passing show.   Finding a book that greatly interested him, he devoured it in silence, and plunged into the abyss of thought.   On his return home, he declared that he had neither seen nor heard the slightest occurrence of the public exhibition that passed before him.

The Right Rev. Charles Walmesley, Vicar Apostolic of the London District, who consecrated Bishop Carroll of Baltimore, was a very distinguished scholar, as well as a devoted Prelate. In 1750, he was, on the recommendation of Buffon, D'Alembert, and other eminent scientists, elected a Fellow of the Royal Society of Great Britain. He was, also, a member of the Royal Academy of Berlin. When England determined to adopt the Gregorian Calendar, he was one of the learned men consulted by the British Government to arrange the new Calendar.

It is said that, one day, while celebrating Mass, the bishop's mind became unconsciously absorbed by a mathematical subject, and, forgetful of the sacred function he was performing, he seized the paten for a pencil, used the altar cloth for paper, and set to work to solve the problem. After spending several minutes abstracted in meditation, he suddenly realized the situation, and so much was he shocked by his ill-timed investigation that, when Mass was over, he ordered his servant to lock up his mathematical books, resolved to discontinue those studies in the future.

There is no royal highway to the mountain of knowledge. The only way is the rugged road of labor. Learning comes not to any one by heredity or descent. The father may bequeath to his son the temporal possessions he has accumulated, but he cannot transmit to him his acquired wealth of lore. Erudition cannot be bought with gold. Minerva will not be lured by bribes to discriminate in favor of any of her votaries. No man can contend by proxy in the arena of intellectual strife. He cannot win glory by purchasing a substitute. He must fight his own battles. Every toiler in the field of letters must plough his own field and plant his own seed, if he hopes to reap the harvest of learning.

The classical scholar of to-day may have at his disposal handier instruments of labor, and greater facility for obtaining them than his ancestors; but it is much to be feared that the multiplication of text-books and works of reference, together with the copious notes and translations at his side, while smoothing his path, have weakened his energies in the pursuit of knowledge. He may cover more ground, but he is apt to plough less deep and to reap a smaller harvest than his fathers, who plodded without the aid of labor-saving machines.

A scholar, fired with laudable ambition, should not be dismayed because he does not hope to rival the intellectual giants to whom reference has been made. He will not aspire to emulate Burke or Webster in forensic oratory, or Bossuet and England in pulpit eloquence. His muse will not lead him to those giddy heights of Parnassus which have been attained by Dante and Milton. He will not push his scientific researches as far as Newton and Faraday. He will never be a Michael Angelo in sculpture, or a Raphael in painting. But between the summit of the mount and its base, there are many intervening resting places, many points of vantage-ground, which it is honorable to gain. A man can be an able lawyer without aiming to become a Marshall or a Taney; he may be a learned theologian without presuming to be a St. Augustine or a St. Thomas. If we have not been favored with ten talents, let us make the best possible use of the one or the five that we have received. Our responsibility to God and to society will be measured by the use we shall make of the talents that have been given to us.

Our American authors of distinction are not so numerous as they should be, because they write in too much haste. Fast eating makes us dyspeptic; fast travelling makes us nervous; fast working shortens our life; and hasty writing gives an ephemeral character to our publications.

If America is to become a successful rival of Europe in the field of letters, as she already is in the commercial and scientific world, her sons must work with more painstaking diligence, and burn more freely the midnight oil.

CHAPTER XIX.

Sources of Discouragement in the Pursuit of Knowledge.

SOME students after perusing the examples given in the foregoing chapter, may be convinced, indeed, of the triumph of industry, but their zeal in the pursuit of science may be dampened by obstacles or difficulties personal to themselves. They may be deterred by the consciousness of their own slowness and dulness in acquiring knowledge, or discouraged by a feeble constitution, or some organic complaint; or they may be appalled by the multifarious occupations that distract and bewilder them.

Let us take up these objections categorically, confront them resolutely, and see whether or not they are insurmountable.

1°. Some one will say : I am naturally dull of comprehension; my mind is slow and sluggish. I experience great difficulty in grasping a subject, while many of my colleagues are blessed with extraordinary facility. They run so fast that I cannot keep pace with them. In my first efforts at public speaking, I was timid and bashful, I nearly lost my head, and I have never since regained my composure when addressing an audience. I am, therefore, downcast and dispirited. I entertain but faint hopes of success from any exertion I may continue to make in the paths of learning and of oratory.

This is not an unusual source of disheartenment. I have known a zealous and venerable priest who was seized with stage-fright on delivering his first sermon, and who never afterward could summon courage to preach. If he had forced himself to face the congregation a second and a third time, he would have conquered his timidity.

For the comfort of backward and diffident minds, I will observe that some of the most learned scholars and most successful orators were at the foot of their class in the early stage of their studies. The consciousness of their natural defects far from depressing, stimulated them to greater ardor, while many who possessed innate aptitude for learning, subsequently failed, their very facility proving a dangerous and fatal gift, which led them to indulge habits of indolence.

The first sermons of Savonarola, the great Dominican, disappointed his hearers, both in Ferrara and Florence. His diminutive size and harsh voice, his homeliness of speech and embarrassment of manner told against him. But instead of sinking under the humiliation, he resolutely kept on preaching to peasants and children, meanwhile practising elocution in his room, till he became one of the most captivating orators of his age.

When Alban Butler, the learned author of *The Lives of the Saints*, was in the first period of his studies in the English College, at Douay, he was obliged to rise long before the regular hour in order to keep up with his companions in class.

Benjamin Disraeli, in his maiden speech in the House of Commons, was jeered and cried down by the members. Undismayed by their clamor, he said : " I have several times begun many things, and I have succeeded at last.

I shall sit down now, but the time will come when you will hear me." His prediction was fulfilled. He afterward became one of the most brilliant and effective speakers in the British Parliament, and even Prime Minister of England.

Dr. Boyd writes in Longman's Magazine:[1] "The master of the school, Mr. Rawson, declared that Arthur Stanley (the future Dean Stanley), was the most stupid boy at figures that ever came under his care, save only one, who was yet more hopeless, and was unable to grasp simple addition and multiplication. That other stupid boy more hopeless than Stanley, became the great finance minister of after years, William E. Gladstone, who could make a budget speech of three hours' length, and full of figures, which so interested the members of the House of Commons, that they filled the hall standing and sitting till midnight." The incident has this important moral, that a youth may, by hard study, overcome his natural repugnance to a branch of knowledge, and even become an eminent master of it.

The mother of Richard Brinsley Sheridan, when presenting him to his tutor, is represented as speaking of him as an incorrigible dunce. His first speech in the House of Commons was a great disappointment to his colleagues. And yet that which he delivered during the impeachment trial of Warren Hastings, "produced an impression," as Macaulay says, "such as has never been equalled." Mr. Fox assigned to this oration the first place among all the speeches ever delivered in the British Parliament.

Oliver Goldsmith speaks of himself as a plant that flourished late in life.

[1] February, 1894.

14

Sir Isaac Newton, when at school, stood next to the bottom of his class in the early part of his course; but by dint of study and perseverance, he rose to the front rank among his companions.

Daniel Webster tells us that, when a boy at the academy, he could never summon courage enough to declaim before his schoolmates. "The kind and excellent Buchminster," he says, "especially sought to persuade me to perform the exercise of declamation, like the other boys, but I could not do it. Many a piece did I commit to memory and rehearse in my own room over and over again; but when the day came, when the school collected, when my name was called, and I saw all eyes turned upon my seat, I could not raise myself from it. Sometimes the masters frowned, sometimes they smiled. Mr. Buchminster always pressed and entreated with the most winning kindness that I would venture *once;* but I could not command sufficient resolution, and when the occasion was over, I went home and wept bitter tears of mortification."

Chief Justice Taney, referring to his valedictory when graduating, says: "I was sadly frightened, and trembled in every limb, and my voice was husky and unmanageable. I was sensible of all this, much mortified by it, and my feeling of mortification made matters worse. Fortunately, my speech had been so well committed to memory, that I went through without the aid of a prompter. But the pathos of leave-taking from the professors and my classmates, which had been so carefully worked out in the written oration, was, I doubt not, spoiled by the embarrassment under which it was delivered."

He thus described his timidity in the first case he had to plead before a court of justice: "I took no notes, for my hand shook so that I could not have written a word legibly if my life depended on it; and when I rose to speak, I was obliged to fold my arms over my breast, pressing them firmly against my body; and my knees trembled under me so much that I was obliged to press my limbs against the table before me, to keep me steady on my feet; yet under all these disadvantages, I determined to struggle for composure and calmness of mind, and by a strong effort of the will, I managed to keep possession of the reasoning faculties, and made a pretty good argument in the case, but in a tremulous and sometimes discordant voice." This same embarrassment, he says, seized him for years afterward, though no one but himself was conscious of it. "Indeed," he adds, "this morbid sensibility was so painful to me in the first years of my practice, that I am not sure that I should not have abandoned it, if I had been rich enough to live without it." [1]

Dr. Milner, the author of *The End of Controversy*, informs us that, when he first went to school he did not get on well, but appeared dull and stupid, and said his lessons very indifferently. One day, when he happened to do well, his master was so pleased with him that he gave him a colored print as a reward and encouragement. "This," he used to say, "was the turning point in my school career; I felt fresh animation and confidence, and ever after studied with success and improved to the satisfaction of my masters." [2] How precious to a diffident

<hr />

[1] *Memoir of Roger B. Taney*, Chap. I.   [2] *Life of Rt. Rev. Dr. Milner.*

student is a word of encouragement and a deed of kindness from his professor.

General Grant in his *Personal Memoirs*, makes the humble avowal that he stood next to the bottom of his class at West Point; and General Sheridan asserts in his *Memoirs* that he "graduated at West Point, number thirty-four in a membership of fifty-two."

A kind-hearted teacher will take a fatherly interest in the backward and timid pupil who is conscientiously striving to succeed, just as the mother has a special tenderness for an afflicted or a delicate child. Dr. Arnold observes: "If there be one thing on earth which is truly admirable, it is to see God's wisdom blessing an inferiority of natural powers, when they have been honestly, truly, and zealously cultivated." At Lakeham, when teaching a rather backward boy, he rebuked him somewhat severely, whereon the pupil plaintively looking up to him, said: "Why do you speak angrily, Sir? *Indeed* I am doing the best I can." Dr. Arnold keenly felt the rebuke, and years afterward he used to say: "That look and that speech I have never forgotten."[1]

2°. Feeble health is another source of discouragement to many an aspiring student; for earnest and diligent application requires physical, as well as mental exertion, and mental exertion is more or less painful to frail constitutions.

But the pupil of a delicate frame will derive much consolation and encouragement from the reflection, that many of the most illustrious scholars in Church and State have labored under the disadvantage of a diseased or infirm body.

[1] *Self-help*, Samuel Smiles.

To begin with the great Apostle of the Gentiles :—The Corinthians said of him, " His bodily presence is weak, and his speech contemptible."[1] And still what fatigues were undergone by that weak body ! " In journeying often, in labor and painfulness, in hunger and thirst, in fastings often, in cold and nakedness."[2] And the echoes of that " contemptible " voice have resounded in thundering tones throughout the world, and have made princes tremble on their thrones. Nor can it be doubted that the sermons of St. Paul were the fruit of study, as well as of prayer. His Epistles give intrinsic evidence of a cultivated, as well as of an inspired mind.

Timothy, notwithstanding his " frequent infirmities," was a diligent student of the Holy Scriptures, as St. Paul testifies ;[3] and the Apostle, while prescribing for his disciple's physical maladies,[4] exhorts him not to desist from study, but to continue to apply to *reading,* to exhortation, and to doctrine.[5]

What life has been more active or more fruitful in the Church than that of Pope Gregory the Great ? The bare enumeration of the Councils he convened, of the nations he converted, of the letters he wrote, the works he edited, the sermons he preached, and of the deeds of charity he performed during the thirteen years of his Pontificate, fills us with amazement ; and yet Gregory suffered during his life from frequent ailments and habitual infirmity of body.

St. Basil was a confirmed invalid. In one of his Epistles,[6] he says that, in his best physical condition, he was weaker than patients usually are whose recovery is

---

[1] II. Cor. x. 10.   [3] II. Tim. iii. 15.   [5] Ibid. iv. 13.
[2] Ibid. xi. 26, 27.   [4] I. Tim. v. 23.   [6] *Epis.* 257.

despaired of by their physicians. When Modestus, in
the name of the Emperor Valens, threatened to torture
and banish him if he did not conform to the Arian
heresy, Basil replied : " I fear not your torments. My
emaciated body cannot hold out long under them." With
all his infirmities, Basil was a close student. He excelled
in the liberal arts, in natural sciences, in philosophy and
poetry, as well as in theology and sacred eloquence; and
although charged with the government of an important
diocese, he has left six octavo volumes rich in intellectual
and spiritual treasures.

The austerities practised by St. John Chrysostom in
his youth, the privations he endured during his six years'
sojourn in the mountains near Antioch, together with his
incessant preaching, impaired his lungs and made him
the victim of many distempers. Yet though he ruled the
Patriarchal See of Constantinople, and was harassed by
the persecutions of temporal and spiritual princes, the
productions of his pen are so copious as to fill thirteen
folio volumes.

St. Bernard was rarely exempt from some corporal infirmity. From a habit of excessive abstemiousness, his
stomach could hardly retain solid food ; yet he never
seemed to take any rest. He was indefatigable in preaching the word of God, in inditing letters, and in composing
spiritual treatises, all marked by evidences of profound
meditation. They display so intimate an acquaintance
with the Scriptures, that almost every page is dovetailed
with passages from the Sacred Text.

During the last thirty-four years of his life, St. Alphonsus suffered from constant distempers, which became
aggravated with time; but he never permitted his ail-

ments to interrupt his ministerial or literary labors. The formidable vow which he took and faithfully kept, of never losing a moment of time, serves to explain to us how so many learned works could be written by him amid physical suffering so continuous. His contemporaries justly compare him in this respect to St. Jerome, of whom it is said : " *Morbos perpetua lectione et scriptione superabat.*"

Cardinal Newman never enjoyed robust health. His letters reveal a constant solicitude on the score of overwork and its consequences. His constitution, indeed, showed singular powers of continuous application all through his life; but there was not, even in his early days, the sense or aspect of exuberant health. In his busiest years, toothache was a constant source of suffering; indeed, it seems to have been somewhat abnormal.[1]

Cardinal Manning was the most emaciated prelate I ever met. His bloodless face was almost transparent. Owing to his weak digestion, he habitually ate very sparingly of the simplest food. When obliged to dine out, he partook only of a biscuit and a glass of water, for he never indulged in wine even in his feeblest condition. He was most indefatigable in active labors, and a close student as well. When travelling, he read and even wrote. In the notice of his *Religio Viatoris*, he states that "being for many days on a journey without work or books, I thought that it might be a fair time to write down, in fewest words, the reasons for what I believe." The little book remains as he then penned it. This is a fair sample of his habit of improving every hour, and of studying and writing while others under

[1] John H. Newman's *Letters and Correspondence*, by Anne Mozley.

similar circumstances would feel justified in taking rest.
Archbishop Spalding said to him in my presence, during
the Vatican Council : "I know not how Your Grace can
work so hard, for you scarcely eat or drink or sleep."

Archbishop Spalding, of Baltimore, was not only a
laborious missionary, but also a diligent student, a pro-
lific writer, and an indefatigable preacher and lecturer.
I never knew him to decline an invitation to preach even
during his much-needed summer vacation. Wherever he
was sojourning, the people, without distinction of faith,
were eager to hear him. Though a man of untiring
energy, he was, during the last twenty-five years of his
life, a chronic sufferer from an acute form of bronchial
and gastric affection.

Andrew Lang says that Sir Walter Scott wrote *The
Bride of Lammermoor* and *Ivanhoe* amid spasms of a pain
so severe, that he was insensible to the burning applica-
tions made on his flesh.

Of the Rev. Frederick W. Faber, the author of so
many popular Catholic works, the Rev. John Edward
Bowden writes : "With regard to his occupations at
Oxford, the friend who knew him intimately during
the whole of his undergraduate career, can attest to the
innocence and joyousness of his life, and to the determination with which, in spite of severe and often of excruciating headache, he formed those habits of study which
were the foundation of his future learning." The malady
of Father Faber's youth clung to him through life. In
the Preface to one of his books, he tells us that he wrote
for the most part in feeble health.

Cicero informs us that, when a young advocate, he was
compelled to suspend his professional labors, as he felt

himself unequal to the exertion of public speaking. He spent two years in Greece to repair his shattered health.[1] "He was lean and meagre, and had such a weakness of stomach, that he could take nothing but a spare and thin diet, and that not till late in the evening." [2]

Virgil, also, was of a delicate frame and a feeble constitution.

The violence and variety of the complaints with which Gibbon, the historian, was afflicted in his youth, necessitated his frequent absence from Westminster School. A distressing disease contracted his nerves, and produced the most excruciating pain. He continued to be an invalid till his sixteenth year.[3]

The History of the German People, by Dr. Janssen, is regarded as one of the most searching historical productions of this century; yet its author was always in poor health. He suffered from weakness of the eyes and general debility. He had frequent hemorrhages and, on eight different occasions before his last illness, his death was expected; but he was never deterred by his bodily infirmities from prosecuting his literary labors.

Dr. Samuel Johnson was born with a diseased constitution. He was the victim of malignant scrofula, which permanently affected his sight and hearing. In the first years of his literary career, he wrote in the midst of privations, and was obliged to dine most economically.

Alexander Pope was a life-long invalid, as Dr. Johnson tells us. For several years before his death, he was afflicted with asthma and other diseases, which baffled the skill of his physicians.

---

[1] *De Clar. Orat.,* 91.   [3] Gibbon's *Memoirs,* Vol. I.
[2] Plutarch's *Life of Cicero.*

3°. How many others, also, have stamped their name on the pages of history as legislators, poets, historians, and orators notwithstanding their serious organic complaints! Some were afflicted with an impediment of speech, others with total or partial blindness, and others with deafness.

When Moses was chosen to be the leader of the Hebrew people, he interposed as an obstacle his hesitancy of speech : " I beseech Thee, Lord, I am not eloquent from yesterday and the day before : and since Thou hast spoken to Thy servant, I have more impediment and slowness of tongue. The Lord said to him : Go, therefore, and I will be in thy mouth, and I will teach thee what thou shalt speak." [1]

Demosthenes, the prince of orators, was a youth of weak and delicate health. He was so emaciated in appearance that his companions nicknamed him *Batalus* from an attenuated contemporary of that name.[2] On account of serious defects in his voice and delivery, he made so unfavorable an impression on his audience in his first effort, that they ridiculed and interrupted him. But instead of yielding to despondency, he subjected himself to a severe discipline with the view of overcoming his natural impediment of speech. He was accustomed to recite several verses without interruption with pebbles in his mouth while ascending a steep grade. He used, also, to declaim on the sea-shore, to inure himself to the tumultuous shouts of the multitude.

St. Augustine says that the voice of St. Ambrose was weakened by very little speaking, and yet he preached every Sunday.[3]

[1] Exod. iv. 10–12.   [2] Plutarch.   [3] Confessions, B. vi.

St. Charles Borromeo overcame by incessant labor and attention his natural impediment of speech, and it was only after repeated disputations and discourses, that he subdued his bashfulness and timidity in preaching the Gospel.

John Philpot Curran, on account of his stammering habit at school, was commonly called by his fellow-students, "Stuttering Jack Curran." He succeeded in correcting his defective enunciation by reading aloud every day with emphasis and distinctness, passages from the best English authors, and he overcame his native awkwardness of manner by speaking and gesticulating before a mirror.

Milton dictated the poems of *Paradise Lost* and *Paradise Regained*, when he was totally blind, distracted by pain, and tortured by domestic infelicity.

William H. Prescott, the American historian, even from his college days, was a victim to impaired sight. During the latter half of his life, his eyes were so weak that he could read only for a few moments at a time, and he could hardly see distinctly enough to write at all. Yet he spent ten years in the study of modern languages as a remote preparation for his historical works. He afterward devoted ten years more to the composition of his *History of Ferdinand and Isabella*; then six to *The Conquest of Mexico*; and, lastly, four to *The Conquest of Peru*. During this toilsome period of thirty years, he had to employ the services of a reader and amanuensis.

Beethoven suffered from almost total deafness when he composed his greatest musical works.

While we are filled with admiration for these persevering men who, undeterred by physical infirmities, have risen to intellectual eminence, we cannot lose sight of the fact, that sound health is the greatest of earthly blessings. If so many leaders in the republic of letters have attained such distinction though hampered by bodily ailments, we may reasonably suppose that they would have won still greater laurels, had they been endowed with a vigorous and healthy frame. It behooves all students, therefore, while diligently engaged in the pursuit of knowledge, to beware of sowing the seeds of disease by excessive or indiscreet application. *Mens sana in corpore sano*, is a maxim always to be kept in view. Though St. Paul declares that " piety is profitable for all things," he asserts also that " bodily exercise is useful." [1] For the promotion of bodily health, it were much to be desired that gymnasia and other means of healthful exercise were established in all our collegiate and academic institutions ; and it is gratifying to observe that much attention has of late years been given by the heads of colleges to the important subject of physical culture.

4°. But the most formidable obstacles that confront a clergyman in the pursuit of study, are the multitudinous and distracting cares and duties of the ministry. As the devoted father and counsellor of the people, he is liable to be interrupted at any hour of the day or night, and new and unforeseen obligations are thrust upon him in an endless chain of succession. When a leisure hour comes to him, he may find it hard to control his wandering imagination, to compose his mind, and to concentrate his thoughts on serious literary subjects.

Yet strange to say, the most voluminous writers in the Christian world have been actively engaged in the sacred

[1] I. Tim. iv. 8.

ministry. Nearly all the Fathers of the Church were
bishops charged with the government of large dioceses.
I have already spoken of the studious habits of Gregory,
Chrysostom and Basil.

During the five and thirty years that St. Augustine ruled
the See of Hippo as its chief pastor, he was habitually
engaged in preaching the Gospel, in visiting his diocese,
and in administering the Sacraments. When we consider
the activity of his public life, there would seem to be but
little room left for composing books; and yet we cannot
but marvel at the extent of his literary labors when we
contemplate the nine volumes in folio which are the fruit
of his brain.

St. Augustine gives us a touching and graphic picture
of Ambrose, Archbishop of Milan, employing in deep
study the brief and uncertain intervals at his disposal
between the numerous business calls that were made on
him. "Often," he says, "when we entered his room
unannounced (for it was permitted to all to do so), we
silently observed him reading, and never otherwise engaged; and after remaining for a considerable time, we
quietly withdrew, without having the heart to disturb
him from the meditations in which he was absorbed." [1]

Alfred the Great was twelve years of age before he was
taught to read, and forty before he began the study of
Latin. Reckoning from that period to the time of his
death, which occurred in his fifty-second year, he could
claim but twelve years for scholastic pursuits. Yet he was
regarded as the best poet, the ablest writer, and probably
the most learned man of his kingdom. Edmund Burke
says of Alfred: "One cannot help being amazed that a

[1] St. Augustine's *Confessions*, B. VI.

prince who lived in such turbulent times, who commanded personally in fifty-four pitched battles, who had so discordant a province to regulate, who was not only a legislator, but a judge, and who was continually superintending his armies, the traffic of his kingdom, his revenues and the conduct of all, could have bestowed so much time on religious exercises and speculative knowledge." The secret of his success is found in his estimate of the value of time, and in his methodical distribution of the hours of the day.

It would be difficult to find any churchmen who have been more diligently engaged in apostolic labors than the celebrated Bishop Challoner. His vicariate included the city of London, and during his eventful life he had to contend with poverty and religious persecution. He was a melancholy spectator of the Lord George Gordon anti-Catholic riots of 1780, which involved the demolition of so many of his chapels and which hastened his death. We wonder how, notwithstanding his busy public life, he found time to publish so many works. Besides issuing a revised translation of the Sacred Scriptures with explanatory notes, he wrote some twelve books covering a wide range of doctrinal, historical, and devotional literature, the titles of which are still familiar to the English Catholic reader.

Bishop Hay, who was a contemporary of Bishop Challoner, endured in Scotland the same trials and tribulations that his venerable colleague had to suffer in England. His jurisdiction embraced about one-half of Scotland. It is hard to realize how, amid his incessant journeyings, labors and correspondence, he had sufficient leisure to write the three learned works he has left us,—so cogent

in reasoning, and so replete with scriptural quotations,—
The Sincere Christian, *The Devout Christian*, and *The
Pious Christian*.

The United States can also furnish some notable examples of prelates and priests who, notwithstanding the
distractions and interruptions of missionary life, have
enlightened posterity by their pen, as they instructed
their own generation by their apostolic labors.

The diocese of Bishop England, of Charleston, comprised the three States of South Carolina, North Carolina,
and Georgia. As those States did not contain a single
railroad in his day, he was obliged to traverse the immense
area of his jurisdiction in vehicles or on horseback. He
was habitually engaged in preaching at home, or in some
other part of the country. Owing to the scarcity of
clergymen in his diocese, he had frequently to perform
the ordinary duties of a missionary priest. He opened a
seminary in Charleston where he himself taught theology.
He established a Catholic periodical of which he was the
editor-in-chief, and sometimes, through dearth of funds,
he even had, also, to set the type. We could hardly
imagine that a bishop, engrossed by ministerial labors so
varied, would have time for serious study and writing,
had we not the evidence before us of his intellectual pursuits in six volumes covering a wide field of historical,
polemical and liturgical literature.

Few prelates have been more indefatigable in missionary duties than Archbishop Kenrick, of Baltimore. And
yet his literary labors are so copious and profound that
they would do honor to a professor exempt from the cares
of the ministry. His works comprise a *Moral and Dogmatic Theology*, a new *Translation of the Sacred Scriptures*

with explanatory notes, the *Primacy of the Apostolic See*, and *A Vindication of the Catholic Church*, besides several minor productions. So collected and concentrated was his mind, and so industrious his habits that, on returning home after several days' visitation, he would sit at his desk and resume his pen without even laying aside his travelling dress.

Rev. Simon Gabriel Bruté, afterward Bishop of Vincennes, used to walk from Emmittsburg to Baltimore, a distance of sixty miles, reading during the journey some classical author, or the Scriptures, or some historical work, and making critical notes all the while.

During the sixty-five years of his ministry, Wesley is said to have travelled about 270,000 miles, or an average of nearly 4,200 miles a year, and he delivered over 40,000 sermons besides numerous addresses and exhortations. He was withal a voluminous writer, and his works cover a wide range of subjects.

I venture to affirm that there are few clergymen in the country, no matter how extensive their parish, how numerous their flock, how pressing their ministerial duties; no matter how much they may be pre-occupied by materia. constructions, or how deeply immersed in indispensable financial operations,—there are few, I maintain, who cannot have at their disposal as much opportunity for earnest study as the Challoners and the Mannings, the Englands and the Kenricks could command in their day. Though oppressed by the cares inseparable from pastoral life, they are less handicapped than was Dr. Johnson who often wrote for a living when the wolf was at his door. This great author says: " Give an hour a day to serious reading steadily and perseveringly for ten years, and you will be a learned man."

If the priest from the time of his ordination contracts the habit of devoting an hour to study each day, he will find the labor easy and delightful; but if the practice is neglected at the close of the seminary career, diligent application will become an irksome task for him, and he will readily discover pretexts to pretermit altogether this important and sacred duty of his sacerdotal life.

CHAPTER XX.

IF two men of equal strength, prowess, and agility
engage in conflict, the one wielding a blunt and
cumbersome sword, the other a sharp and well pointed
blade, victory is almost sure to crown the combatant who
is the better armed.

The weapons of the Christian warrior are his books.
Thrice armed and thrice happy is the priest who has learnt
to make a judicious selection of a few choice books that
are to be his daily associates, and who is not easily beguiled from their society by a multitude of others whose
chief recommendation is often the charm of novelty. One
trusty friend is more precious than a score of casual ac-
quaintances.

Works with ambitious titles and an attractive exterior,
are thrown on the market in such boundless profusion as
to bewilder the unwary searcher after knowledge who,
like a hungry man sitting before a variety of food, will
be tempted to pass hastily from one dish to another at the
expense of his mental digestion.

The book that I recommend to the minister of Christ,
first and last and above all others, is of course the word
of God. The Bible is the only book of study that is
absolutely indispensable to a priest, and hence it is appro-

226

priately called by St. Ambrose, "*Liber sacerdotalis.*" He might be familiar with the whole range of ancient and modern literature, and yet his sermons would be lamentably cold and defective, if he happened to be ill-instructed in the Sacred Volume. On the other hand, if he is well versed in the Holy Scriptures, though a comparative stranger to human science, he will preach with edification and profit. The clergyman that draws his inspiration from the Sacred Text, is easily recognized by the sweet unction that flows from his lips.

The word of God is an inexhaustible treasury of heavenly science. It is the only oracle that discloses to us the origin and sublime destiny of man, and the means of attaining it. It is the key that interprets his relations to his Creator. It is the foundation of our Christian faith and of our glorious heritage. Its moral code is the standard of our lives. If our Christian civilization is so manifestly superior to all actual and preexisting social systems, it is indebted for its supremacy to the ethical teachings of Holy Writ.

Viewed as an historical chronicle, it is the most ancient, the most authentic, the most instructive and interesting record ever presented to mankind. It contains the only reliable history of the human race before the Deluge, embracing a period of more than fifteen hundred[1] years from the creation of Adam to the time of Noe. Were it not for the Hebrew annalist, the ante-diluvian world would be a complete blank, a subject of mere speculation to all succeeding generations. The Decalogue is seven hundred years older than the jurisprudence of Lycurgus,

---

[1] Upward of two thousand, according to the Septuagint Chronology.

two thousand years older than that of Justinian, twenty-seven hundred years older than the Magna Charta, thirty-three hundred years older than the Code Napoléon, and almost as many years older than the American Constitution ; and yet the Decalogue is better known to-day and more generally inculcated than any laws ever framed by the hand of man.

It is an historical monument that has remained impregnable for thousands of years, and has successfully withstood the violent shocks of the most formidable assailants. There is not a single arch or column or key-stone in the sacred edifice that does not show some marks of a foreign or domestic assault. But there it stands as firm as the Pyramids, unshaken and unriven by the upheavals and revolutions of centuries.

It gives us the narrative of the most memorable and momentous events, and of the most eminent men that have ever figured in the theatre of the world.

There is scarcely a notable incident recorded in Scripture that may not serve as a text for some moral reflection. Bible facts are sermons as well. Read Massillon's discourses and you will perceive the truth of this assertion. If "history is philosophy teaching by example," this definition is specially applicable to the word of God, for the Apostle says, "What things soever were written, were written for our learning."

There is not a single virtue that is not embellished by the luminous example of some patriarch or prophet, or Apostle, or king, or matron in the Sacred Book.

If you look for an exemplar of unshaken faith and hope in God, where will you find it more beautifully portrayed than in Abraham? In David you have a conspicuous model of tender piety toward God, and of magnanimity toward an enemy. Chastity and filial affection shine forth in the life of the Patriarch Joseph. Tobias and Job are held up as types of patience and resignation in adversity. Martial heroism is strikingly exhibited by Josue, Gedeon, and the Machabees; domestic affection, by Jacob and Ruth. Susanna is a sublime pattern of conjugal purity; and St. Paul, of burning zeal and apostolic courage.

Where shall we find a more graphic and impressive historical picture than that of Paul, his face emaciated after two years' imprisonment, led in chains to the audience hall of Felix, the governor at Caesarea? Felix is presiding, his adulterous wife beside him. The Apostle, with uplifted, manacled hands, preaches to Felix on "righteousness, on chastity and the judgment to come." Felix, stung by the words of Paul and oppressed by a guilty conscience, trembles before his prisoner and hastily withdraws from the chamber. Ah, well might he tremble! for to righteousness he was a stranger, chastity he had violated, and the judgment to come he had reason to dread. What a striking instance is this of the supremacy of innocence enchained over guilt enthroned! What an example to the minister of God to be fearless in the denunciation of iniquity!

While those great luminaries shine forth like stars in the firmament, guiding the wayfarer in the path of rectitude, the lives of others recorded in Holy Writ, who had fallen from their high estate, serve as beacon-lights, warning us to shun the rocks, which occasioned their destruction.

Saul's disobedience; Samson's and Solomon's licentiousness; the vengeful spirit and cruelty of Jezabel, with the awful retribution that followed; the treachery of Judas;

the falsehood of Ananias and Saphira,—these and other examples of the kind are striking object-lessons in the hands of God's minister, supplying him with forcible arguments to show that no crime can be committed with impunity, and that "what a man soweth, that shall he reap also."

√ The Bible is the only book that our Saviour is known ever to have read or quoted in the whole course of His public ministry. He makes no allusion whatever to the classic literature of Athens or Rome that flourished in His day.

It is the unfailing fountain at which theologians, Doctors, and the Fathers of the Church have copiously drunk. Who have surpassed in pulpit eloquence the Fathers of the third, fourth, and fifth centuries? There is a freshness, a virility in their sermons which have rarely been equalled and never excelled by modern preachers. Their giant strength was the result of the invigorating nourishment on which they fed. The only book of divinity they consulted, was the word of God. Origen had studied the Bible from his youth. It was his daily practice to commit to memory and recite to his father some passages of the Scriptures, and to sound their hidden meaning.

Basil and Gregory Nazianzen spent thirteen years in solitude, where they devoted themselves to the study of the Sacred Volume to the exclusion of secular authors. No week passed in which Chrysostom did not peruse the fourteen Epistles of St. Paul.

"To be ignorant of the Scriptures," writes St. Jerome, "is to be ignorant of Jesus Christ." "Read the Scriptures," he adds. "Let sleep overtake you while holding the Sacred Volume, and let the inspired page support your drooping head." He tells us that the young priest, Nepotien, by assiduous reading and daily meditation, had made his heart the library of Christ.

The Venerable Bede says: "At the age of seven, I entered a monastery where I consecrated my whole life to the meditation of the Scriptures."[1] He died in the act of translating the last chapter of St. John's Gospel.

St. Bernard's sermons are a scriptural mosaic. In fact, the Sacred Text is so interwoven with every fibre of the discourses and writings of the Fathers, that if the Bible were lost, it would be almost fully recovered in their works.

The favorite authors of Bossuet were Isaias and St. Paul, besides Homer and Tertullian. His mind was so penetrated with the two inspired penmen, that we can trace in his sermons, the majesty and sublimity of the prophet with the energy and conciseness of the Apostle. Mr. Wallon, a French writer, has published a separate volume of Bossuet's quotations from the Bible, with the view of demonstrating the fact, that he had incorporated in his works a very considerable portion of the Sacred Scriptures.

They who have read the speeches of the leading English and American statesmen and orators, cannot fail to observe what frequent use some of them have made of scriptural passages. Biblical parables and historical allusions, allegories, precepts, maxims, and other striking phrases from the Old and the New Testament are freely employed to illustrate and adorn their discourses. The Earl of Chatham and Lord Brougham, Patrick Henry and Daniel Webster are indebted for their richest thoughts

[1] *History of the Anglo-Saxon Church.*

to the pages of Holy Writ. In a single speech of Webster, I counted over a dozen references to the Word of God. One of his finest perorations is a paraphrase of the hundred and thirty-eighth Psalm.[1]

If it would be a shame for a statesman to be exceeded by a churchman in the science and discussion of statecraft and of the civil Constitution, it would be no less humiliating to a churchman to be surpassed by a statesman in the knowledge and application of the Scriptures, which are the groundwork of the divine Constitution of the Church.

Apart from its inspired character, the Bible is a model of literary excellence. What classic author, ancient or modern, can excel Isaias and St. John in sublimity of conception? or the Books of Samuel or those of Kings, and the Gospels in the charm and conciseness of historical narrative? or Jeremiah's Lamentations in pathos and tenderness? or Paul in eloquence? or the Apocalypse in descriptive power? or Job in majestic and terrible images? or David in elevation of poetic thought?

The grandest poetic creations of human genius pale before the Psalmody of the Royal Prophet. Milton and Dante have borrowed their noblest images from the pages of the Sacred Writings.

The simplicity of Hebrew pastoral life is portrayed in Ruth in a style so charming and so true to nature that it is not excelled by any passage in Homer, or in the Eclogues of Virgil. Dr. Johnson once read to some friends in London a manuscript copy of a pastoral story. They were delighted with the narrative, and desired to know the author's name. Imagine their surprise when he in-

---

[1] cxxxix. according to the Hebrew version.

formed them that it was an ancient document written 2,500 years before the discovery of America; in fact, that it was no other than the Book of Ruth. Had it been composed by an English author of note, selections from it would have found a place in our choice classical literature.

"An essay has been written to prove how much Shakespeare has been indebted to the Scriptures. The Red Cross Knight in the *"Faerie Queene"* of Spenser, is the Christian in the last chapter of the Epistle to the Ephesians. Pope's *"Messiah"* is only a paraphrase of some passages in Isaias. The highest strains in Cowper's *"Task"* are an expansion of a chapter of the same Prophet. The *"Thanatopsis"* of Bryant is indebted to a passage in the Book of Job."[1]

But the Bible should be read for a higher motive than for the sake of its style. It should be perused for the light and consolation which it imparts. When you open the portals of this temple of divine knowledge, you should not stop to admire the ornaments and decorations of the interior, but you should rather meditate on the words of wisdom that are inscribed on its walls, and contemplate the hallowed portraits looking down upon you, that you may venerate them, and hold them up to the imitation of the faithful.

St. Augustine says, "He who negligently receives the word of God is not less guilty than he who, through his own fault, would permit the sacred Host to fall on the ground."

The Ark of the Covenant was carried by the Hebrew people with great reverence, because it contained the tables of the Law, a portion of the Manna, and other emblems

[1] See *Men and Books*, Phelps.

of God's mercy.   With what awe and devotion should not
we handle the Ark of the Bible, containing the Commandments and the spiritual Manna of the Gospel, which has
nourished millions of souls for centuries.

Are not the words which Christ spoke nearer to Him,
and more profitable to us than the Cross on which He
lay? and should they not be prized accordingly?   Constantine the Great and his sons Constantius and Constans,
wrote a joint letter to St. Antony, recommending themselves to his prayers, and requesting a reply.   St. Antony,
observing the surprise of his monks, said to them without
emotion : " Do not wonder that the Emperor writes to
us ; rather be filled with admiration that God himself
should have written to us, and that He has spoken to us
by His Son."

When Francis Xavier was in India, he was in the habit
of reading the letters of St. Ignatius, not sitting or standing, but on bended knees, so great was his reverence for
his Superior.   With what a profound sense should not
we meditate on the Holy Scriptures, which are letters sent
to us by our Father in heaven !

We have all the more need of this admonition, as our
official duties bring us daily into contact with the word
of God when we celebrate Mass, and recite the Breviary,
as well as when we announce the Sacred Text to the
faithful on the Lord's day.   There is danger that familiarity may blunt our reverence.

Plutarch informs us that it was the habit of Alexander
the Great to sleep at night with a copy of Homer and a
dagger under his pillow.   You who are a chosen captain
of Christ, should certainly have as much attachment for
the Book of books as Alexander had for the Greek poet.

If you rest on your pillow, armed with "the sword of the Spirit, which is the word of God,"[1] you will find in it the best sedative for allaying mental troubles and feverish excitement; you will repose in peace and security; for, in the language of the Psalmist, "He shall overshadow thee with His shoulders, and under His wings thou shalt trust. His truth shall compass thee with a shield. Thou shalt not be afraid of the terror of the night, nor of the arrow that flieth in the day."[2]

When St. Charles Borromeo was advised to take some recreation in his garden every day, he replied that the Scriptures were the garden in which he delighted to recreate his soul. You have the same mission that Charles had. Visit daily this spiritual garden, cultivate it, partake of its delicious fruit, and pluck its flowers. By diligently tilling it, your spirit will be invigorated; its fruits will nourish you; and the choice flowers that you may gather will be a fragrant and healthful bouquet, diffusing its sweet odor, and serving as the best disinfectant to counteract the poisonous atmosphere that may surround you.

Like the Prophet Ezechiel, who was commanded by the Lord to eat the Book of the Law,[3] you should mentally consume and digest the Sacred Volume, until it becomes bone of your bone and flesh of your flesh, and is intertwined with every fibre of your heart.

We should apply to the Scriptures the advice which Horace gives about perusing the Greek models: "*Exemplaria Græca nocturna versate manu, versate diurna.*"

Let us become so assiduous in meditating on the word of God, that we may be said to live and move in that

[1] Eph. VI. 17.   [2] Ps. XC. 4–6.   [3] Ezech. III. 1.

spiritual world which the sacred writers have portrayed for us.

While you are yet young, when the memory is fresh and retentive, you would do well like Origen to learn by heart some striking passages of Holy Writ, which you can afterward use to advantage.

✓ "All Scripture, inspired of God," says the Apostle, "is profitable to teach, to reprove, to correct, to instruct in justice, that the man of God may be perfect, furnished to every good work."[1] You are always sure of your ground when you stand on a scriptural rock. You are always orthodox, always instructive; you are never false or exaggerated, never tedious or verbose, never frivolous or aimless; you are never preaching yourself, but always "Christ, and Him crucified."

Your sermons will be a torch that warms while it enlightens. You will not only captivate the minds, but you will also subdue the hearts of your hearers. "The people will be in admiration," not of you, but of your doctrine, because like your Master you will speak "as one having authority," and not as an actor or a rhetorician in the persuasive words of human wisdom. You will speak with an apostolic freedom of speech that will impart a supernatural force and energy to your eloquence. Your speech, like that of the Apostle, will be "not in word only, but in power also, and in the Holy Ghost, and in much fulness."[2]

Like the children of Israel, who "wept, and fasted, and prayed before the Lord,"[3] when they heard the words of the Law from the lips of Baruch, the prophet, your congregation will be filled with compunction of heart

[1] II. Tim. III. 16, 17.   [2] I. Thess. ١. ٥.   [3] Bar. ١. ٥.

when they receive from your mouth the words, not of man, but of God.

There is a grace in the Inspired Word, both to the speaker and the hearer, and an efficacy such as no human production can possess: " for, the word of God is living and effectual, and more piercing than any two-edged sword, and reaching unto the division of the soul and the spirit, of the joints also and the marrow, and is a discerner of the thoughts and intents of the heart." [1]

[1] Heb. IV. 12.

CHAPTER XXI.

THE STUDY OF THE FATHERS.—DOGMATIC AND MORAL THEOLOGY.—CANON LAW.—HISTORY. —GREEK AND LATIN CLASSICS.— ENGLISH CLASSICS.

IN laying so much stress, in the foregoing chapter, on the study of the Sacred Scriptures, and in giving that subject the leading place, I am far from underrating the vital importance to the ecclesiastical student of other departments of knowledge.

The writings of the Fathers of the Church are an inexhaustible storehouse of spiritual treasures. They are the best and the most approved commentators on the Holy Scriptures. As jurists and constitutional lawyers are not content with mastering the text of the Constitution and the organic laws of the country, but study also its ablest and most authorized expounders, so will the diligent disciple of Christ be amply rewarded by the luminous expositions of the word of God which are set before him in patristic literature.

The writings of the Fathers will assist the student in fathoming the hidden meaning of the Sacred Text, and will disclose to him a copious fund of interpretations which his own unaided efforts might fail to discover. The Fathers are models, not only as writers and commentators, but also as preachers. Their sermons are conspicuous for unction and earnestness, as well as for brevity.

Dogmatic Theology is a scientific study of Revelation. It is a digest of the grounds of Christian belief. Its province is to group together and arrange in methodical and logical sequence the various arguments from Scripture and tradition, from history and reason, in support of some particular doctrine of faith. It points out the relation and connection between the different articles of the Creed.

It sets before the reader in harmonious order the oracles of God, uttered at divers times, and scattered over the voluminous pages of the Bible. It marshals and coördinates these numerous sacred texts bearing on a particular dogma. It makes one Bible quotation supplement and confirm another. Text is added to text, like stone piled on stone in a building, each adjusted in its place, each strengthening and sustaining the other, till the majestic edifice of Christian faith is constructed from the exhaustless quarry of the Scripture.

Viewed separately, the passages quoted might appear less conclusive; but welded together in compact form, they have a cumulative weight, and an irresistible force of conviction. Take, for instance, the Primacy of Peter as an illustration. One might cavil at the proof based on a single text; but let all the passages bearing on his supreme jurisdiction be adduced from the Gospels, the Acts and the Epistles, and no honest inquirer can gainsay their convincing power.

Apart from the knowledge obtained, there is still another great advantage derived from the study of Theology. One cannot fail to observe the natural order, the rational method and sequence which the compiler of Theology pursues in arranging his proofs of a given proposition. The student thus acquires almost unconsciously systematic habits of mind for the collocation of his ideas in preparing a discourse or a treatise, and this logical precision of thought becomes a valuable aid to memory.

But the greatest advantage of a comprehensive Theology is found in the weapons of defence with which it supplies the Christian apologist against the adversaries of Revelation. The *Summa* of St. Thomas and the treatises of other learned theologians propose and refute more subtle and specious objections against religion than are met in the pages of the most formidable opponents of Christianity. These champions of the faith surveying the battle-ground of Christendom, are able to group together every form of attack from the beginning of the Christian era. They detect old errors constantly reappearing under a new guise, and they enable the student to be prepared at all points.

Some time ago, a Unitarian clergyman delivered a sermon against the divinity of Christ, which attracted much attention, as its arguments were regarded as the most plausible and effective that could be presented against this fundamental doctrine of Christianity. It was afterward discovered that he had borrowed his weapons of assault from the armory of St. Thomas, having presented *seriatim* all the objections found in the *Summa*, without referring to their triumphant refutation by the Angelic Doctor.

Should any one be disposed to attach less importance to the study of systematic theology, in view of the assertion made in the preceding chapter, that the Fathers of the Church were the most eloquent of pulpit orators, though the Bible was their only book of sacred study, I would answer that it is time enough for him to offer this excuse when he has acquired the mental grasp and patient industry of the Fathers. As well might a farmer of the present century reject the modern steam-plough, the sowing and reaping machines, on the ground that his forefathers were successful tillers of the soil, though they labored with the hand-plough and the sickle. While an adequate knowledge of the Scriptures is a pre-requisite for the study of dogmatic theology, it does not exempt us from the duty of devoting ourselves to this indispensable branch of ecclesiastical science. "These things ye ought to have done and not to leave the other undone."[1]

Next in importance to dogmatic Theology is the study of *Moral Theology*, which instructs the divinity student how to estimate the moral character of human actions by their conformity or non-conformity to Christian Revela-tion, to the positive teachings of the Church, and to the natural standard of ethics.

A Catholic priest is liable to be called upon every day, especially in the tribunal of Penance, to give a prompt and practical decision for the moral guidance of others. He has to decide whether an act is right or wrong, a mortal or a venial transgression; whether it is harmless or dangerous; and if dangerous, whether it is remotely or proximately an occasion of sin. He has also to deter-mine whether the offence committed demands reparation or restitution. In a word, every pastor of souls is a local spiritual judge. He is charged with the duty of inter-preting the divine Law for those committed to his care,

[1] Luke XI. 42.

16

just as the district judge is appointed to decide questions of a civil or criminal nature.

To be capable of giving a satisfactory solution to questions of this kind, a priest must not only be possessed of a judicial temper of mind, but he should also be acquainted with the complex cases of conscience involved in the Decalogue, as well as with the positive laws of the Church. The aim of Moral Theology is to enlighten the student on these points, and to support and illustrate its decisions by copious examples and rulings of Church authorities, particularly by the judgments of the Holy See.

Canon Law is another prominent branch of ecclesiastical science. The Church, like all other human societies, has her own laws and discipline for the good government of her hierarchy and people; and this disciplinary legislation is comprised under the head of Canon Law.

It were much to be desired that in every diocese there were found a select number of accomplished canonists, and it is to be hoped that a fair proportion of our clergy may pursue this branch of knowledge in the Catholic University of Washington, and in other advanced seats of learning.

All the clergy engaged in the sacred ministry should possess, at least, an elementary knowledge of Canon Law, especially in its practical application, and this result can be obtained by the study of the Third Plenary Council of Baltimore. The decrees of this Council embody the legislation of the preceding National and Provincial Synods of the United States.

The peculiar merit of the Baltimore decrees lies in the fact, that they are not like "new wine in old bottles." They do not contain a single obsolete law or canon, but all are eminently adapted to the times and country in which we live. They should not only be carefully studied in the seminary, but should be afterward reviewed, at least once a year.

It is gratifying to know in what high esteem the *Baltimore Council* is held by leading churchmen in Europe, and that even the Holy See has been pleased to recommend it as a model to the hierarchy of other countries.

The study of *History*, both sacred and profane, is one of the most delightful and instructive occupations that can engage the attention of the minister of religion. History is philosophy teaching by example. As history deals with concrete facts, they are easily retained both by the speaker and the hearers; and as nearly all great historical incidents are suggestive of some moral reflections, the wholesome lessons which they convey, are stamped without effort on the heart and memory. An interesting event of history is like a garment which adorns, while it affords warmth; it clothes the mind with useful knowledge, and enriches the heart with salutary reflections.

The student of history will not fail to trace the superintending action of Divine Providence in the birth, the development, and the decline of nations. He will observe that empires, as well as men, are amenable to Divine Justice, and in following the course of commonwealths down the stream of time, he will realize the truth of the Scripture axiom: "Justice exalteth a nation; but sin maketh nations miserable."[1]

In the memorable words of Cicero: "History is the witness of ages, the torch of truth, the life of memory, the oracle of life, the interpreter of the past."

[1] Prov. xiv. 34.

They who have leisure to cultivate the *Greek and Latin Classics,* will be amply rewarded by the treasures of natural wisdom, and charmed by the poetic fancy in which they abound. When we peruse them in mature life, our ripened experience enables us to appreciate their varied excellence far better than when the study of them was imposed as a task on our undeveloped mind.

No truth is profane to the Christian. All truth is appropriated and sanctified by religion, for its Author is the Source of truth.

Moses was instructed in the wisdom of the Egyptians.[1] He was thoroughly versed in the sciences cultivated by them, such as astronomy, physics, and mathematics, also in the literature of the country; and Daniel excelled tenfold in knowledge, all the diviners and astrologers in the whole realm of the Chaldeans.[2]

If Christ never read or quoted any book but the Scriptures, this fact reminds us that the Incarnate Wisdom needed no human instruction; if Moses and Daniel were advanced in the knowledge of the Egyptians and Chaldeans, it teaches us that we are not to despise, but to cultivate secular learning.

Cyprian and Ambrose, Basil and Gregory Nazianzen, Chrysostom and Leo, Jerome and Augustine, formed their style on the great orators and poets of Greece and Rome. No casket in their judgment was too precious to serve as a receptacle for the gems of Gospel truth.

As our Christian temples are not profaned by being designed after pagan patterns, neither is Christian eloquence desecrated by following the great models of Greece and Rome. Those nations will ever remain the standards

[1] Acts VII. 22.   [2] Dan. I. 20.

of literary excellence, as they are to this day the highest exemplars of architecture and sculpture. The orations of Cicero and Demosthenes, in point of style and construction, will always continue to be the best models for Christian oratory.

Solomon decorated the temple of the Lord with the gold of the Gentiles, and Judas Machabeus suspended from its walls, the trophies of the conquered infidels.

The Fathers of the Church declare that, as the Hebrews were authorized by Almighty God to despoil the Egyptians of their household treasures, so are Christians allowed to appropriate to themselves the intellectual wealth of the Gentiles, to adorn and illustrate the teachings of the Church. To-day the eloquence of ancient Greece and Rome is in possession of the Christian world, while Paganism and Mohammedanism are in intellectual decay.

It is no exaggeration to say that a clergyman's influence for good is vastly increased by a mastery of the English tongue, which can be acquired only by a familiar acquaintance with the English classics. He might possess the theological knowledge of St. Thomas, and yet labor under a serious disadvantage, if he cannot express his thoughts with precision, ease, and elegance. David encased in the ponderous armor and girded with the sword of Saul, was unwieldy and ineffective; while with merely his sling, he conquered Goliath.

Our English literature abounds in profound natural truths. It is marked by a masculine force and a sturdy common sense that appeal to the reason and judgment of mankind. I may add that our standard prose and poetical writers, with few exceptions, exhibit commendable reverence for religion and familiarity with the Sacred

Scriptures, from which they borrow many of their noblest thoughts and images.

But the most attractive feature of these authors is their exquisite style, which delights the fancy and captivates the understanding, by the happy and judicious form of words in which their ideas are expressed. The Protestant minister, notwithstanding his doctrinal errors, has succeeded in gaining the public ear by the charm of his speech, while the herald of truth has been too often handicapped, because his heavenly message was not conveyed in an inviting dress. The poet, indeed, has well said that

"Truth needs no color,—beauty no pencil."

But in order to attract the gaze of the spectator, truth must be clothed in a becoming garb.

It may be objected that the vast majority of our leading British and American writers are heterodox in faith. But if we can peruse Pagan authors with impunity, why not Protestant authors? If we can be proof against unbelief, why not against misbelief as well? Newman and Manning, Faber and Allies, with scores and hundreds of other converts, had drunk deep from their youth at the fount of English classical literature; yet we have never heard any of them declare that their daily intercourse with the masters of English style, was a bar to their conversion.

When President Lincoln was reproached for allowing the Southern national air to be played in his presence, he replied: "*Dixie* is ours since we have conquered the Confederacy." So can we say: All truth is ours. Truth, like the air of heaven, is the heritage of all. Our province is to seek the gold of truth, like diligent miners, and sift it from the dross of error. We should, like the bee, extract the honey of wisdom from the flower, and leave the poison behind. The student that is afraid of inhaling the poison with the honey, has not the moral vigor to grapple with the world.

I am speaking, of course, not to children, but to men who are, or are to be, the leaders of men, to men of tried virtue who have a wholesome dread of heresy, and whose sole object in the pursuit of knowledge, is to enrich the mind with the ornaments of heavenly wisdom.

If the great bulk of English authors are hostile or un-friendly to the Catholic religion, does not the same remark apply to many of the leading writers in Catholic nations? Whatever may be said of the doctrinal errors of the liter-ary celebrities of England and America, their moral tone is usually healthier than that of the average French and Italian writers of note. Addison, Johnson and Gibbon, Milton and Wordsworth, Tennyson and Longfellow are remarkably free from the taint of licentiousness.

While the English classical writers have been, for the most part, aliens to the Catholic faith, we can claim as our own, at least two of the most eminent poets of the post-Reformation period,—I refer to Dryden and Pope. Shakespeare, also, has been sometimes classed among the adherents of the ancient Church ; and certainly few dramatists have portrayed Catholic thought more hap-pily, or described Catholic Ritual more correctly than he has done.

We have reason to rejoice that the present century has produced several British and American authors of literary ability, sound in doctrine and unexceptionable in morals.

Cardinals Wiseman, Newman, and Manning, Doctors Lingard and Brownson (not to speak of living writers), have enriched our noble tongue by their erudition, and illumined it by their faith. They have presented their ideas in vigorous and idiomatic language, and clothed them in a graceful and attractive style.

CHAPTER XXII.

THE STUDY OF MEN AND THE TIMES.

AFTER the Bible, the study of mankind is the most important and instructive pursuit for the ambassador of Christ. The aim of his ministry is to enlighten and convince, to persuade and convert his fellow being, and to elevate him to a higher plane of moral rectitude.

The first step toward the accomplishment of this noble aim is to obtain a thorough knowledge of man, his springs of action, his yearnings and desires, his passions and emotions, his vices and temptations, and the arguments and motives, as well as the means that are best calculated to promote his spiritual progress.

Now, the knowledge of the mysterious kingdom of the heart is more accurately acquired by going to the original than by seeing it described in the pages of a book. An artist makes a better portrait from a living subject than from his photograph. We view objects in the abstract in books, but in the concrete in living men.

"No book," says Cardinal Newman, "can convey the special spirit and delicate peculiarities of its subject, with that rapidity and certainty which attend on the sympathy of mind with mind, through the eyes, the look, the accent and the manners, in casual expressions thrown off at the moment, and the unstudied turns of familiar conversation. . . . The general principles of any study,

249

you may learn by books at home; but the detail, the color, the tone, the air, the life which makes it live in us, —you must catch all these from those in whom it lives already."[1]

Books describe human beings as existing in times and countries, or under circumstances different from our own ; but in studying the race that surrounds us, we contemplate man just as he is to-day.

We see him, not as reflected through the mind of another, but as viewed by ourselves. Human nature, it is true, is everywhere radically the same, but it receives a coloring and an impression from its environments. Man is influenced and modified in temperament and habits of thought by the social and domestic circle in which he moves, and by the political institutions under which he lives. By a knowledge of his own times and people, the speaker can accommodate his remarks to the special needs of his hearers.

An exhortation that would be admirably suited to a French or Spanish congregation, might not be adapted to an American audience. A discourse against the evils of divorce, which is so vital a subject with us, would scarcely find any application in Ireland or in the Tyrol, where divorces are almost unknown. A sermon that would be most appropriate to a fourth or fifth century congregation, might be out of place in our time and country, as the prevailing errors and vices of those times are not the predominant errors and vices of to-day. St. John Chrysostom's arraignment of the voluptuous Court of Constantinople in the beginning of the fifth century, would be a libel if applied to-day to the White House at Washington. His denunciations of the theatre in that city,

[1]*Historical Sketches.*

could not be justly repeated from an American pulpit without some important reservations.

They who have a long experience in the ministry, cannot fail to observe the faults into which young clergymen are sometimes liable to fall, whose knowledge is chiefly confined to books, and who have had as yet little opportunity to commune with their fellow-men. They are apt to attach undue weight to matters of minor importance, and to treat lightly, subjects of grave moment. Or they may be strained, fanciful and unreal, and talk over the heads of the people. They may denounce in unmeasured or exaggerated terms, a social plague scarcely known by the congregation.

I once listened to a visiting clergyman condemning, in vehement language, low-necked dresses where their use was utterly unknown, and where the censure had as little application as it would have had among the inhabitants of the arctic regions. I heard of a young minister of the Gospel who delivered a homily on the ravages of intemperance before an audience composed exclusively of pious, unmarried ladies who hardly knew the taste of wine, and still less that of stronger drink. I heard of another who preached on the duties of married life before a community of nuns and aged inmates.

Some of our separated clerical brethren are not unfrequently betrayed into similar errors in ascribing to their Catholic fellow-citizens, religious doctrines and practices which they repudiate. A caricature instead of a true picture is held up to the public gaze, because the information is drawn from books, or hearsay, or tradition, and not from contact with living men.

Another advantage which we derive from a discreet study of men, is the habit of moderation in our judgment

of them. We will find that few men are altogether perfect, and few, also, totally depraved. Blemishes will be
discovered in the most exemplary character, and traits of
genuine goodness in the most abandoned and perverse.
This two-fold experience will teach us to use sobriety of
speech in praising virtuous men and women, including
even canonized saints, and to avoid excessive harshness in
reproving sinners; for if we paint righteous men without
a single fault or imperfection, we tempt the objects of our
eulogy to vanity, should they be within our reach, and we
discourage those who are earnestly aspiring to virtue. If
we describe the vicious as absolutely bad, we drive them
to despair.

This subject is forcibly illustrated by the different
methods pursued in writing the lives of men conspicuous
for Christian or civic virtues. Some authors portrayed
the saint, leaving out the man. They gave us the light
without the shadow. There was no background to their
picture. They exhibited an ideal character entirely free
from human foibles. Many readers regard these biographies as one-sided and unreal, and take no pleasure in
studying them. Others, accepting them as true, derive
little consolation or encouragement from their perusal, as
the model is beyond their reach.

Leo XIII. once remarked to Cardinal Manning: " It
has been too much the fashion in writing history, to omit
what is unpleasant. If the historians of the last century
had written the Gospels, for example, we might never have
heard of the fall of Peter, or of the treachery of Judas."[1]

The same Pontiff in his letter on Historical Studies
teaches that " the first law of history is never to dare to

[1] *London Tablet*, July 6th, 1895.

speak falsely; its second, never to fear to declare the truth."

Of late years, I am happy to say, we are treated to memoirs that aim at being true to life, that represent to us men of flesh and blood, as well as of spirit;—men of strong faith, virility of soul, genuine charity, magnanimity of character, and self-denial, but not exempt from some of the imperfections incident to humanity. The merit of these biographies is, that the author has either studied his subjects from life, or he represents them to us in their true light as portrayed in their own actions and writings. The public man, whether churchman or layman, who has never committed an error of judgment, or who was never betrayed into any moral delinquency, will hardly ever be credited with any great words or deeds worthy of being transmitted to posterity.

The best models of biography are the inspired penmen. They give us a faithful and accurate portrait of their most sacred subjects, without any effort to hide their moral deformities or defects. David's sin, Peter's denial, Paul's persecution of the early Church, the worldly ambition of the sons of Zebedee, the incredulity of Thomas, are fearlessly recorded without any attempt at extenuation or palliation. The delinquencies of those men arouse our compassion without diminishing our reverence for them, and serve by contrast to lend additional lustre to the halo of their subsequent lives.

St. Cyril uttered severe language against St. John Chrysostom, and yet both are honored on our altars. Who thinks less of Augustine and Jerome, because he sees them engaged in earnest theological controversy which almost snapped asunder the bonds of charity? Who finds his veneration and love for Basil and Gregory cooled, because of the melancholy estrangement which followed a long and tender friendship? What names are more venerated in France than those of Bossuet and Fenelon, although they were long involved in a heated controversy? Whoever would omit these episodes on the plea of edification, would mutilate their glorious lives. He would remove the shading which presented the picture in a bolder light. "Hath God any need of your lie," says the prophet, "that you should speak deceitfully for Him?"[1] Neither have God's saints any need of having their faults suppressed. They are not whited sepulchres, and they fear not the light.

The alienation between Burke and Fox at the close of their career, though much to be deplored, does not diminish our admiration for these two statesmen. It brings out in stronger relief, the inflexible character of Burke, who sacrificed friendship on the altar of truth. It shows us that upright men may sometimes differ in conclusions, without violating conscience, or incurring the unfavorable judgment of posterity.

Modern biographers, while dwelling with pride on the civic and military virtues of Washington, avoid the language of hyperbole in which some of his contemporary eulogists indulged toward the Father of his Country. They seemed to be so dazzled by the lustre of that great luminary before he descended below the horizon, that they could detect no shadow in the object of their adulation.

Webster, too, shortly after his death, was lauded with extravagant encomiums as a man above reproach. The

[1] Job XIII. 7.

dispassionate testimony of Mr. Bryce,[1] who says that his splendid intellect was mated to a character open to censure, will be acquiesced in by the judgment of impartial readers. Yet the American people admire and cherish none the less those two illustrious personages, notwithstanding the more discriminating verdict and less fulsome praise of modern critics. The spots discovered in these effulgent suns, serve only to disclose in clearer view the splendor of their achievements. "Paint me as I am, warts and all," said Cromwell to Cooper, the artist.

The first living book that a student should read is his own heart, which is a little world in itself, and a miniature of the great heart of humanity. "Know thyself," is a primary maxim of Christian, as well as of pagan, philosophy. Massillon was once asked how he could delineate so faithfully the emotions and rebellions of the human heart, and especially the intrigues, the ambitions, and the jealousies of the Court, which he so rarely frequented. He replied that he drew his knowledge from the study of his own heart.

The searcher after knowledge will also find an open and instructive book, full of object lessons, in the mass of human beings that he may encounter in the daily walks of life. He can pick up useful bits of information from his companions during his college course, and afterward from the persons he will meet on the streets, on the farm, in the workshop, the counting-room, the social circle, on steamboats and railroad cars.

Sir Walter Scott says that a man of active mind cannot talk to the boy who holds his horse, without obtaining some new thought.

[1] *The American Commonwealth*, Vol. II.

But it is especially while making his daily rounds through the parish, that the clergyman acquires profitable instruction and subject-matter for his sermons. He learns then the intellectual and moral standard of the people confided to his care. He is made acquainted with their virtues and vices, and with the sources of their temptations. He observes their patience and fortitude in poverty and sickness, and their Christian resignation in the presence of death. He will often contemplate in the cottages of the lowly domestic peace and content, which compensate them for their temporal privations, and which are too often wanting in the homes of the rich. I have found striking evidences of genuine piety and gratitude even among the inmates of our penitentiary.

All this personal experience will enable the minister of God to speak in a manner intelligible and attractive to his audience, and to embellish his discourse by allusions to the incidents of daily life like our Lord, who habitually instructed in parables and drew His illustrations from the surrounding landscape, and from the habits and occupations of the people.

This intercourse with living men not only enlightens the mind, but also quickens the sympathies and fires the heart of the speaker in the pulpit far more powerfully than abstract learning; for what is seen, affects us more sensibly than what is read, and the earnestness of our words is proportioned to the strength of our impressions.

The more the man of God studies the inner life of the people, their hopes and fears, their joys and sorrows, the more persuasive and moving will be his exhortations. He will come down to the level of his flock, he will be in touch with them, and they will recognize that his heart is in his work. He will retain his hold on the masses without neglecting the classes. But if the preacher has not the sympathy that is born of a knowledge of the people; if he cannot say with his Master: "I know Mine, and Mine know Me," he may enlighten without warming them; and his words, like oil poured on water, will not mingle with their hearts' blood.

These remarks apply to statesmen and lawyers, as well as to ministers of the Gospel. O'Connell's influence over the people of Ireland was such as no man in his generation ever exerted on any other nation. Playing on every chord of their heart, he could sway the multitude, and move them to tears or laughter. The secret of his empire over his countrymen was that he had sprung from the peasantry, had lived among them, knew their grievances and aspirations, and sympathized with them in their wrongs and sufferings.

Gladstone would never have attained his acknowledged eminence as a public speaker, without his vast experience in the House of Commons. It was in that great university of politics, that he learned the art of a consummate debater.

Daniel Webster was not more indebted to his book-learning for his success at the bar, than to his keen discernment of human character, and to his power to conciliate and control it. The following anecdote of him was related in my presence at a dinner in Washington.

He and Rufus Choate were once pitted against each other as opposing counsel in a lawsuit concerning an alleged infringement of a patent right on locomotive wheels. The wheels were before the jury. Rufus Choate

17

as counsel for the defendant, expended his legal acumen in a learned and labored mathematical essay, going to prove that there was an essential difference between the wheels and, therefore, no infringement on the patent right. Then Webster, who had gauged the character of the jurors, spoke for the plaintiff. "Gentlemen of the Jury," said he, "you have heard an elaborate scientific disquisition upon those wheels. I have nothing of the kind to give you. There are the wheels. Look at them." The jury looked at them, and gave him the verdict. A judge, who attended the dinner, confirmed the truth of the anecdote, remarking that he happened to be engaged in that suit as junior counsel. The difference between these two great lawyers was this: Choate bewildered the jury by the intricacies of a vocabulary above their comprehension; while Webster measured the intelligence of the jury, and gained his case by appealing to their common sense.

Napoleon, though a poor shot, was the greatest general of his age. He said with truth of himself: "I know man." He owed his success to his insight into human character, which enabled him to make a judicious selection of his military officers and State officials.

I have heard of distinguished lawyers, when they had an important case in hand, studying the habits, dispositions, and mental calibre of every member of the jury, and addressing to each one in succession a few pertinent remarks, calculated to convince his judgment, conciliate his good will, and gain his confidence.

Clergymen at the time of their ordination are, I think, as a rule, more thoroughly grounded in sacred science than graduating lawyers are in the abstract knowledge of their profession, because the curriculum of the former covers a

longer period of time than that of the latter. But what
a jurist may lack in book-lore, is compensated by his
greater readiness of speech and felicity of expression.
His faculties are sharpened by the contact of mind with
mind in the courts, and by his habitual intercourse with
the members of the bar, the jury, and the spectators.
The earnest pleadings of his distinguished and experienced
seniors, are the strongest incentives to his intellectual activity and honorable emulation.

The soldier of Christ, on the other hand, on emerging
from the seminary, is sometimes unwieldy. He is oppressed by the weight of his theological armor, till he has
acquired practice in the arena of Christian warfare. This
disadvantage on the part of clerical students, would be
overcome, at least partially, by the more general establishment and cultivation of debating societies for the senior
classes in our colleges and seminaries, where they would
learn to acquire ease and fluency of expression, and to
wield with dexterity the sword of the word of God.

They should, besides, profit by every opportunity to
hear and observe practised speakers; for as a person may
read the most elaborate manual on politeness and etiquette,
and yet be awkward and embarrassed in company if he
does not occasionally appear in refined society; so the
student may peruse the most approved treatises on elocution without much profit, unless he is brought face to face
with recognized orators, and feels the subtle and inspiring
influence of the living voice.

The learned men of ancient Greece and Rome did not
consider their education complete till they had travelled
abroad, and acquainted themselves with the habits and
manners of other people and climes; and I am informed

that, in our own day, a few of the leading universities of England and America have already a limited number of travelling scholarships.

Herodotus, the Father of Grecian History, derived most of the information embodied in his work from extensive travel and converse with men.

Plato, after being eight years a disciple of Socrates, spent twelve years in the pursuit of knowledge in foreign parts, before he returned to his native Athens.

Edmund Burke says of Homer and Shakespeare that "their practical superiority over all other men, arose from their practical knowledge of other men,"—a knowledge which Homer acquired by frequent journeys abroad, and Shakespeare by studying mankind at home.

Cicero improved his sojourn in Greece and Asia, by studying oratory under the best masters that then flourished in those countries.

St. Jerome, the most eminent Hebrew scholar of his age, visited various cities of Gaul and Greece, Antioch and other places in Asia Minor, Palestine, Constantinople, Rome, also Alexandria and other centres of learning in Egypt, where he consulted the men most conspicuous in those times for erudition and piety. When his own fame for learning was spread abroad, scholars flocked to him, as to an oracle, from all parts of the civilized world.

Sir Walter Scott's charming novels are remarkable for their accuracy in the portraiture of the Scotch character and of the scenes that he describes. He obtained his information by traversing Scotland, living and conversing with the people, treasuring up their bits of local traditions, and afterward interweaving them with his historical romances. "I have read books enough," he says, "and conversed with splendidly educated men in my time; but, I assure you, I have heard higher sentiments from the lips of poor, uneducated men and women than I have ever met with out of the pages of the Bible."

It is well known, that while Milton is read by the few, Dickens is read by the million. He made personal visits to the prisons, the insane asylums, reformatories, and boarding-schools of England. He frequented the haunts of poverty, suffering, and wretchedness in London. His sense of indignation is aroused against official insolence, cruelty, and injustice; and his warmest sympathy is quickened in behalf of the victims of legalized oppression and tyranny. He draws his scenes from actual life; he deals with the men and women of his own time, and he gains the popular heart.

I was never more impressed with the impulse given to knowledge by contact with learned men, than during the Vatican Council, when prelates of world-wide experience and close observation were assembled in Rome. Each bishop brought with him an intimate acquaintance with the history of his country, and with the religious, social, and political condition of the people among whom he lived. One could learn more from a few hours' interview with those living encyclopaedias, than from a week's study of books. An earnest conversation with those keen-sighted churchmen, on the social and moral progress of their respective countries, was as much more delightful and instructive than the reading in print, as a personal inspection of an International Exposition would be in comparison with a description of it in the pages of an illustrated periodical. The living words left an indelible impress on the heart and memory.

It is scarcely necessary to say that the student who aspires to improve his knowledge by travel, should already possess maturity of years and of judgment, and should have laid the foundation of the science which he desires to cultivate and develop.

Above all, he must be a man who has acquired the habit of close observation. Take, for instance, two companions returning from a journey made together. The mind of the one is stored with useful facts gleaned on the way, while the other has scarcely a single practical incident to relate.

It may be objected to literary tourists, that the knowledge which they gather, is sometimes purchased at the expense of piety; for Kempis says, "They who travel much abroad are rarely sanctified." This axiom is true, indeed, of those that make excursions solely for pleasure's sake, but not of the diligent pilgrim who starts on his journey bent on plucking the fruits of wisdom on the roadside. David gave proofs of self-denial during his warlike expeditions,[1] and he sinned in his own home. Jerome's pilgrimages were blessed with an increase of sanctity and knowledge.

As the minister of Christ is preëminently the friend and father of the people, he cannot be indifferent to any of the social, political, and economic questions affecting the interests and happiness of the nation. The relations of Church and State, the duties and prerogatives of the citizen, the evils of political corruption and usurpation, the purification of the ballot-box, the relative privileges and obligations of labor and capital, the ethics of trade and commerce, the public desecration of the Lord's-Day,

---

[1] II. Kings, or Samuel XXIII.

popular amusements, temperance, the problem of the colored and Indian races, female suffrage, divorce, socialism, and anarchy,—these and kindred subjects are vital, and often burning questions on which hinge the peace and security of the Commonwealth.

Politics has a moral, as well as a civil, aspect; the clergyman is a social, as well as a religious, reformer; a patriot as well as a preacher, and he knows that the permanence of our civic institutions rests on the intelligence and the virtue of the people. He has at heart the temporal, as well as the spiritual, prosperity of those committed to his care. They naturally look up to him as a guide and teacher. His education, experience, and sacred character give weight to his words and example.

There is scarcely a social or economic movement of reform on foot, no matter how extravagant or utopian, that has not some element of justice to recommend it to popular favor. If the scheme is abandoned to the control of fanatics, demagogues, or extremists, it will deceive the masses, and involve them in greater misery. Such living topics need discriminating judges to separate the wheat from the chaff.

And who is more fitted to handle these questions than God's ambassador, whose conservative spirit frowns upon all intemperate innovation, and whose Christian sympathies prompt him to advocate for his suffering brethren every just measure for the redress of grievances, and the mitigation of needless misery?

The timely interposition of the minister of peace might have helped to check many a disastrous popular inundation, by watching its course, and diverting it into a safe channel, before it overspread the country.

Nor can it be affirmed that the temperate and seasonable discussion of these problems, or at least of those phases of them that present a moral or religious aspect, involves any departure from evangelical and apostolic precedent. There is hardly a subject of public interest that has not been discussed, or alluded to by Christ or His Apostles. I may cite a few examples.

Our Saviour speaks of the relations of Church and State in His memorable declaration : " Render, therefore, to Caesar the things that are Caesar's, and to God, the things that are God's." [1]

When the ancients asked our Lord to confer a favor on the Centurion, they appealed to His patriotism, as well as to His zeal for religion. " He," they said, "is worthy that thou shouldst do this for him. For, *he loveth our nation*, and he hath built us a synagogue." [2]

John the Baptist gave this excellent advice to certain officers of the law who had consulted him : " Do violence to no man, neither calumniate any man, and be content with your pay," [3]—a counsel that all public officials would do well to take to heart.

St. Paul eloquently treats of the duties and privileges of citizens : " Let every soul," he says, " be subject to higher powers ; for there is no power but from God. . . . Render, therefore, to all men their dues ; tribute, to whom tribute is due ; custom, to whom custom ; fear, to whom fear ; honor, to whom honor." [4]

When the commander ordered him to be scourged, Paul protested against the outrage, and asserted his dignity as a Roman citizen, saying : " Is it lawful for you

---

[1] Matt. XXII. 21.　[2] Luke VII. 4, 5.　[3] Luke III. 14.　[4] Rom. XIII. 1, 7.

to scourge a man that is a Roman and uncondemned?"[1]
The same Apostle treats with admirable tact and apostolic
charity, the delicate race question, both from a religious
and social standpoint.[2]

St. James devotes a portion of his Epistle to Labor
and Capital. He denounces the injustice and oppression
of the employer in language which, if uttered in our time
from a Christian pulpit, might be censured as a direct
assault on the rich, and an incentive to sedition.[3]

The reigning Pontiff, Leo XIII., in his usual masterly
manner and luminous style, has, in a series of Encyclicals,
enlarged on the great social and economical questions of
the day.

In his Encyclical of January, 1895, addressed to the
Hierarchy of the United States, His Holiness says · "As
regards civil affairs, experience has shown how important
it is that the citizens should be upright and virtuous. In
a free State, unless justice be generally cultivated, unless
the people be repeatedly and diligently urged to observe
the precepts and laws of the Gospel, liberty itself may be
pernicious. Let those of the clergy, therefore, who are
occupied with the instruction of the people, *treat plainly
this topic of the duties of citizens, so that all may understand
and feel the necessity in political life of conscientiousness,
self-restraint, and integrity; for that cannot be lawful in
public, which is unlawful in private affairs."*[4]

Of course, the kingdom of God and the salvation of
souls are the habitual theme of the minister of religion,
the burden of his life-long solicitude; and the subjects to
which I referred, are, in the nature of things, exceptional

[1] Acts XXII. 25.
[2] Gal. III. 28. and Philemon 15, 16.
[3] James v. 1–5.
[4] Longinqua Oceani Spatia.

and incidental. They should be handled, moreover, with great prudence and discretion, with a mind free from prejudice and partisan spirit, and in the sole interests of Christian charity, social order, and public tranquillity.

Words inspired by motives so lofty, will strengthen the hands of the civil authorities; they will be "like apples of gold on beds of silver;"[1] they will be the oil of religion poured on the troubled waters of popular commotion; and the apostle of Christ, raising his voice in season, will merit the benediction of Heaven and the approval of all good men. "In the time of wrath," he will be a minister of peace and "reconciliation."[2]

---

[1] Prov. xxv. 11. [2] Ecclus. xliv. 17.

CHAPTER XXIII.

The Priest, the Herald of the Gospel.

MUCH has been written to prove that the ascendency which oratory formerly wielded over popular assemblies, has not only declined since the days of Demosthenes, but that its power has been practically superseded by the press, which enables millions calmly to read what only a few could hear from the living voice some hours before.

While it must, indeed, be admitted that the influence of public speaking has been weakened, it has by no means been supplanted by the newspaper. The personal magnetism of the orator is still felt whenever he has a subject of vital interest to discuss, especially in a nation like ours, in which popular government prevails, and political debates are so eagerly listened to.

What more striking evidence can we have of the persuasive and overwhelming force of eloquence than that furnished by Mr. Bryan's speech at the National Democratic Convention, held in Chicago, July, 1896?

The burning words of the orator spread over the surging mass before him with the force and rapidity of a prairie fire in his own Western country. The effect was electrical. The audience of fifteen thousand persons was swayed by the irresistible power of his eloquence, as the trees of the forest bend before the storm. The young

267

speaker, comparatively unknown to fame, became the idol of the hour. All competitors fell before him, and he was enthusiastically nominated for the Presidency.

Eloquence is, therefore, not a lost art. But whatever inroads the secular press may have made on political and forensic oratory, the newspaper can never be a substitute for sacred eloquence.

It is a divine ordinance, that the Gospel is to be propagated by oral teaching ; and that ordinance has never been, and it never will be rescinded. While the press will always be a powerful auxiliary for the publication of political speeches, it cannot be expected to render the same measure of aid in the dissemination of pulpit discourses. It is our duty, indeed, whenever we can, to avail ourselves of the press as a vehicle of Gospel truth ; but as the daily journal naturally deals with current topics, and not with facts of revelation, the publication of political speeches will be the rule, and that of sermons, the exception. Scarcely one Sunday discourse, out of five hundred delivered, is ever reproduced in the morning paper.

Hence, there is no reason or excuse that pulpit oratory should decline, or be less assiduously cultivated to-day than in any preceding age of Christianity, since it has as wide a scope and as sublime a mission now as it ever had.

The priest is the consecrated herald of the Gospel. How exalted is his message to the people ! how general its applicability ! how awe-inspiring his authority ! how profound the reverence paid to him ! how far-reaching and indispensable his influence ! how tremendous his responsibility and the interests at stake !

How glorious is the message that the minister of Heaven has to communicate! The preacher is charged with the most vital and momentous themes that man has ever been commissioned to announce to his fellow-being. He does not discuss from the pulpit subjects of a political or transitory nature, unless some moral issue be involved in them. The same Decalogue that Moses gave to the Hebrew people on Mount Sinai; the same solemn warnings that the prophets uttered on the hills and plains of Judea; the same Gospel that Christ preached on the Mount and along the coasts of Galilee; the same evangelical precepts that the Apostles proclaimed throughout the Roman Empire,—this is the message that the shepherd of the Lord has to declare to his congregation.

He speaks of God and His attributes. He speaks of a God infinitely holy, powerful, just, and merciful, of a God whose superintending providence watches over the affairs of nations, as well as of men. He speaks of man with his intellectual and moral endowments, of his relations to God and to his fellow-being, of his dignity and responsibility, of his origin and destiny, and of the means of attaining it. He speaks of death and its consequences, of a judgment to come, of the retribution of the wicked, and of the recompense of the righteous.

He discourses on these eternal truths, which have engaged the profound attention of sages and philosophers of every age and country and religious belief. These truths, however, were problems which philosophers and sages could not solve. They were "ever learning and never attaining to the knowledge of the truth."[1]

[1] II. Tim. III. 7.

But while the message of the Catholic preacher primarily deals with God and the spiritual and eternal interests of man, it contributes more than any other influence to the happiness and welfare of society. The Gospel is not oil flowing on the surface of life's turbid waters without commingling with them, but a leaven penetrating, fermenting, and purifying the social mass. The code of doctrine which the priest has to expound, is a vindication of social order, and a protest against anarchy and disorder. It upholds the legitimate authority of the civil magistrate and enjoins on him, the duty of even-handed justice. It inculcates on the citizen the obligation of obedience to the civil, as well as to the divine, law. It promotes the cause of good government and public tranquillity, of domestic peace and fellowship, of charity and benevolence, and of social and family purity. It sets its face against sedition and disloyalty, strife and bloodshed, against avarice, lust, and heartless cruelty ; against iniquity in high and low places, and against every turbulent element that would paralyze or disturb the tranquillity of the Commonwealth. In a word, the Gospel that he preaches, is the embodiment of the reign of law, the strongest bond that keeps together the diversified members of the national family, and the most potent factor in the development of the highest and purest type of our Christian civilization.

Another distinguishing feature of the Gospel, is its universal applicability. There is a marked difference between the political speech of a statesman and the sermon of a priest. The politician submits opinions that are often qualified by a variety of circumstances. They are, consequently, more or less convincing according to the party bias of his hearers, and they are received by many with some reserve. The speech of Mr. Bryan, which was hailed in Chicago with shouts of applause and adhesion, was derided in New York and London as a tissue of specious and dangerous sophisms. Even the fundamental principles of our republican form of government, which are so warmly and so justly cherished by all our citizens, without distinction of party lines, and which are regarded by us as self-evident political axioms, would neither find favor nor be admitted among several of the European nations. The genius of the British Constitution would be ill-suited to the people of the Chinese Empire.

But the Gospel which the priest announces is not weakened or affected by any circumstances of time or place or person. It is independent of State lines, of national boundaries, and of the forms of political government. It has the same force of truth in Tokio and in Pekin that it exerts in New York or Paris; it is never obsolete nor antiquated: it appeals as strongly to the present, as it did to the first century of Christianity, because the doctrines of religion which it embodies, are founded on the eternal and unchangeable Law of God. The pastor delivers a revelation which his hearers have the liberty, indeed, to reject, but not the right to gainsay or to controvert.

The message of the pastor is marked, also, by the stamp of unerring authority. The trumpet of the priest, unlike the voice of the Pagan philosophers, gives no uncertain sound. He can exclaim with all the confidence of the prophets: "Thus saith the Lord." Like his Master, "he speaks as one having authority, and not as the scribes and Pharisees;" for he is clothed with the panoply of

Christ, and is furnished with credentials as authentic as those communicated to the Apostles themselves. "As the Father hath sent Me, I also send you;"[1] "He that heareth you, heareth Me,"[2] says Christ to His ministers. With St. Paul, the priest can affirm that his speech "is not yea and nay;" but that "Jesus Christ yesterday, and to-day, and the same forever,"[3] is the steadfast and unvarying burden of his message to the people.

When the priest ascends the altar or the pulpit to preach, he is looked upon not as an ordinary man, but as the oracle of Christ. He can address his congregation in the language of the Apostle: "When ye had received of us the word of the hearing of God, you received it not as the word of men, but (as it is, indeed,) the word of God."[4] He is, therefore, listened to with a respectful attention and reverence rarely paid to a public speaker. How much more favored in this respect is the ambassador of God than our representatives in Congress! When a statesman rises to speak in our halls of national legislation, he is usually exposed to repeated contradictions and interruptions, and bewildered by noise and distractions:—pages are running to and fro on the floor of the House; groups of members are chatting together; others are reading, writing, or nodding in their seats; and sometimes he is speaking to almost empty benches.

I was once in company with a number of Senators, in Washington. Senator Bayard, afterward our Ambassador to London, happened to be one of the guests. I expressed to him my surprise and admiration that some of his colleagues could exhibit so much physical and mental endurance as to prolong their discourse for several con-

[1] John xx. 21.   [2] Luke x. 16.   [3] Heb. xiii. 8.   [4] I. Thess. ii. 13.

secutive hours, and even days, on the same subject. Then Mr. Bayard made me this reply: "Ministers of religion like yourself have a great advantage over us. You can talk as long as you please, you can say what you please, you can upbraid if you please, and you are heard with silent respect without fear of contradiction, while we are liable to be interrupted by frequent rejoinders and inter- pellations." I playfully retorted that we have a clear field because we are always expected to tell the truth, the whole truth, and nothing but the truth.

The remark of Mr. Bayard made on me at the time a deep impression, and suggested the following reflection, which I did not then express:

Since the members of the congregation have so much reverence for their pastor that they will not presume to admonish him of his faults in the pulpit, and since even his brothers in the priesthood will not assume the un- grateful task of reproving him, should not his own con- science and sense of duty be a stern monitor to him? for, "the just is first accuser of himself."[1] Is it not a crime against religion for an ambassador of Christ to abuse this exemption from public criticism which he enjoys? Imagine a clergyman strutting into the pulpit and, in the sacred precincts of the temple, before a hushed con- gregation, delivering himself in a tiresome and perfunctory manner of some commonplace remarks, which the people have heard over and over again; or becoming a *Jupiter tonans*, making up for lack of ideas by a thundering and aggressive voice; or talking throughout of dollars and cents, without any allusion to the Gospel; or indulging in general vituperation; or venting his anger on some

[1] Prov. XVIII. 17.

18

particular parishioner under a thin disguise of language which many of his hearers, as well as the object of his assault, can easily penetrate. I can hardly conceive a spectacle more cowardly and contemptible than that of an anointed minister taking unwarrantable advantage of the immunity which his sacred office bestows on him, protected by the armor of his priestly robes, sheltering himself behind the breastworks of the pulpit, and pouring forth volleys of offensive language that he would not dare to utter to a gentleman on the streets. Such license must arouse in every honest breast sentiments of righteous indignation. The people came for bread, and they received a stone. They came for peace and consolation, and their hearts were filled with sadness and irritation.

I would hesitate to use such strong language if I were not supported by prophetic authority: "Son of man," says the Lord to His prophet, "prophesy concerning the shepherds of Israel : . . . Thus saith the Lord God : Wo to the shepherds of Israel, that fed themselves. Should not the flocks be fed by the shepherds? You ate the milk and you clothed yourselves with the wool ; . . . but My flock you did not feed. The weak you have not strengthened, and that which was sick you have not healed, that which was broken you have not bound up. . . . Neither have you sought that which was lost. But you ruled over them with rigor and with a high hand." [1]

The herald of the Gospel should make it a rule of his life never to degrade the pulpit by intruding into it his alleged personal grievances. Christ gives him authority to preach His Gospel of love, not the gospel of hate or of pelf. The preacher that substitutes the gospel of selfish greed

[1] Ezec. XXXIV. 2–4.

for the Gospel of Christ, desecrates the House of God like the money-changers whom our Lord drove from the temple; he dishonors his ministry; he detracts from the reverence which is due to his sacred profession; he is a usurper, and not an ambassador of Christ.

But do not the prophets frequently denounce in vehement language, the rebellious children of Israel, and does not St. Paul instruct the minister of Christ to "reprove" and "rebuke," as well as to "exhort" and "entreat" his congregation? Does not the Apostle himself severely reprehend the Corinthians and Galatians? I grant it. But if the Apostle tells Timothy to rebuke his hearers, he immediately adds that the rebuke is to be administered with "all patience and doctrine." And if he inflicts a wound in one sentence, he heals it in the next. He says to the Corinthians: "I did regret seeing that my Epistle saddened you although for an hour. Now I rejoice, not because ye were made sad, but because ye were made sad to penance. For ye were saddened according to God."[1] This is the language of a kind father whose words of reproach are inspired by love and not by vindictiveness. He gravely chides the Galatians and calls them "senseless;" but before laying down his pen, he thus addresses them with all the tenderness of a mother: "My little children, of whom I am in labor again, until Christ be formed in you."[2] Surely, the dullest hearer can easily distinguish between the reproofs that are prompted by fatherly love and zeal, and the denunciations that are fomented by passion. The former produce sorrow unto repentance, as the Apostle himself says; while the latter inflict bitter feelings and provoke resentment.

[1] II. Cor. VII. 8, 9.   [2] Gal. IV. 19.

You will say again : Are not our pastoral clergy obliged to discuss monetary subjects from the pulpit? For our churches are frequently burdened with debt, and in this country, where there is no union of Church and State, the pastor has to rely entirely on the voluntary contributions of the faithful. Most assuredly. Indeed, I have known some noble priests to whom even the most legitimate and urgent appeal for contributions was very distasteful, and who erred rather from defect than excess in the matter. But the pastor's efforts to meet his financial obligations will be rendered most successful, not by habitual complaints and persistent demands, but by a calm and dispassionate statement made in season. Our people are proverbially generous. They will never fail to respond to the reasonable demands of their devoted clergy.

It is needless to say, that God sanctions the reverence paid to His priests, not to gratify their personal vanity, but to render their ministry more fruitful and effective; for the word of God acquires additional lustre and persuasive force when it is proclaimed by men who are honored with public esteem and veneration.

This leads me to the consideration of the far-reaching, all-pervading and indispensable influence of the priest in fostering and perpetuating among the people, the light of Christian truth. The priest is the *one* essential agent in the diffusion and conservation of Christianity; and the preaching of the Gospel through him is the divinely-appointed means for the accomplishment of that result. "How, then, shall they call on Him in whom they have not believed? Or how shall they believe Him, of whom they have not heard? And how shall they hear without a preacher?"[1] If each parish may be called a little world in itself, the apostolic man is the sun of that world. His beams radiate through every family. To borrow the idea of the Royal Prophet: His sound goeth forth into all the land within his orbit, and his words into the bounds thereof. There is no one who is not cherished by his heat.[2] This luminary has, indeed, many satellites, but they are all subordinate to him, and receive their light through him, as the moon borrows her light from the sun. I am far from underrating the salutary influence in Christian life and piety that is exerted by parental instruction, by the atmosphere of Christian homes, by the catechism taught in the week-day and Sunday schools under the guidance of devoted men and women, by the circulation of Catholic periodicals, and the diffusion of sound religious books. But after giving full credit to these and other valuable auxiliaries, it must be admitted that the waters of grace, flowing through these channels, will generally move sluggishly, and may eventually be dried up, if they are not replenished and quickened by the fountain springing from the pulpit. Moreover, in almost every large congregation there is a considerable number of members who never receive any refreshment from these minor sources. They breathe no religious air at home, they read nothing but the daily papers, they are engrossed by the labors and solicitudes of daily life. The only opportunity they have of hearing the word of God is at the Sunday Mass, and if they are not nourished on that day by the food of the Gospel, they are doomed to a spiritual famine for the rest of the week. They are worse off than were the children of Israel in the desert, who had

[1] Romans x. 14.   [2] Ps. xviii. 5-7.

to fast all day if they did not gather the manna in the morning.

The Fathers of the Third Plenary Council, profoundly impressed with these facts, command in addition to the usual sermon delivered at the late Mass, "that all those who have the care of souls, shall on Sundays and Feast-days, not excepting the summer season, at all Masses read distinctly in the vernacular, the Gospel of the day, and if time permits, instruct the people in the Law of the Lord for five minutes, all customs and pretexts to the contrary notwithstanding."[1]

So essential, indeed, to the preservation of Christianity is the ministry of preaching, that, if the voice of the Evangelist were hushed in a district or city for fifty years, the light of the Gospel would be well-nigh extinguished in that region. We have abundant examples to confirm this statement. When, in the sixteenth century, the leaders of the Reformation determined to abolish the Catholic religion in Denmark, Norway, and other parts of Scandinavia, they adopted the most effective method for accomplishing their designs. " The Catholic clergy were commanded under penalty of death to quit the kingdom, and the same punishment was decreed against those who might harbor them."[2] The Catholic laity and their descendants were subjected, indeed, to many pains and disabilities, but they were allowed to remain in the country. The enemies of the ancient Church knew that by silencing the pastors, the lamp of faith would soon die out in the hearts of the faithful ; and their efforts were so successful that, up to the present century, scarcely any vestige of Catholicity remained in those lands. The last surviving priest could say in the pathetic language of the

[1] Dec. No. 216.   [2] Alzog III. 190.

Prophet Elias : " With zeal have I been zealous for the Lord God of hosts; because the children of Israel have forsaken Thy covenant. They have destroyed Thy altars, they have slain Thy prophets with the sword, and I alone am left, and they seek my life to take it away." [1]

Daniel Webster in his memorable speech in the Girard will-case, delivered in the Supreme Court at Washington, eloquently and forcibly demonstrates the fact, that, from the days of the Apostles to our own time, the religion of Christ has never been propagated and perpetuated in any part of the world, except by the agency of the Christian ministry. "Where," he asks, "was Christianity ever received, where were its truths ever poured into the human heart, where did its waters, springing up into eternal life, ever burst forth, except in the track of ministers of the Gospel? Does history record an instance of any part of the globe christianized by lay preachers? And descending from kingdoms and empires to cities and countries, to parishes and villages, do we not all know that wherever Christianity has been taught by human agency, that agency was the agency of ministers of the Gospel?"

But it is hardly necessary to say that the vast influence which the priest exerts, involves tremendous responsibility. It is not enough for the minister of God to be the depository of the law, and to announce it to the people. He must labor with all diligence in bringing the Gospel home to the minds and hearts of his hearers, by persuading them to make it their religious and moral guide. Like a diligent husbandman, he must not only plant the seed, but endeavor to reap an abundant harvest. He should speak to them " not in the persuasive words

[1] III. Kings xix. 14.

of human wisdom, but in the showing of spirit and power," for he knows that it is in vain for him to preach to full churches, if he leaves the souls empty.

What was said by Simeon of Christ, may be justly applied to every pastor of souls: "He is set for the fall and for the resurrection of many in Israel, and for a sign which shall be contradicted."[1] For under God, it largely rests with him whether they shall accept the living faith, without which it is impossible to please God. Like his Saviour, though in a subordinate sense, he is "an advocate with the Father" for the people, and an advocate with the people for the Father.

And never did any counsel in civil or criminal court occupy so responsible a position as the Catholic preacher when upholding the cause of righteousness in the pulpit. God's interests are at stake. Man's immortal soul is on trial. Each individual conscience has to decide the issue for himself. It is the duty of the priest to vindicate God's honor, majesty, sovereignty, and supreme dominion, His justice and sanctity, and to insist on man's submission to the divine Law.

He has to convince the people that the narrow road, which their inclinations abhor, is to be followed, and that the broad road, which their passions and self-love desire to pursue, is to be shunned. With the prophet of the Lord, the priest says to them: "I call heaven and earth to witness this day, that I have set before you life and death, blessing and cursing. Choose, therefore, life that both thou and thy seed may live."[2]

To be successful in his pleading, he requires no small degree of learning, tact, and argumentative persuasion,

[1] Luke II. 34. [2] Deut. xxx. 19.

especially when we consider the three astute advocates arrayed against him;—the World, the Flesh, and the Devil, who will present the most specious and insidious arguments on the opposite side. "Son of man, I have made thee a watchman to the house of Israel, and thou shalt hear the word out of My mouth and shalt tell it to them from Me. If when I say to the wicked: Thou shalt surely die; thou declare it not to him, nor speak to him, that he may be converted from his wicked way and live: the same wicked man shall die in his iniquity, but I will require his blood at thy hand. But if thou give warning to the wicked, and he be not converted from his wickedness, he indeed shall die in his iniquity, but thou hast delivered thy soul."[1]

Mr. Gladstone, being asked what sort of sermons he liked best, wrote that, in his opinion, "the clergymen of the day were not, as a rule, severe enough upon their congregations. They do not sufficiently lay upon the souls and consciences of their hearers, their moral obligations, or probe their lives and bring them up to the bar of conscience; the sermons most needed are those similar to the one that offended Lord Melbourne when he complained that he was obliged to listen to a preacher who insisted upon a man's applying his religion to his private life. This is the kind of preaching men need most and get least of."

Those sermons are the most effective in which the people are so much absorbed by what they hear that they lose sight, as it were, of the preacher.

You may always hope to preach with fruit by observing the following simple suggestions: 1°. In every sermon

[1] Ezec. III. 17–19.

you deliver, have a definite object in view, such as the vindication of some special truth, the advocacy of some virtue, or the denunciation of some vice. Let every sentence in the discourse have some relation to the central idea, and help to illustrate and enforce it.

2°. Borrow as freely as possible, your thoughts and even your expressions from the pages of Scripture, especially of the New Testament.

3°. Master your subject to the best of your ability. Commit to memory at least the leading facts logically arranged.

4°. Be intensely earnest in the delivery of your discourse. Thus your hearers will be convinced that your heart is in your work. They will be in sympathy with you, they will catch your spirit, and will be warmed by the sacred flame issuing from your mouth.

The Gospel message conduces most to edification and spiritual profit when conveyed through the medium of direct and simple language. High-sounding phrases may tickle the ear, and gain admiration for the speaker, but they will not excite compunction of heart in the hearers. Affectation of style and manner, or straining for effect, makes a preacher unnatural and pedantic. It is a desecration of the pulpit.

Plain speech that needs no effort to be understood, is not only necessary for the masses, but is the most acceptable even to cultivated minds. Men listen to sermons not for the sake of abstract information, but for religious and moral improvement. The true aim of a discourse is not so much to enlighten the mind as to move the heart, not so much to convince us of our duty as to impel us to fulfil it; therefore, the appeals best calculated to rouse the conscience, are straightforward and to the point, un-encumbered by ponderous phraseology. This is genuine eloquence, because it fulfils the legitimate end of preaching, namely, the spiritual progress of the hearers.

The most sublime thoughts may be embodied in the plainest words. What is more elevated in sentiment than Paul's exhortation on Charity, and yet what language is more clear and transparent than his? Any mental exertion required to follow the preacher and seize his thoughts, is painful to the audience, and chilling to the spirit of devotion. Daniel Webster used to complain of this kind of discourses. It involved too severe a strain on the intellect to be in harmony with the spirit of worship. In the House of God, he said that he wanted to meditate " upon the simple verities, and the undoubted facts of religion," and not on mere abstractions or speculations.

Except on extraordinary occasions, a sermon should not be lengthy. A discourse occupying from twenty to thirty minutes, if judiciously prepared, will contain abundant matter to instruct and edify without fatiguing the congregation. A surfeit of spiritual, as well as of corporal, food is hurtful to those who partake of it.

St. Francis de Sales approved extremely of shortness in sermons and said that lengthiness was the most general defect of the preachers of his day. "When the vine," he said, " produces a great deal of wood, then it is that it bears the least fruit. A multitude of words never produces a great effect. Observe all the homilies and sermons of the ancient fathers—how short they are, but O how much more efficacious they were than ours! The good St. Francis of Assisi in his rule, enjoins upon the preachers of his Order to be brief. Believe me, I speak from experience, and from very long experience; the more you say, the less will be remembered; the more you say, the less will your hearers profit. By dint of overloading their memory you make it break down, as lamps are put out by too much oil, and plants are stifled by too much watering. When a sermon is too long, the end makes us forget the middle, and the middle, the beginning."

"Preachers of very moderate powers are endurable provided they are brief, while such as are excellent become burdensome when they are too long. A preacher cannot have a more offensive fault than lengthiness. You must say little and that good, and inculcate it diligently, not making the least account of those fastidious minds who are displeased when a preacher repeats a thing, and goes over the same ground again. What! is it not necessary in making a work of iron, to heat it over and over again, and in painting, to touch and retouch repeatedly? How much more, then, is it needful, in order to imprint eternal truths on hearts confirmed in evil, and on hardened intellects?"[1]

---

[1] *Life of St. Francis de Sales*, by Robert Ornsby.

...ERMONS.—EXTEMPORANEOUS
...ACHING.

... of a sermon usually depend
...d on its composition. The
...wo-fold, the remote and the

...is the work of a whole life.
...t of knowledge that has any
...y, and includes all sources of
... to a newspaper paragraph

...re the mind is stored with
... more abundant will be the
...can dispense to the people.
..., " maketh *a full man;* con-
...ference, a ready man; and writing, an exact man." In a
word, remote preparation is the raw material out of which
the apostolic workman will construct a discourse fitting
the intellectual and moral stature of his congregation.

I would strongly advise young clergymen to provide
themselves with a repertory, or memorandum book, alpha-
betically arranged, in which to note down any striking
idea or passage that will be suggested during their professional studies and discursive reading. Many a precious
ray of thought will flash across the student's mind, like

the transit of a planet in the heavens, but will be irrevocably lost to his vision, unless photographed on the spot, and recorded on paper. The best of our English, as well as of French, writers have been accustomed to catch those fleeting visitors before they vanished into the regions of oblivion. Bacon left after him copious manuscripts which he called *Sudden Thoughts set down for Use.* For more than thirty years, the Count de Maistre was accustomed to jot down whatever subject of particular interest he met in his reading, accompanying his extracts with comments. He recorded, also, before they were extinguished from his memory, those sudden scintillations of thought that shot through his mind.

We are all familiar with the two volumes of exquisite matter left us by Father Faber, and which are published under the title, *Notes on Doctrinal and Spiritual Subjects.* They are gems of the first water, and we shall ever regret the setting that would have been given them by the mind that conceived them, had God willed to spare him a little longer. As they are, they afford to the serious thinker ample food for meditation on some of the most exalted truths of our holy faith.

Besides the remote preparation, the minister of God should devote a reasonable time to the proximate and immediate construction of his discourse, by a profound and prayerful consideration of the subject-matter on which he intends to speak, as well as on the class of people he will have to address. This important preliminary survey will enable him to preach with clearness and precision, with order and method, as well as with confidence and fruit. By neglecting this preparatory exercise, the majority of speakers will betray a rashness or a diffidence of manner; they will indulge in tedious repetitions, and will inflict on their hearers an ill-arranged discourse.

The conscientious legal practitioner does not trust to his general knowledge of jurisprudence in pleading the cause of his client; but in each particular case, he studies the law and the facts bearing on the question in dispute, and he formulates a brief which may be called a legal sermon.

When a trustworthy physician is consulted on a serious case, he first makes a thorough diagnosis of the patient before him, and then applies to the invalid the general principles of medical science which he has mastered as a student, as well as the special knowledge he has since acquired in the most recent development of his profession.

The cause of the defeat of the French in the Franco-Prussian war is ascribed to the fact, that, while both nations were warlike and had vast military resources, Germany was actually prepared for the conflict, but France was not. The first Napoleon, perhaps the greatest military genius of the century, though having under his command well-equipped armies, never risked an important engagement without elaborate preparation. He mapped out a plan of campaign, carefully surveyed the field, and acquainted himself, as far as possible, with the strength and position of the enemy. He posted his men on the best vantage-ground, and threw his most reliable troops on points where their charge would be most effective and decisive.

The Christian leader, armed " with the sword of the Spirit which is the word of God," should in like manner diligently set before himself the nature of the spiritual adversaries against whom he has to contend. He should arouse to action his intellectual and moral forces, and arrange them in the most judicious order, if he hopes to succeed in routing the enemy and in conquering for his Master the citadel of the soul. Should he recklessly hazard an assault without this preliminary study, he may fire at random, and engage in a desultory warfare, which will inflict few wounds on sin and gain few conquests for Christ.

The priest who ascends the pulpit without due premeditation on occasions which could easily have been foreseen, is tempting Providence and dishonoring his ministry; he is lowering the dignity of the Gospel message, and exposing himself to well-merited humiliation and criticism. Several years ago, a certain clergyman delivered a discourse in the Baltimore Cathedral, in presence of some distinguished Prelates, including Archbishop Hughes. At the dinner which followed, the preacher remarked : "Upon my word, until I entered the pulpit, I had not determined on the subject of my sermon." "I thought as much when I heard you," quietly rejoined the Archbishop of New York. The speaker had hoped to be complimented on his impromptu effort; but instead of praise, he received a just rebuke, for he had had ample leisure to arrange his thoughts and study his sermon. He was guilty of rashness if he had not prepared the sermon ; or of vanity and falsehood if he had previously studied it, while pretending that the discourse was improvised.

The length of time to be devoted to the preparation of a sermon largely depends on local circumstances, as well as on the talents and experience of the priest. Bishop McGill, of Richmond, one of the most scholarly and logical Christian apologists of his day, was accustomed to begin the composition of the Sunday discourse on the preceding Thursday.

Father Lacordaire, as one of his colleagues informed me, made it a rule not to deliver a set sermon without receiving at least one day's notice. "I have too much respect," he said, "for the word of God, for my hearers, as well as for myself, to preach without due preparation." He referred, of course, to preachments delivered on the regularly appointed days, or on extraordinary occasions which could have been foreseen. For I have no doubt that, in an emergency, the illustrious Dominican would have spoken at an hour's notice, rather than deprive the congregation of the blessing of God's word. Nay, he would several times a day cheerfully "give to them that asked him," and "would deal his bread to the hungry," rather than "send them away fasting;" for like St. Francis de Sales, he would say: "God will graciously multiply the loaves."

Some zealous pastors have adopted the practice of determining on the subject of the weekly discourse, and of constructing its framework, or skeleton, at the beginning of the week. This skeleton gradually and imperceptibly assumes a living soul, with flesh, and bones, and nerves, form and development. New ideas spring up, and arrange themselves almost unconsciously in the mind, even while the priest is taking some recreation, or while engaged in his daily pursuits. Fresh thoughts are suggested by the perusal of a book, and by habits of observation. By the end of the week, he has before him a clear and well-defined picture of the theme he intends to announce to the congregation.

19

As to the manner of preparing a discourse, some are in the habit of writing it out, and committing it to memory; others take extensive notes, while others content themselves with profoundly meditating on the subject, and arranging the thoughts in their mind. Without presuming to assert which of these is the best method, I will simply say that deep consideration is as essential to the merit of a sermon, as contrition is to the integrity of the Sacrament of Penance. Each should follow the genius and bent of his own mind. But it is universally conceded that young clergymen should, for some years after their ordination, write their sermons and study them by heart, so as to acquire habits of order and precision of thought together with copiousness and felicity of expression.

But some one to justify himself for not studying his sermon beforehand, may quote the following words of our Lord: "Take no thought how or what to speak, for it shall be given you in that hour what to speak."[1] "Does not this text warrant me in trusting in the inspiration of Heaven, rather than in my own intellectual efforts? and do I not pay a higher homage to God by relying more on His promised light, than on my own industry for the success of my exhortations?"

This oft-quoted and much abused passage refers, as the context clearly shows, to those critical and perilous times when the Apostles were brought before kings and governors, and when they were exhorted to proclaim their faith in Christ at the risk of their life. It has no application, therefore, to the ordinary preaching of the Gospel, and it cannot be justly cited as a plea for exempting us from

[1] Matt. x. 19.

the obligation of studious application before announcing the Word of God.

Again, I may be told that the Apostle despised "the persuasive words of human wisdom," that divine truth needs no embellishment, that it is most attractive when presented in its native simplicity, that it is best adorned when adorned the least, and that to clothe the living word in the vesture of studied phrases is as useless as

"To gild refined gold, to paint the lily, to throw a perfume on the violet."

But who can deny that the gem of heavenly truth ought to have an appropriate setting? The Gospel message should be presented not, indeed, with meretricious ornaments, but dressed in language that will exhibit it in all its grace and beauty; now, this cannot be accomplished without human skill and labor.

Another will say: "I am so much preoccupied by other engrossing duties of the ministry that I have scarcely a leisure moment to prepare the usual Sunday sermon." No one, on the plea of want of time, can reasonably exempt himself from the composition of the discourse for the Lord's-Day. A clergyman of systematic habits, who judiciously economizes the hours of the day, will ordinarily find ample space for the faithful discharge of all his ministerial works, among which the preaching of the Gospel holds the first rank. It should not, therefore, be relegated to a subordinate place. When the Apostles were compelled for want of time to pretermit a portion of the duties that had devolved on them, they specially reserved for themselves that of preaching, and committed other functions of the ministry to the deacons.[1]

[1] Acts VI.

It will, indeed, not unfrequently happen that the minister of God will be called upon to deliver a discourse though with little opportunity for a previous consideration of the subject. To consent to speak words unto edification in such contingencies, when charity and zeal demand it, is the mark of an apostolic man. On such extraordinary occurrences, he can confidently apply to himself the words addressed to Moses: "Go, therefore, and I will be in thy mouth, and I will teach thee what thou shalt speak."[1]

If he feels a sense of humiliation from the consciousness of not having acquitted himself to his satisfaction, the sacrifice will be well-pleasing to God. His personal reputation sinks in value before the salvation of his neighbor. It is far better for him to serve his brethren with spiritual bread hastily prepared, than to send them away empty. Instead of finding fault with him who ministered to them, they will admire and bless him in their heart, as the multitude blessed our Lord for feeding them in an emergency in the desert with plain, but nutritious food.

The conduct of St. Francis de Sales on such occasions is a safe guide for the ambassador of Christ to follow: "When I was provost," says Francis, "I used to preach on every occasion, whether in the Cathedral or the parish churches, down to the smallest confraternities; I never refused any one. 'Give to them that ask.' My dear father used to hear the bells ringing, and asked who preached? 'Who but your son?' was the reply. At last, he took me aside and said: 'My son, indeed you preach too much; even on week days, I hear the sermon bell going, and it is forever the provost, the provost!

[1] Exod. iv. 12.

In my time it was very different; sermons were much rarer, but goodness knows what real preachments they were;—so studied, so learned,—more Latin and Greek in one of them than you stick into a dozen! Everybody was edified and delighted; they trooped to listen as if they expected to pick up manna. But now you make sermons such everyday matters, that nobody thinks much of them or of you.' You see, my father said what he thought; you may believe that it was from no lack of love to me; but he went by the world's maxims. Believe me, we don't preach half enough: '*Nunquam satis dicitur, quod nunquam satis discitur.*'"

With regard to discourses and phrases which have been popularly classified as extemporaneous, or spoken on the spur of the moment, I may remark that they were either carefully prepared immediately beforehand, or the ideas they contained were the fruit of long and deep study.

Sheridan had the reputation of being a great impromptu orator. But those who were familiar with his private life, declare that he was accustomed to polish and repolish with the most diligent attention those brilliant passages which fascinated the House of Commons, and which had all the appearance of improvised flashes of thought.

Edward Everett, on one occasion, delivered an address to the students of Harvard University. In the course of his remarks, he upset, apparently by accident, a glass of water that sat before him. Instantly he apostrophized the drop that had adhered to his uplifted finger, and dazzled his audience by an eloquent allusion to the power and utility of water. His hearers entertained no doubt that the digression was entirely spontaneous and unpremeditated. When the exercise was over, the speaker had the candor to avow to the students that the spilling of the water was intentional, and that every word of the apostrophe had been prepared with the greatest care.

"I was informed," says Goodrich, "by a member of Monroe's Cabinet, that he heard Pinkney, about five o'clock of a winter morning, reciting and committing to memory in his own room, the peroration of a plea which he heard delivered the same day before the Supreme Court."[1] This peroration was regarded at the time as an extemporaneous outburst.

The extraordinary ability which some orators have displayed in improvising discourses, is due to their long and earnest habits of study. The words of our Saviour may be applied to them : "The scribe instructed in the kingdom of heaven, is like to a man that is a householder, who bringeth forth out of his treasure new things and old."[2] The genius of these men does not consist in suddenly conceiving and giving expression to new thoughts in the heat of an oration, but rather in drawing out the intellectual forces from the well-furnished citadel of their mind, and in promptly marshalling them for the occasion. Sometimes in the glow and fervor of delivery, when all the powers of the mind are aroused to their highest energy, a beautiful idea long since forgotten, or a charming picture which had almost faded from the mind, will spontaneously reappear before the mental vision, and be eagerly seized to enrich and illustrate the argument of the speaker. But these are "angels' visits, few and far between."

Bishop England, of Charleston, was perhaps the ablest pulpit orator that has ever appeared before an American

---

[1] Personal Recollections, p. 776.　　　[2] Matt. XIII. 52.

Catholic audience. After a few moments' notice, he could speak for several consecutive hours on any subject within the range of the religious domain; and so eager were the people to hear him, without regard to their convictions of faith, that he was often solicited to address a congregation on arriving in a town or city after a fatiguing journey. Having been invited to preach at the dedication of St. John's Church, Frederick, in 1839, he reached that town on Sunday morning after travelling all night in the stage-coach from Baltimore. When the sexton went for him to the Sacristy at the appointed time, he found the bishop buried in profound sleep. The discourse, however, was worthy of the orator. Being once questioned by a priest how he could preach extempore with so much facility, clearness, and force, he gave this answer: "For many years after my ordination, I not only carefully composed my sermons, but I even wrote them out, and committed them, at least substantially, to memory. My ministerial life has been a continuous preparation for the pulpit." He was a diligent student up to his last illness.

The speech of Daniel Webster in the United States Senate in reply to Hayne, is often quoted as a marvellous effort of impromptu oratory. Hayne's speech was in response to a previous oration of Webster. His argument was regarded by his friends as invincible, whilst Mr. Webster was thought to have exhausted his ammunition in his previous discourse. Hayne's address was made on the 25th of January, 1830, and as Webster was known to have spent that evening in the social company of friends, he had no time to study his reply except on the following morning. He spoke for several hours on the

26th and 27th of January, and competent critics consider his rejoinder the ablest forensic effort ever pronounced in the American Senate. If this oration, delivered in an emergency, abounds in so much wealth of constitutional knowledge, it was the fruit of the accumulated labor of many years. It was subjected after its delivery to a long and careful process of revision before it was given officially to the public.

Mr. Winthrop asserts that it was Webster's practice to prepare himself long beforehand for extraordinary contingencies, so that when the occasion presented itself he was ready to strike. In his speech on the *Presidential Protest*, he refers to England as "a power which has dotted over the surface of the whole globe with her possessions and military posts, whose morning drum-beat following the sun, and keeping company with the hours, circles the earth with one unbroken strain of the martial airs of England." Being asked whether that elegant passage was an impromptu, "An impromptu!" he exclaimed with an expression of surprise. "Why that idea first occurred to me twenty years before, while I was standing on the Heights of Abraham in Quebec, and I have been trying to work it into shape ever since. But I have never succeeded to my satisfaction till now."[1]

In his oration at the laying of the corner-stone of the Bunker Hill Monument, he thus begins to apostrophize the surviving soldiers of the Revolution who sat before him: "Venerable men! you have come down to us from a former generation." The entire passage, containing about five hundred words, was also considered as the expression of a sudden thought inspired by the sight of

[1] Robert C. Winthrop, in *Scribner's Magazine*, Jan., 1894.

the veterans in front of him.   But his son declared that, some time before the speech was delivered, he heard his father declaiming to himself these words while fishing at Cape Cod.

Cardinal Wiseman's range of studies was so extensive that, on a few moments' notice, as Cardinal Vaughan informed me, he could instruct and entertain an audience for half an hour on any subject proposed to him, embracing literature, science, art, or religion.   His brain, like a melodious organ, was so rich in harmony of thought and so well attuned, that it readily responded to the touch of its master mind.

The following instance of the Cardinal's wonderful power of improvisation is given by one who was present on the occasion.

In 1855, His Eminence visited Roulers College, near Bruges, in Belgium.   To do him honor, the professors with Belgian hospitality gave a grand dinner, followed by an Academia and Public Reception.   During dinner, the conversation turned on extempore speaking, and Mr. Joseph Algar, the English professor, who knew the Cardinal's wonderful power in this respect, mentioned it at table, and it became the subject of general conversation.   The professors, anxious "to see for themselves," begged His Eminence to say a few words at the Reception. He consented, leaving it to them to name the subject. For a few minutes, the matter was eagerly discussed amongst them, when at last the Professor of Mathematics wickedly suggested the word "*Logarithms.*"   It was caught up immediately.   The Cardinal did not hesitate, and the company repaired to the College Hall for the Academia and Public Reception.

The élite of the town were there.   Many distinguished professors from Bruges, some of them mathematicians, had come to pay their respects to His Eminence, and all the College professors and students were in their places, for the whisper had gone round that the English Cardinal's address was to be delivered in French, and was to be a test of his powers of extempore speaking.   In fifteen minutes the distinguished guest was ready.   The company were in a little flutter of excitement.   The Cardinal was not.   He rose quietly and thoughtfully, and after the usual college cheering had subsided, to the astonishment of everybody, he lectured for three-quarters of an hour on the subject of *Logarithms.*   Clearly and concisely, he first explained his terms, and then proceeded to discuss the whole subject.   On sitting down, he was greeted with thunders of applause.   Everyone was amazed at the depth of his knowledge of the subject, and scarcely less surprised at the beautiful language in which he had clothed his ideas.

I was informed by Mr. Blaine shortly after the Presidential election of 1884, in which he was defeated by Mr. Cleveland, that during the campaign he had spoken four hundred times in forty days, or on an average ten times a day.   Nearly all these speeches were, of course, improvised, and they who heard or read them, could not fail to be impressed with the variety of the subjects discussed, as well as with the immense resources, and magnetic power of the orator.   His inexhaustible fund of information, and his marvellous ease and felicity of expression were the recompense of close study, and of the experience and observation of twenty years spent in both Houses of Congress.

The conclusion to be drawn from the foregoing remarks is this, that no speaker can hope to pour out a copious and steady stream of improvised declamation with credit to himself, unless he has drunk deep and long at the fountain of knowledge.

CHAPTER XXV.

The Priest as a Catechist.

THE catechism is the abridgment of Scripture doctrines. It contains more solid food than is found in many pretentious volumes.

Chief Justice Taney said that the little Catechism which he learned in his youth, formed the basis of his legal knowledge.

It is not only to the congregation assembled in the house of God that Christ's ambassador is required to preach the truths of salvation. He has, also, to catechize the children in the churcn or scnoolroom; for like the Apostle, it is his duty to give milk to the "little ones in Christ,"[1] as well as "meat" to the strong. The instruction of children is the most imperative, as well as the most fruitful, work of the ministry; and therefore, to the man of God, it is the most congenial and delightful of occupations. The best argument and the strongest incentive which God's minister can have for teaching children, is furnished by the example of Christ. It is chiefly by grouping together the various texts of the Gospel in which our Lord refers to the young, that we can adequately realize His special predilection for them.

[1] I. Cor. III. 1.

300

"I give praise," He says, "to Thee, O Father, Lord of heaven and earth, because Thou hast hidden these things from the wise and prudent, and hast revealed them to little ones."[1] "And Jesus calling unto Him a little child, set him in the midst of them, and said : Amen I say to you, unless you be converted and become as little children, you shall not enter into the kingdom of heaven. Whosoever, therefore, shall humble himself as this little child, he is the greater in the kingdom of heaven. And he that shall receive one such little child, in My name, receiveth Me. But he that shall scandalize one of these little ones that believe in Me, it were better for him that a mill-stone should be hanged about his neck, and that he should be drowned in the depth of the sea."[2] "Then were little children presented to Him, that He should impose hands upon them and pray. And the disciples rebuked them. But Jesus said to them : Suffer the little children, and forbid them not to come to Me; for the kingdom of heaven is for such. And when He had imposed hands upon them, He departed from thence."[3] "And the chief priests and scribes seeing . . . the children crying in the temple, and saying : Hosanna to the Son of David, were moved with indignation, and said to Him : Hearest Thou what these say ? And Jesus said to them : Yea, have you never read : Out of the mouth of infants and of sucklings Thou hast perfected praise ?"[4]

Our Saviour tells us here that children's innocence, simplicity, and humility render them fit depositories of God's revelation, and worthy heirs of His kingdom. He tenderly embraces and blesses them ; He threatens with

[1] Matt. XI. 25.
[2] Matt. XVIII. 2–6.
[3] Ibid. XIX. 13–15.
[4] Ibid. XXI. 15, 16.

the most severe reprobation those who scandalize them; He rebukes His disciples for trying to repel them from Him; He quickens the pastors' zeal for them by declaring that the fatherly affection bestowed on them, He regards as shown to Himself; and while He shrunk from the plaudits of men, and fled when they would make Him their King, He receives with complacency the praises of children. As the holocaust of a lamb was most pleasing to the Father, so are the hosannas of the younglings of the Christian flock most grateful to the Son.

With the beautiful example of Christ before them, we are not surprised to find that the most learned and eminent fathers, bishops, doctors and apostolic missionaries of the Church have been particularly devoted to the Christian instruction of youth.

One of the first literary works of St. Augustine after he was raised to the episcopate, was his admirable treatise *De Catechizandis Rudibus*, written for the use of a deacon of Carthage.

It was at the urgent request of the Fathers of the Tridentine Synod, that Pius IV., the reigning Pope, ordered the compilation of the Catechism of the Council of Trent.[1] The supervision of this valuable work was assigned to St. Charles Borromeo. And the same Council directs all pastors of souls to have children instructed in catechism on Sundays and holidays of obligation. St. Charles was one of the first prelates to carry out this provision of the Council. He enjoined on all parish priests the duty of teaching catechism every Sunday, and he established throughout his vast diocese of Milan 740 schools of Christian doctrine, which were attended by

[1] Sess. XVII.

40,000 scholars, and superintended by upwards of 3000 catechists.

Not less zealous than St. Charles in the instruction of youth was Don Bartholomew, Archbishop of Braga, in Portugal, one of the most conspicuous lights of the Council. Prior to the Tridentine Synod, on the occasion of a visitation of his diocese, he observed a shepherd boy during a violent storm remain at his post regardless of shelter, lest the wolves and foxes, which abounded there, should snatch any of the sheep or the lambs committed to his care. The sight deeply touched him, and elicited from him this reflection : " How much more watchful a pastor of souls ought to be in protecting his flock from the snares of the enemy !" Eight years before his death, he resigned his see and consecrated the remainder of his life to the cherished occupation of teaching the young in the villages lying in the neighborhood of his convent.

St. Ignatius, though charged with the government of a new Religious Order, found time to catechize children in the rudiments of Christian faith. Even while in Rome he gave lessons in catechism in one of the churches. His imperfect knowledge of Italian was amply redeemed by the fervor with which he taught. Such is the charm of genuine apostolic speech, though unadorned with elocutionary art, that canonists, theologians, and men of rank came eagerly to hear him. The fatherly love of his heart was expressed on his countenance ; and there was a sacred fire in his simple, earnest words that shed warmth, as well as light, on the souls of his hearers.

When St. Francis Xavier arrived in Goa, he found the Portuguese Christians in a state of deplorable ignorance and vice. Their pernicious example was an almost in-

superable barrier to the conversion of the native infidels.
He began his apostolic labors with the rising generation.
He walked through the streets of Goa, bell in hand, and
implored parents and masters to send their children and
slaves to catechism in the church. He instructed the
little ones in the elements of Christian faith, and they, in
turn, became young evangelists in their respective homes,
edifying their parents by their piety and example, so that
the words of the Psalmist were fulfilled in them : " Out
of the mouth of infants Thou hast perfected praise."

The scholarly and pious Cardinal Bellarmine, Archbishop of Capua, who was the most formidable champion
in his day against the antagonists of the Church, did not
disdain to stoop to children and to feed them with the
milk of Christian knowledge. He is the author of one
of the best catechisms ever compiled. He personally instructed the young in his cathedral and in other churches
of the diocese, and enjoined the same duty on all pastors
under his charge.

St. Vincent de Paul took pains in mature years to learn
the *patois* in vogue in the country districts that thus he
might reach the hearts and minds of the young, and
impart to them the principles of Christian faith.

The first care of St. Francis de Sales on taking charge
of his diocese, was to institute catechetical instructions,
which he enlivened and illustrated by examples and comparisons frequently repeated under different forms, in order
to impress them on the mind. The holy bishop never
dispensed himself from this duty unless his other occupations rendered it absolutely necessary to do so. " I had
the happiness of assisting at these blessed instructions,"
said a cotemporary, " and never before did I witness such

a sight. The good and gentle Father was seated on a raised chair, his little army around him. It was charming to hear how familiarly he explained the rudiments of faith. At each step, numerous comparisons fell from his lips. He looked at his little crowd, and his little crowd looked at him. He became a child with them in order to form in them the perfect man according to Jesus Christ." Not only the young, but persons of every age and rank frequented these instructions. The bishop's grace and simplicity while explaining the most profound mysteries of faith, greatly interested his hearers, enlightened the ignorant, edified the learned, and did good to all.

His mother, Madam de Boisy, was very assiduous in her attendance whenever she visited Annecy. Her son, telling her one day that it was a distraction to him to see among his little ones her from whom he had first learned the catechism, she replied: "My son, I taught you *the letter*, but from your lips I learn the hidden meaning of our sacred mysteries in which I have been very ill instructed." He directed his clergy to give catechetical lessons every Sunday for two hours before Vespers.

I might also speak of Gerson, the famous Chancellor of Paris, and of Bossuet, one of the greatest pulpit orators that France, or perhaps any other nation, has ever produced. Both of these eminent men felt that they were honoring their sacred ministry and themselves, also, by consecrating their declining years to the instruction of youth.

A little reflection will enable us to understand why those illustrious churchmen, following the example of the Incarnate Word, were so assiduous in the training of the young.

20

A child is susceptible of impressions at an earlier age than is commonly imagined, and first impressions last the longest. Train up a child in the way he should go, "and when he is old he will not depart from it."[1] Pope conveys the same idea when he says:

> "'Tis education forms the common mind;
> Just as the twig is bent, the tree's inclined."

This thought is more tersely expressed in the axiom: "The child is father to the man."

It is, therefore, a matter of supreme importance whether the kingdom of the youthful soul shall be under the dominion of the angel of light or of the angel of darkness. It is of vital moment to the child's future career whether the maxims of Christ or the maxims of the world shall be first inscribed on the *tabula rasa* of his heart. The first inscriptions recorded on the tablet of the soul, though afterward blurred and partially defaced by sin and the dust of neglect, are apt in the long run to come to light again when exposed to a healthy religious atmosphere. I am aware, indeed, that many have ended in the flesh who "had begun in the spirit," while many others after a bad beginning, have ended well. But these are the exceptions, not the rule. I knew a gentleman in North Carolina who had received an excellent Christian training in Baltimore, but who afterward drifted away from the faith of his fathers. He declared that he was frequently haunted by the image of the venerable pastor who had instructed him, and the early admonitions of the priest often rose up in judgment against him. He found no peace till, like the Prodigal, he returned to his Father's house.

[1] Prov. XXII. 6.

✓ "It is good for a man," says the prophet, "when he hath borne the yoke from his youth."[1] The Gospel precepts become sweet and easy when inculcated in early life. But we know what a heavy, and even an intolerable, burden they appear to many to whom they are proposed in mature years.

The instruction of children becomes a grateful task to the pastor when he reflects that he is casting the seed of faith in virgin and fruitful soil where there are no briars or weeds of doubt to choke it. The child is naturally innocent and artless, open and ingenuous, affectionate and confiding. He accepts without misgiving the truths that are taught him. The pastor has, therefore, an open and solid foundation on which to rear the edifice of faith and piety. He has no rubbish of false doctrines to clear away before he begins to erect the building. He has no obstacles to remove, no sophistries to encounter, no prejudices to overcome. In the words of St. Peter, his pupils "as new-born babes" receive "the rational milk without guile that thereby" they "may grow unto salvation."[2] They have no more suspicion of any poison of error in the food of knowledge given them than the infant that is nourished at the breasts of its mother.

Another consoling thought to the apostle of youth is the consideration, that the child of to-day is the man or the woman of to-morrow. In a dozen, or at most in a score of years, the scholars he has catechized, become husbands and wives, fathers and mothers, and heads of households. The words of the Wise Man will be fulfilled in him: "Cast thy bread upon the running waters, for after a time thou shalt find it again."[3] He will have the

---

[1] Lament. III. 27. [2] I. Pet. II. 2. [3] Eccl. XI. 1.

supreme satisfaction of being surrounded in church by a
well-instructed and edifying congregation whom he himself has trained to virtue, and to whom he can say with
St. Paul: When ye were "little ones in Christ I fed
you with milk;"[1] and now ye are "my joy and my
crown."[2]

But the shepherd of souls has not to wait for fifteen or
twenty years to witness the salutary effects of his catechetical instructions on the adult portion of his flock.
He already gains the heart of the parents through their
offspring; for the children whom he teaches, react on
their elders and become unconscious, though fruitful,
missionaries in their respective families. They repeat at
home the lessons they have been taught; they speak of
the loving kindness of their spiritual father; they exhibit the premiums and other tokens of appreciation and
affection they have received from him; and thus they
become the instruments of heaven in attaching their
parents more closely to their pastor, to their church, and
to their God.

When young Tobias had returned from his long
journey, he related to his father the untiring solicitude
of his guide, the Angel Raphael, disguised as a man.
"Father," he said, "what wages shall we give him? or
what can be worthy of his benefits? He conducted me
and brought me safe again. He delivered me from being
devoured by the fish. *Thee also he hath made to see the
light of heaven;* and we are filled with all good things
through him."[3] Such, also, is the sentiment, if not the
language of filial and parental gratitude for the pastor's
devotedness. He is not only a benediction to the child,

[1] I. Cor. III. 1, 2.   [2] Phil. IV. 1.   [3] Tobias XII. 2, 3.

but he often opens the eyes of the father himself to the light of practical faith.

The establishment of a parochial school is, indeed, of supreme importance, and no parish is complete without it, as will be demonstrated in a subsequent chapter. But even where a parish school exists there will be usually found, as we know from experience, a certain proportion of children who will not frequent it. Some will be absent through parental neglect, others will attend the public schools, and others will play the truant.

But whether they attend a public or a private school, or no school at all, the heart of the priest should never be indifferent toward them, much less steeled against them. They should ever be the objects of his vigilant care in the catechetical instructions. Indeed, the more vicious and refractory they are, the more they have need of his tender forbearance and fatherly solicitude. Did not David love the unruly Absalom as well as the dutiful Solomon? When the former rebelled against his father, the king gave this order to Joab, the general of the army: "Save me the boy Absalom." And when he heard of his son's death, he wept and cried out: "My son Absalom, Absalom my son: who would grant me that I might die for thee, Absalom my son, my son Absalom."[1]

✓ I can find no words strong enough to express my reprobation of the priest who would despise and ostracise these erring little ones. A pastor may be eloquent and effective in the pulpit; he may be zealous in the confessional; he may be fervent at the altar; but these good qualities will not atone for his neglect of the wayward youths of his flock. If it is a fault not to seek for them

[1] II. Kings XVIII. 33.

when they wander away ; if it is a reproach to be harsh and cold toward them when they do come ; how shall we characterize the act of repelling them from the fold like infectious lambs when they do present themselves, and of treating them as Pariahs and outcasts from the circle of the Sunday School ? The mission of the priest, like that of his Master, is to heal the wounded and to save that which was lost. With the Apostle he must say : " The Lord hath given me power unto edification and not unto destruction." [1]

Did not Christ send His servant " to compel the poor, the feeble, the blind, and the lame," that is, the frail and despised members of the flock, to come to His supper. Did He not Himself seek the lost lamb and leave the ninety-nine in the desert ? Did He not rebuke His disciples for their rudeness to the children that were presented to Him ? Did He not welcome back the Prodigal Son, and even go to meet him ? We should remember, after all, that attendance at the parish day-school is a means, and not an end ; and if that means cannot be availed of in behalf of all the children, every other method that paternal instincts will suggest, should be employed in bringing those less favored ones to the knowledge of Christ.

Apart from the signal blessings which the pastor confers on children by his catechetical instructions, he is at the same time deriving great benefit for himself by improving and enriching his mind. The logical arrangement and sequence of subjects, the clearness of ideas and accuracy of statement, the familiarity of style and felicity of illustrations which mark his lessons to the young, serve

[1] II. Cor. XIII. 10.

to develop and strengthen in himself habits of order and precision of thought which are of incalculable benefit to him in the pulpit. In addressing adults, his language will be unconsciously characterized by a directness and simplicity of expression and practical sense that will not fail to interest and edify the congregation. He will be as much at home and at ease with them as he was with the junior members.

Bishop Dupanloup informed a friend of mine that whatever success he had attained as a preacher and a writer, was chiefly due to his long experience as a catechist.

It is worthy of note, also, that many of the seminarians educated by the Sulpicians in Paris, who afterward acquired distinction in the ranks of the French hierarchy, had been catechists in the church of St. Sulpice while pursuing their studies in the seminary.

A word in conclusion may be added on the manner of instructing children. The successful compilation of a catechism is acknowledged to be a most arduous task. The Rev. Dr. McCaffrey, a former President of Mount St. Mary's College, Emmittsburg, one of the most accomplished scholars of his day, spent several years in writing a catechism; and yet, while it is justly admired by many able critics, it failed to receive the commendation of the Second Plenary Council of Baltimore, on account of its alleged obscurity in certain passages. He was charged with the fault to which Horace refers:

" *Brevis esse laboro, obscurus fio.*"

But if it is difficult to write a good catechism, it is not an easy work to teach it well.

By a cheerful and benevolent disposition, the pastor will put his young pupils at their ease; he will gain their affection and confidence, and make them more attentive to his instructions.

The mind of a child is undeveloped, and his capacity for acquiring knowledge limited. He is not yet accustomed to abstract reasoning, and he can grasp but one subject at a time. The instructions, therefore, will be more profitable if they are imparted in the simplest and the most familiar language. One truth should be explained under different forms before another is introduced. The instructions, also, should be reasonably short; otherwise the child may forget at the end what was said in the beginning of the discourse. Even to adults, long sermons are usually distasteful; but to children, they are positively oppressive, because they overload the mind with more intellectual food than can be digested and assimilated.

As the imagination of children is strong and vivid, an instruction conveyed in the form of imagery is always most grateful to them. Their attention is aroused by the picture, and, while the image remains stamped on their memory, it is inseparably associated in their mind with the religious truth, the moral sentiment, or the sacramental rite which it is intended to embellish.

The mysteries of religion are, therefore, best communicated to the youthful mind through the medium of a parable, an anecdote, an historical fact, or an incident of daily life. These narratives awaken the interest of the child; they are listened to with pleasure, and remembered without much effort.

The Holy Scripture is an inexhaustible source from which the zealous catechist can draw his illustrations.

He will find in its pages copious examples to enforce every truth he conveys, every virtue he enjoins, and every vice he has to condemn.

The other volume that I should particularly recommend to priests, is the great Book of Nature written by the hand of God Himself, and which is ever open and intelligible to all. It is the first book unfolded to the admiring gaze of the child, and its ever-varying pictures are contemplated by him with renewed awe and delight. Every object in nature is calculated to illustrate some attribute of the Divinity, for, " the heavens show forth the glory of God and the firmament announces the work of His hands."

The splendor of the sun, the countless multitude of the stars, the illimitable expanse of the firmament, the beauty of the landscape, the ever-flowing river, the boundless ocean, will serve as object-lessons typifying and vividly portraying the majesty, the omnipresence, and the omniscience of God, His almighty power and immensity, the glory of heaven, the fleetness of time, and the never-ending duration of eternity. In fact, every striking work of creation is an illuminated manuscript from which the child can learn " to look through nature up to nature's God."

CHAPTER XXVI.

The Home and the Sunday School.

THERE are three great Schools of Christian Doctrine for youth, namely, the Home, the Sunday School, and the Parish Day-School. They are the fruitful nurseries of the Lord's Vineyard. The efficacy of these schools largely depends on the zeal and pastoral vigilance of the spiritual shepherd. Under the influence of his careful supervision and exhortations, they become powerful auxiliaries in the growth of Christian faith; whereas without these accessories, his sermons in the temple of God, how eloquent and persuasive soever they may be, will commonly fail to produce results commensurate with the labor expended.

A congregation of men and women who have drunk in early life at these three fountains of religious science, is like a well-ploughed field which is prepared to receive the seed of God's word; while an audience bereft of these advantages, is like an arid and uncultivated soil covered with weeds and briers. It is slow to catch the inspiration, and to feel the warmth of the preacher's words, because its religious training has not been developed.

I.

The Home.

The home is the primeval novitiate. Its beneficent agency is the most far-reaching and enduring of all schools.

The parental fireside was the only seminary which the Patriarchs Abraham, Isaac, and Jacob frequented, and in which they received and transmitted, in turn, the knowledge and worship of Jehovah.

The pious Christian home is the best and most hallowed of all academies, and the mother is the oldest and the most cherished of all teachers. The devout Christian mother is called to be an apostle. The family circle is her field of labor; the members of the household are the souls committed to her ministry.

No teacher can adequately supply the place of the mother. No one has the same hold that she maintains on the intellect and affections of her child. She is not only an authority whose right to rule is never questioned, but also an oracle that is implicitly believed.

The words and example of a parent, especially of a mother, exert a life-long influence on the child. The seed of righteousness, sown in the youthful mind by the maternal hand, usually bears abundant fruit. The salutary lessons the mother has taught, are seldom effaced from the memory. They are engraven on the heart in luminous characters, and the sacred image of the mother herself stands before us silently, but eloquently, pleading the cause of God. The tablet of the soul, like a *palimpsest*, may afterward receive impressions that will hide from view the original maternal characters written upon it, but the waters of compunction, and the searching rays of divine grace, will bring them to light again.

There is no exaggeration in saying that the hope of America is in the rising generation, and the hope of the rising generation is in its Christian mothers. The individual and national character may be traced to the training imparted under the domestic roof, and its beneficial or baneful influence may be gauged by the religious and moral standard of the family circle.

" It is true, indeed," says the Count de Maistre, " that women have written no *Iliad*, nor *Jerusalem Delivered*, nor *Hamlet*, nor *Paradise Lost*. They have designed no church like *St. Peter's Basilica*, composed no *Messiah*, carved no *Apollo Belvidere*, painted no *Last Judgment*. They have invented neither algebra, nor telescope, nor steam engine; but they have done something far greater and better than all this, for it is at their knees that upright and virtuous men and women have been trained,— the most excellent productions of the world."

It is worthy of note that those men and women who have shed lustre on the world by their moral or civil virtues, have been usually the fruit of an exemplary parentage. Samuel and Tobias, the seven Machabean brothers, John the Baptist, and Timothy, were born of parents distinguished for their virtues. The Scripture pays a beautiful tribute to the father and mother of Susanna, declaring that they were " just," and " had instructed their daughter according to the law of Moses."

The patience and prayers, the example and instructions of Monica rescued her son Augustine from the thorny path of sin and error, and led him to the sublime heights of faith and sanctity. She exercised over his strong and turbulent nature a sway that no earthly teacher could have wielded.

Anthusa, the mother of St. John Chrysostom, became a widow at the age of twenty years. She divided her time between the care of her family and her exercises of devotion. She instilled into her son from the first dawn of reason, the most exalted maxims of Christian piety. His future teacher, a celebrated pagan sophist, was so profoundly impressed with the influence exerted on Chrysostom by his mother, that he exclaimed : " What wonderful women the Christians possess ! "

St. Basil refers with admiration and gratitude to his childhood days, spent under the guidance of his excellent parents, and saintly grandmother.   The pure and invigorating atmosphere he then breathed, the order and tranquillity that reigned in the household, and the lessons of heavenly wisdom he imbibed, were a potent antidote against the moral and intellectual poison of the schools of Athens which he afterward frequented.   They moulded the character and conduct of his whole life.

The parents of St. Gregory Nazianzen are both honored in the Calendar of the Church.   Gregory profited as much as did his friend Basil, by the hallowed environments in which his youthful days were spent, and by the living models of virtue he daily contemplated.

Louis IX., King of France, is largely indebted for his magnanimity as a ruler, and for his virtues as a saint, to his mother Blanche.   Though occupied during the minority of her son with the affairs of state, she had time to devote to the religious instruction of her child.   " I love you tenderly, my son," she said to him, " but sooner would I behold you a corpse at my feet, than that you should tarnish your soul by any grievous transgression." If this queen could pay so much attention to her son's education, notwithstanding her engrossing cares in the administration of public affairs, surely there are many mothers who cannot excuse themselves on the plea of want of time, from discharging a similar duty to their offspring.

George Washington, the Father of his Country, exhibited in an eminent degree during his public life the natural virtues of heroic courage, love of truth, magnanimity, pure patriotism, and a rare disinterestedness. He glories in confessing that he was indebted in a large measure for these traits of character to the assiduous vigilance and methodical habits, to the wholesome instructions and example of his excellent mother.

John Randolph, of Roanoke, is quoted as having once remarked : " I should have been an atheist, if it had not been for one recollection ; and that was, the memory of the time when my departed mother used to take my little hands in hers, and cause me on my knees to say, ' Our Father who art in heaven.' "

Anne Lemarchand des Noyers, the mother of Monseigneur De Cheverus, first Bishop of Boston, and afterward Cardinal Archbishop of Bordeaux, was one of those rare women who thoroughly understood the education of children. Sedulous in inspiring her offspring by example as well as by precept with the fear of God, the habit of prayer, the love of their neighbors, and the admiration of all that is good, generous, and virtuous, she equally well knew how to make herself feared and beloved. She never indulged in those severe reprimands which sour the disposition, instead of correcting it, still less in those corporal chastisements which compel outward obedience without changing the heart.[1]

There is no name better known and more revered in North Carolina than that of Judge Gaston. He succeeded in eliminating from the new State Constitution, framed in

---

[1] *The Life of Cardinal De Cheverus*, by Rev. J. H. Doubourg.

1835, the clause excluding Catholics from the privilege of holding public office. Like Noemi in the land of Moab, Mrs. Gaston with her family lived alone among a people who were strangers to the faith of her fathers. Judge Gaston was always fond of referring to his pious Christian mother, to whom under God he attributed not only the heritage of his faith, but also those sterling moral and civic virtues which had endeared him to his fellow-citizens.

Chief Justice Taney pays this beautiful tribute to his mother: "She was pious, gentle, and affectionate, retiring and domestic in her habits. I never in my life heard her say an unkind word to any of her children, nor speak ill of any one. I remember and feel the effect of her teaching to this day."

Would to God that this eulogy could be pronounced on all American Christian mothers! If they were faithful to their sacred trust, there would be less need in our day of insisting on religious education in the schools, and the perplexing problem that agitates our country would be practically solved.

I need not say that adequate home-training involves much more than the lessons in Christian Doctrine which are to be taught to the children. The home should be pervaded by a religious atmosphere. It should be a temple of domestic peace, sobriety, conjugal love, parental affection, and solicitude. Above all, it should be a sanctuary of family prayer. *Lex orandi, lex credendi*. Prayer is the most secure guardian of Christian faith. The blight of infidelity never falls on a household that assembles for daily communion with God; for "the Author and Finisher of our faith" has declared: "Where two or three are gathered together in My name, there I am in the midst of them."

The more earnest and successful the pastor is in impressing on parents the duty of religious training in the family, the more easy, more grateful, and more efficient will be his ministerial labors; for he will find in the heads of families most valuable helps to promote the reign of sound morals and healthy piety throughout the parish.

II.

The Sunday School.

The Sunday School is another helpful agency for inculcating the elements of Christian Doctrine. The catechism classes, taught by zealous young men and women of the parish under the pastor's supervision, are productive of a two-fold advantage: they benefit not only the children, but also the teachers themselves.

The Sunday School invests the Lord's-Day with a sacred character distinct from other days of the week, by associating in the children's mind the Christian Sabbath with the religious exercises which form the subject of their studies. It also secures their more faithful and regular attendance at the celebration of the Mass, which usually precedes or immediately follows the catechetical exercises.

The instructions imparted to the pupils, are better adapted to their undeveloped intelligence than the sermon preached to the congregation during divine service.

They are taught the principles of Christian faith and morals in their simplest form, and they learn, besides, to chant the popular sacred hymns and canticles of the Church.

Though some of the teachers may be only imperfectly qualified for their task, the children under their guidance can, at least, learn by heart and retain without much effort the answers to the questions proposed in the Catechism; and even though they may not comprehend as yet the full meaning of the words they express, their knowledge imperceptibly grows in proportion as their mind becomes matured and developed.

The Sunday-School exercise is, also, of great utility to the teachers themselves. They are withdrawn from the danger of dissipation and profane amusements on the Lord's-Day; they are confirmed in the science of Christian Doctrine, because one of the best methods for learning a thing, is to teach it; they have a grateful sense of the confidence reposed in them, and of the mission assigned them; they become active and useful subordinate helpers of the pastor in the work of the ministry, and are inspired with greater zeal for the interests of religion. The pastor can rely on the ready and cheerful coöperation of the Sunday-School teachers for the promotion of any good work he may inaugurate in the parish.

CHAPTER XXVII.

Parish Schools.

ONE of the most effective instruments for the expansion and perpetuity of the religion of Christ, is the Catholic day-school. It was a favorite saying of Archbishop Bayley, that no parish is fully equipped without a parochial school.

Christian education is as essential to the development and permanence of Christian life as pure air and food are for the health and growth of the physical man.

If the generations yet unborn are to be Christian, they will be indebted for their faith not to natural propagation and inheritance, but to the religious instruction which they will severally receive. Christianity is not transmitted like physical life from father to son. "Faith cometh by hearing," not by generation. A father may have the sturdy belief of a Sir Thomas More, or of a Montalembert, and yet, if his son grows up under adverse influences, he may be utterly alien, if not even hostile, to his father's religious convictions.

Now, the question arises, How is the child to be instructed in the tenets of his religion? How is the seed of Christianity to be implanted in his breast? How is the heritage of faith to be transmitted?

First, indeed, by his parents, who are his divinely-appointed teachers, as I have said. But are there not many parents who have not the capacity or ability to instruct their children? Are there not many others who have not the time at their disposal? And are there not still more who lack the inclination and disposition to impart the principles of Christian knowledge to their offspring?

Secondly, by the Sunday School. The Sunday School indeed, as has been observed, is productive of excellent results, and is a most salutary aid to Christian home-training; but it is hardly adequate to satisfy the spiritual needs of youth, or to counteract the downward and materializing tendencies of every-day life.

Thirdly, Christian traditions, Christian sentiment, and public opinion. Christian laws and literature now dominant among us, may be appealed to as another factor for ingrafting the religion of Christ on the youth of the country. But this public sentiment derives its strength and vitality from the faith of the individual. The religious sentiment of the nation is the reflex of the faith of the units that compose it. The stream does not rise above its source. The force of traditional Christianity and of sound literature may be neutralized by the anti-Christian ideas and opinions, and the demoralizing literature that confront our youth at every step.

I need not refer to our system of public schools as an element for the diffusion of Christian knowledge, as they do not even profess to include religious doctrines in their curriculum of studies.

It is but just to say that, if Christian doctrine is not embraced in the course of public-school studies, its absence is not due to any hostility toward the Catholic religion on the part of the State or municipal authorities; nor does

it imply a subserviency to any anti-religious public sentiment.   But in view of the conflicting religious convictions
of the pupils, the introduction of positive dogmatic teaching would be beset with difficulties not easy to surmount.

Let us hope that the American people, so deeply imbued
with reverence for Christian revelation, so conspicuous for
justice and fair play, so resourceful in solving perplexing
social and political problems, will discover some practical
method for reconciling the general diffusion of elementary
education with a proper regard for the sacred rights of
conscience.

If, then, parental instruction, the Sunday School, Christian traditions, and literature leave a void to be filled, and
are found from experience to be usually insufficient for
transmitting to youth the blessing of Catholic faith, we
are forced to the conclusion that, if we desire to make our
children partakers of the inestimable heritage of divine
truth, we must avail ourselves of the day school, where
secular science is combined with sacred instruction, and
where they will daily inhale a healthy religious and moral
atmosphere.

The best criterion for estimating the value of a Catholic
school, is to compare the religious progress of two parishes
some years after their formation.   Let us suppose that
both parishes had, at the time of their foundation, equal
advantages as to the wealth and number of their members,
and in all other respects, with this single exception, that
one was furnished with a school while the other had none.
At the expiration of a decade of years, it will very probably be found that the parish destitute of a Catholic school
has been marked by a very slow growth, or has barely
held its own, or in some instances, notwithstanding the

earnest efforts of the Rector, may even have retrograded. The ranks in the house of God that were depleted by the death of parents, have been but partially filled up by their children.

On the other hand, the parish that was blessed with a Catholic school, beholds springing up a new generation well-grounded in the principles of religion and virtue, docile and obedient to the law of God and the teachings of the Church, the hope and joy of the minister of Christ.

Of course, there are many happy exceptions to the unfavorable results arising from the absence of a Catholic day-school. I know several country parishes too small or too poor to sustain a parochial school, which, nevertheless, exhibit a healthy and steady growth by reason not only of the natural increase, but also of numerous conversions, which far more than compensate for the leakage occasioned by defections or religious indifference.

In a subsequent chapter, I shall speak of the zeal which should be exercised in instructing and receiving converts. But it is evident, that the fruit derived from adult accessions to the Church, can bear no proportion to the normal influence of the school.

The number of converts added to the fold compared with the army of youthful confessors of the faith, growing in spiritual life, and equipped with the panoply of religion in the school, is proportionately as small as were the ears of corn gleaned by Ruth in comparison with the harvest gathered by the reapers before she entered the field.

It is gratifying to see a statesman so profound, an intellect so gifted, a witness so disinterested, an American so typical as Daniel Webster insisting on the importance of associating religious with secular knowledge in juvenile training. It is true, that, in the speech to which I shall refer, he is alluding to a boarding-school; but it is manifest, that the principles he lays down, can be applied with almost equal force to a day-school.

In the celebrated Girard will-case, Mr. Webster denounces with his usual power and eloquence the provisions of the will which excluded Christian ministers and religious instructions from the institution founded by Girard. The orator declares that it is cruel and heartless to rob children of the blessings of religion, more precious than life; that there can be no morality without religion, and no religion without the basis of doctrinal truths or tenets; that a school for the instruction of the young which sedulously omits Christian science, is a violation of Christian charity; that the sin is aggravated since this advantage is withheld from them at a period of life in which they are so susceptible of impressions that are most lasting; and that a legacy bequeathed under such terms, would prove a curse instead of a blessing.

He proceeds to say: "The earliest and the most urgent intellectual want of human nature, is the knowledge of its origin, its duty, and its destiny. 'Whence am I, what am I, and what is before me?' This is the cry of the human soul so soon as it raises its contemplation above visible, material things. . . . And that question nothing but God and the religion of God can solve. Religion does solve it, and teaches every man that he is to live again, and that the duties of this life have reference to the life which is to come. And hence, since the introduction of Christianity, it has been the duty, as it has been the effort of the great and the good, to *sanctify human knowledge*, to bring it to the fount, and to *baptize learning unto*

Christianity, to gather up all its productions, its earliest and its latest, its blossoms and its fruits, and lay them all upon the altar of religion and virtue."

Much has been written regarding the loss of faith in this country during the present century. Some writers, no doubt, have exaggerated the number of souls that, in different parts of the country, have drifted away from the religious moorings of their fathers.

Without attempting to give an estimate of the leakage, two facts must be conceded: 1°, that the loss is appalling to all those who value the precious gift of Catholic belief; 2°, that the greatest injury has resulted from the neglect of early Christian education. Archbishop Kenrick, of Baltimore, a prelate never suspected of exaggeration, once remarked in my presence that, as a result of his personal experience and observation, hundreds, nay thousands had been bereft of their sacred heritage, because their youthful training had been overlooked. They were sent to schools in which their religion was either studiously ignored or openly assailed. They had neither the knowledge to refute the misstatements of their opponents, nor the courage to resist their shafts of ridicule,—the most overwhelming of all arguments to sensitive youth. The result was, that they abandoned their faith in the Christian religion altogether, or they passively conformed to the prevailing sect of their environment.

Is the child that has been trained in all branches of science save that of the knowledge of his Maker and his own eternal destiny, the only one to be held responsible in after life for the acts that infringe the laws both of God and of man? Can we expect generations reared without religion, without even the first notions of God and their own soul, to become men and women fitted to take their place in later years as honorable and useful members of society? Such was the thought of that lawyer who, when his youthful client was about to be sentenced for some crime, addressed the judge and jury in scathing words, summoning them before the bar of Divine justice for condemning one from whom the godless education of the day had withheld the clear and intelligent appreciation of right and wrong.—"You banish God and His Commandments from the schoolroom," he cried, "you let the boy grow up as he will, and when, as the outcome of such an education, he violates the laws of the land, you arraign him for his crime, you find him guilty, and you condemn him to punishment. Is this right? Is this just?"—Then raising his hand toward heaven, he exclaimed: "God of justice, I adjure Thee, by the Blood of Jesus Christ, to judge the injustice of these unreasoning and unjust men!"

I am not unmindful of the fact, that the maintenance of a Catholic school involves a great burden on a congregation, and that its weight is felt to be all the more irksome and oppressive, since our Catholic citizens, besides voluntarily bearing the expense of a parish school, are taxed for the support of the public system of education.

But the essence of Christianity consists in a spirit of self-sacrifice. As we are not called on, like the Apostles and our forefathers in the faith, to surrender our life, we should be willing to make at least some renunciation of our goods for conscience' sake. The more generous we are in the cause of evangelical truth, the more we will appreciate and love it; while we ordinarily set small value on what costs us little or nothing.

Liberality has been the distinguishing trait of those who are of the household of the faith, from the primitive Christians who laid the price of their goods at the feet of the Apostles, to their medieval brethren who erected those temples of worship that are the admiration of posterity. And the faithful of our day will not be less open-handed in building and sustaining temples of Christian knowledge than were their fathers in constructing and adorning houses of prayer.

It may also be objected that the State, with the vast resources at its disposal, can impart a more thorough course of studies than a school supported by private contributions, is able to supply. It should be the aim of the zealous minister of God to see that the house of learning under his supervision, if inferior to the public schools in the cost and elegance of its material structure, will compare favorably with them, at least in the more essential element of literary and scientific merit.

I am acquainted with several parish schools which equal, if they do not excel in this particular, the best educational institutions sustained by public patronage. What they lack in extension, they gain in condensation.

It is to be hoped that ere long, school sinking-funds from the surplus revenues of the church, will be established in several of the city parishes. This step would inaugurate a movement tending to make Catholic education free, and would preclude or diminish the necessity of appeals to the congregation. The healthy progress of a parish will be promoted wherever this wished-for result can be attained.

It is almost needless to say that our colleges and academies, under the guidance of men and women who consecrate their lives to higher Christian education, should be warmly encouraged and patronized by the Catholic laity.

The plea of poverty, often alleged by many parents for withholding their children from the day-school, can seldom exist in reference to our boarding-schools, which are usually frequented by the sons and daughters of parents in affluent or easy circumstances.

As it is gratifying to a man who invests his money in enterprises where the principal and interest are secure, so is it a supreme consolation to a father when he has the undoubted assurance that the cherished heirs of his name and fortune will return to him from the collegiate institution to which he consigned them, enriched with intellectual knowledge, and confirmed in the principles of Christian faith.

The education of our American youth would be manifestly incomplete, if lessons on the civic virtue of patriotism were not inculcated. The divine Founder of Christianity has ennobled and sanctified loyalty to country by the influence of His example, and the force of His teaching. In these memorable words: "Render to Cæsar the things that are Cæsar's, and to God the things that are God's," He solemnly proclaims to all future generations that, after God, our country should hold the strongest place in our affections.

If the Apostles and the primitive Christians had so much respect for the civil magistrates, in whose selection they had no voice; if they so conscientiously observed the laws of the Roman Empire, which often inflicted on them odious pains and disabilities;—how much more reverence should the juvenile American be taught to entertain for our civil rulers, in whose election he is actively to participate; and with what alacrity he should fulfil the laws, which are framed solely for his peace and protection, and for the welfare of the commonwealth!

Familiar lessons should be incorporated into our text-books, inculcating reverence for our political institutions, and embodying an elementary knowledge of our system of government together with the respective functions of its legislative, judicial, and executive departments, the conditions required for American citizenship, and the duties and rights of the citizen. These lessons should, of course, give a conspicuous place to the memorable events of which our country has been the theatre, and which serve as landmarks in her onward progress. They should include a brief sketch of the nation's heroes, statesmen, and patriots, whose martial deeds and civic virtues the rising generation will be taught to emulate.

The Hebrew people, at the special command of Almighty God, commemorated by an annual festival, their liberation from the bondage of Pharaoh and their entrance into the Promised Land. The history of their redemption from captivity was solemnly recounted, and sacred hymns and psalms were sung, giving praise to the Lord for their providential deliverance.

Among nearly all civilized people, there are certain days set apart to recall some memorable events in their nation's history, and to pay homage to the patriots who figured in them.

Our American youth, in like manner, should be taught to cherish and perpetuate our national festivals. The meaning of each holiday should be brought home to them, so that they may be able to give a rational account of the political faith that is in them.

The public perusal in the schoolroom at stated times, of *the Declaration of Independence* and the *Constitution of the United States,*—an exercise that would occupy scarcely twenty minutes—would be a most profitable and instructive task for the pupils. It would contribute to instil into their minds a strong and intelligent attachment to our system of government, while the chanting of our national songs on appropriate occasions, would nourish in them a healthy enthusiasm and a patriotic devotedness to their country.

CHAPTER XXVIII.

INSTRUCTION AND RECEPTION OF CONVERTS.

THE instruction of converts and their reception into the Church, is a sacred duty, which is specially dear to the heart of every zealous priest. Catholicity is one of the notes of the Church,—a title to which she would have no claim, if she did not aim at bringing all nations and peoples into her fold.

The Catholic Church is not only conservative by reason of her steady and consistent course; she is also aggressive, progressive, and expansive in her career by reason of her indefatigable activity and her missionary spirit. Her family is propagated by accessions from without, as well as by accretions from within. Her constant effort is not only to preserve and cultivate the fields already in her possession, but also to enlarge her bounds and to acquire new territory. Her motto is *onward*. She is militant not merely in the sense that she has to endure assaults and persecutions, but also because her mission is to gain conquests not indeed with the material sword, but with "the sword of the Spirit which is the word of God." Like the Apostle, she becomes all to all men that she may gain all to Christ.

The propagandist feature of Christianity in contrast with the Jewish and Mohammedan religion is clearly sanctioned and imperatively demanded by the commission of Christ to His disciples: "Going, therefore," He says, "teach ye all nations."[1]   "Go ye into the whole world, and preach the Gospel to every creature."[2]   "You shall be witnesses unto Me in Jerusalem, and in all Judea and Samaria, and even to the uttermost part of the earth."[3] "Other sheep I have that are not of this fold; them also I must bring, and they shall hear My voice, and there shall be one fold and one Shepherd."[4]

It is evident from all these texts, that the Apostles were charged to preach the Gospel to nations that were as yet strangers to the religion of Christ.   They were certainly aggressive.   As soon as they left the Cenacle on Pentecost day, they were found preaching the Gospel in Jerusalem to Parthians, Medes, and Elamites, to inhabitants of Mesopotamia, Cappadocia, Pontus, and Asia, Phrygia, Pamphylia, and Egypt, to Cretes and Arabians.   Nor did they restrict their labors to Jewish proselytes.   They parcelled out the Roman Empire among themselves, and their great ambition was to gain new converts among people of every race and tongue and creed.   If they had been instructed to confine their ministry to the Jews, what would have become of us?   We should be groping to-day in the darkness of Paganism; we should be "strangers to the covenants having no hope of the promise, and without God in this world."[5]

But with all their zeal, it is manifest that the Apostles did not personally evangelize all the nations of the earth. They had neither the time nor the capacity to accomplish so formidable a task during their short span of life, and a large portion of the globe remained undiscovered for cen-

[1] Matt. XXVIII. 19.   [3] Acts I. 8.   [5] Eph. II. 12.
[2] Mark XVI. 15.   [4] John X. 16.

turies after their death. Hence, the commission of Christ to His Apostles applies to the ministry of the nineteenth century as well as to them, and the duty devolves upon us to continue the work which they began, of bringing the light of faith to those outside the pale of the Christian fold.

The Church displays to-day the same indomitable energy that marked her career in the early days of Christianity, when Patrick preached in Ireland, Augustine in England, and Boniface in Germany. She manifests her apostolic zeal by sending missionaries to China, Japan, Corea, to Africa and Oceania, and, in fact, to all parts of the habitable globe. It has been remarked that, when the English have an eye on a new territory, with the view of acquiring possession of it, they first send their merchants and then their army, while the French first send their army, which is only sometimes followed by the merchants. But the Catholic missionary is usually found to be in advance of both the soldier and the trader. The rude log chapel has been planted on the soil before the erection of the custom-house or the military fort.

Archbishop Osouf, of Tokio, Japan, while on a visit to this country, was asked by a priest how many Catholics were in his diocese. "Five thousand," he answered. "How many priests?" "Thirty," was the answer. "Well," rejoined his questioner, "your clergy must have little to do." "O but you must remember," remarked the archbishop, "that the diocese includes nineteen millions of Pagans, who have souls to save."

There are fifty-five millions of our separated brethren in the United States, who have a claim on our charity and zeal, and whom we should endeavor to bring to a full participation in the heritage of the Lord. Several years ago a young priest said to me: "I am not concerned about making converts. I am called only to the sheep of the house of Israel." How different were the sentiments of the Apostle of the Gentiles, who said: "I wished myself to be an anathema from Christ for my brethren, who are my kinsmen according to the flesh, who are Israelites, to whom belongeth the adoption of children, and the glory, and the covenant, and the giving of the law, and the service *of God*, and the promises: whose are the fathers, and of whom is Christ according to the flesh, who is over all things, God blessed forever. Amen."[1] When King Agrippa said to him: "In a little thou persuadest me to become a Christian," how noble and self-sacrificing was his reply: "I would to God, that both in a little and in much, not only thou, but also all that hear me this day, should become such as I also am, *except these chains*."[2] If the Apostle had so much concern for the conversion of his Jewish kinsmen, surely we should manifest not less interest in our Protestant American brethren, who are bound to us by national, social, commercial, and often even by family ties.

The question naturally suggests itself here: How are we to attract the attention of our dissenting brethren? how are we to gain a hearing from them? how are we to "compel them to enter?" A priest residing in a city or town can reach many of them by instituting in his church a course of sermons adapted to mixed congregations. A suitable time for such a series of discourses would be during the seasons of Advent and Lent, or on the occasion of a mission. Some weeks beforehand, these sermons might be announced in the church, and even in the local

[1] Rom. ix. 3-5.   [2] Acts xxvi. 28, 29.

papers; and the faithful might be exhorted to influence some of their non-Catholic friends to attend the services. The interest in the sermons would be enhanced if the pastor were to invite a clergyman of tact and marked ability to aid him in delivering them. These discourses could be supplemented by the judicious distribution of catechisms of Christian doctrine, books, and tracts explanatory of the Catholic religion.

Many other opportunities for presenting some leading truths of Catholic faith to our dissenting neighbors, may be judiciously employed to subserve the same end, among others, a marriage ceremony, which is not unfrequently attended by some non-Catholics. When uniting a couple in the bonds of matrimony, the pastor may very profitably make the unity, the sanctity, and the indissolubility of the marriage tie the subject of his discourse. He will have no difficulty in persuading his hearers, whatever may be their religious belief, that this irrevocable bond is indispensable for maintaining the peace and happiness of the married couple, the integrity and cohesion of family life, and the stability and perpetuity of society itself. They will have the candor to admit that both the civil authorities, and the combined influence of the christian organizations outside the Catholic Church have been yielding up one outpost of defence after another until the very foundations of this divine Institution are threatened with being undermined. Marriage, indeed, has come to be regarded by a vast multitude as a virtual compact at will, while the Catholic Church alone has been the consistent and uncompromising vindicator of the principles of Christian wedlock so clearly set forth by Christ in the Gospels and in the Epistles of St. Paul.

22

If conversions do not usually occur after a marriage exhortation, at least the priest becomes better known and more esteemed by his Protestant neighbors. Prejudices and animosities are weakened, or disappear to give way to an honest sentiment of admiration for a religion which condemns divorce and contends for the peace and happiness of the domestic kingdom.

Apart from the extraordinary occasion of a course of sermons, it would, indeed, be a great auxiliary to the diffusion of Christian knowledge, if there were attached to each church a circulating library of well-selected books, for the use of the faithful and of others who might be disposed to seek information respecting the tenets of the Catholic religion.

Numerous examples might be given to illustrate the extraordinary conversions wrought by the distribution of books of instruction. The following incident was related by Archbishop Hughes in 1840. In the spring of 1836, on a bleak night, in the little village of Pompey Hill, N. Y., the family of Colonel Dodge were asked for a night's lodging by a travelling pedler. It was readily granted by the hospitable family. In the course of the evening, they discovered that they were entertaining a Catholic. For a moment, Mrs. Dodge thought of requesting him to withdraw, for prejudices in those days were very strong against the members of the ancient Church. But kindness prevailed over her repugnance. In the morning, before the stranger left, he gave Mrs. Dodge, as an expression of his gratitude, a copy of *Milner's End of Controversy*. After some hesitation, she and her husband read it, and for the first time in their life, they heard the true statement of the Catholic doctrine. They sent afterward to New York for other Catholic books, which brought conviction to their mind. They had never met a Catholic priest, till they presented themselves in Utica for Baptism, in the month of December, 1836. Colonel Dodge was a deacon of the Presbyterian Church, and highly respected in the community. The conversion of the entire family and of some neighbors, numbering in all sixteen, soon followed. Some of their descendants have since been earnest workers in the Lord's Vineyard. One of them, Sister Maria Dodge, died a Sister of Charity at Mount St. Vincent's Academy, New York.

Allow me to quote another little incident of conversion, brought about by what we might call the most casual means, did we not know that God's mighty hand is constantly directing all things, even the most insignificant, to their proper end. The wife of a prominent lawyer received, not many years ago, a box of spring goods, expressed to her from a neighboring city. Several Catholic newspapers had been made use of for wrapping. They presented somewhat of a novelty to the lady's eye, and she laid them aside for perusal. It so happened that one of the papers contained some lines relative to Catholicism, which awoke in her intelligent mind a desire for further inquiry. Suffice to say, that she sought and found in our holy faith what her soul longed for, and in a few months her husband and family were one with her in religious belief.

If the pastor's mission lies in a country district, in which the faithful are few and scattered, and Catholic churches are far between, as is the case in most of our Southern States, he may be called on to preach in private houses, in Protestant churches, in court-houses, or in theatres, like St. Paul who preached in the jailer's apartments and other residences, in Jewish synagogues, in the tribunal of Cæsarea before King Agrippa, and in the Athenian Areopagus. He will have to exercise in such circumstances, that gift of consummate discretion so conspicuous in the Apostle of the Gentiles, by adapting his discourse to the exceptional situation in which he is placed, and to an audience more or less unfriendly and distrustful. He will enlighten without offending his hearers. He will answer inquiries, he will meet objections and dispel prejudices, without adopting a polemical or controversial style of argument, which usually provokes irritation and resistance, while a clear exposition of Catholic principles presented with conscious authority and sincere love, commands the respectful attention of the hearers.

"I have always maintained," says St. Francis de Sales, "that he who preaches with love, preaches sufficiently against heresy, without introducing one word of controversy. Certainly, during thirty-three years in which God has called me to the sacred work of feeding my people with His word, I have observed that earnest sermons on matters of practical holiness are as so many live coals cast among Protestants; they listen, are edified, and become more accessible to doctrinal teaching." [1]

In the Life of this great apostle we learn how fruitful was his ministry of preaching:

"In 1594, when he was sent into the Duchy of Chablais, he found only seven Catholics at Thonon, its capital. He labored there for five or six years, aided by his cousin, Louis de Sales, and in the end brought over to Catholicity between forty and fifty thousand souls. His exertions

[1] *Spirit of St. Francis de Sales.*

seemed to meet with little success for the first four years. He lived in the midst of continual hostility, and sometimes his life was in danger from the fanatical Calvinists in those abodes of heresy; but his angelic sweetness and wisdom carried him through all. A pestilence which raged in Thonon, enabled the servant of God to win the hearts of the people by his saintly charity, assisting the sick and dying at all hours, by day and night, and deterred by no fear of infection. The simplicity and gentleness with which he set forth the Catholic truth gave him such power that, provided only a Protestant allowed him a quiet and peaceable hearing, he would make his objections disappear almost before they were stated. . . . His method was always to have some particular object in his sermons, such as the explanation of a point of faith, or the inculcation of a virtue. He preferred rather to set forth the faith as if he were instructing Catholics only, without controversially disputing against objections. By this means, the heretics, who were very numerous, were gently led to perceive that texts on which they relied to defend their errors, if rightly understood, only proved the truths taught by the Catholic Church."

The missionary in the country districts will be usually greeted by an attentive and respectful, if not a sympathetic audience, as I can avow from personal experience. The people there, irrespective of faith, are eager for the Word of God. They will complain of the brevity, rather than of the length, of the sermons; the more prolonged the discourse, the greater their satisfaction.

The reason is easily found. The visits of the priest to those localities are necessarily at long intervals. The appetite of the people is whetted by a lengthened abstinence from the food of the Gospel, and they have ample time to ruminate and digest the spiritual nourishment served to them, before having an opportunity of partaking of another banquet. Moreover, country folks are perhaps given to more serious reflection than the inhabitants of a city, since they have fewer newspapers, fewer places of amusement to distract and entertain them, and fewer startling incidents to disturb the even tenor of their life.

The Rev. Walter Elliott, a zealous and experienced Paulist missionary, bears testimony to the eagerness with which our separated brethren in country districts listen to Catholic sermons: "I have preached," he says, "over twenty missions to non-Catholics in public halls of small towns, between September, 1893, and the following June. I always had a fair audience of Protestants and, in nearly every place, a full house. They came from first to last, because *they were fond of hearing about religion*. The little hand-bill advertising the lectures, seen in the village post-office, or found in the wagon as the farmer started home, was enough to draw many of them. Others gladly came at the invitation of a Catholic neighbor. The lectures and the answers to questions found in my query box were listened to with absorbed attention, and my leaflets and pamphlets willingly accepted. My experience is that of many priests in all parts of the country. 'Last week,' wrote a priest to me, 'we spoke to a large audience of non-Catholics in a town where there are but two Catholic families.'"

If the ambassador of God is disposed to think that he lowers the dignity of his ministry by preaching in public or private edifices not consecrated to divine worship, he should remember that it is not the place that ennobles the man, but it is the man that ennobles the place.   Christ, our Master, preached not only in the Temple, but also under the canopy of heaven, on the Mount, along the sea-shore, and from the prow of a ship.   The Apostles evangelized wherever they could obtain a hearing.   St. Peter announced the Gospel to his jailers in the Mamertine prison, in Rome, and converted them, as we are informed by authentic records.   St. Paul preached to a number of persons along the river-side just beyond Philippi.[1]   He tells us that he taught the people publicly "from house to house."[2]   Philip, the deacon, converted the eunuch while travelling with him in his chariot.[3]

The missionary priest will derive much comfort, also, from contrasting the apostolic liberty and civic protection he enjoys, with the restraints and legal disabilities imposed on the great Bishop Challoner, of England, who died in 1781.   Dr. Milner, who preached his funeral sermon, tells us that "the retreats in which the bishop was sometimes obliged to preach were so obscure and wretched, that the catacombs were elegant and commodious compared with them."   He says he was often present when the bishop, disguised in secular dress, preached in a cock-pit hired for the purpose, and that occasionally he would address his audience "at some obscure inn where each one present had his pipe, and sat with a pot of beer before him, to obviate all suspicion of the real character of the guests and the purpose of the assembly."[4]   The beer served on those occasions, was called "the bishop's beer," though the bishop himself never partook of it.

There are times even when the pastor will judiciously avail himself of the secular Press to address that larger

[1] Acts XVI.   [2] Ibid. xx. 20.   [3] Ibid. VIII.   *Life of Dr. Milner.*

audience which cannot be reached by other means. The Press is the great vehicle of public thought in our day. It is a colossal engine of truth and of error. It is like the field mentioned in the Gospel, in which good seed and cockle are sown. It is a net that gathers in good fish and bad. We cannot ignore the Press. We are daily confronted by it. It penetrates every walk of life, and its influence and circulation are daily increasing. Even on religious questions, it is regarded by many as an oracle, and it goes far toward moulding the opinion and forming the judgment of millions that have but vague ideas of Christianity.

Through this medium, the minister of God can profitably expound the salient points of Catholic doctrine, or correct an erroneous statement that has been industriously making its rounds, and strike down the foul bird of religious calumny in its flight.

When I resided in North Carolina, I had the consolation of receiving into the Church Dr. Monk, a prominent physician of Newton Grove, Samson County, with his wife and children. As a result of this conversion, upwards of three hundred other persons have since embraced the faith in the same neighborhood. They now form a devout and edifying congregation. The prominence in social and professional position of Dr. Monk contributed to increase the number of converts. The physician lived in an agricultural district, twenty miles from the nearest railroad. There was not a single resident Catholic in his county. He had never read Catholic books, nor entered a Catholic Church, nor held communication with any Catholic clergyman, till he opened a correspondence with me in Wilmington. I was, therefore, naturally curious to ascertain what impelling motive had directed his thoughts toward the Church. In answer to my inquiry, he said: "The first glimpse of light I ever had on the subject came to me from a New York daily paper which contained an admirable sermon on some leading points of Catholic doctrine. Up to that time, I never considered the Catholic Church worthy of serious consideration."

The inquirer after truth, unacquainted as he is, with the time that the pastor may have at his disposal, will call upon him at all hours of the day. Sometimes from necessity or a desire to avoid observation, he will present himself by night, as Nicodemus did, who came to Jesus for fear of the Jews. It is a great act of charity on the part of the pastor to accommodate himself, as far as possible, to the convenience of his visitor. Otherwise, the golden opportunity may be indefinitely postponed, or irretrievably lost, for "the acceptable time and the day of salvation" may never come to him again. The pastor should receive his guest with fatherly benevolence, and make him feel at ease; for when catechumens make their first visit to their spiritual guide, they are usually shy and reserved, embarrassed by the novelty of the situation.

But, perhaps, the clergyman may say: How can I find time to instruct converts, engrossed as I am with the incessant labors of the ministry? I answer that a zealous priest of systematic habits will generally find sufficient time for the discharge of every obligation appertaining to his sacred office. And, certainly, if there is any one duty that is not to be deferred or omitted, but that ought to have precedence, it is the work of enlightening the searcher after truth. Like the good Shepherd, who leaves the ninety-nine sheep in the desert to seek that which was lost, the good pastor will leave for a time in the hands of Providence, the other subjects of his solicitude, till he has diverted the steps of the benighted wayfarer into the path of peace and light.

If you tell me that the labor of instructing those who are of the household of the faith is formidable enough without the additional burden of teaching catechumens, I would reply in the words of our Lord: "These things ought you to have done, and not to leave those undone."[1]

Our Divine Saviour was the busiest of men, and yet we do not read that He ever repelled those that sought His counsel, or excused Himself for want of time from imparting to them words of light and consolation. He not only taught multitudes in the Temple and in the synagogues, in the desert and along the sea-coast, but He gave personal lessons of exhortation to the Samaritan woman at the well of Jacob, to Nicodemus by night, to Magdalen in the house of Simon, to the youth who had asked Him what he should do to possess eternal life, to the man who was born blind, and to many other individuals who daily approached Him.

The unexpected obstacles that the Right Rev. Edgar P. Wadhams encountered when he applied for admission to the Catholic Church, are graphically told by his friend, Father Walworth. These rebuffs might have discouraged a man of less determination and force of character than the future Bishop of Ogdensburg. In 1846, when Mr. Wadhams had resolved to abandon the Episcopalian ministry and enter the Catholic Church, he called at the nearest chapel he could find in his own native Adirondacks; but "after a brief conference with the priest, he

[1] Matt. XXIII. 23.

was allowed to depart without any encouragement. As he turned away, the clergyman said to one of his parishioners: ' Look at that young man. I wonder what he is up to.'

"His second attempt was at Albany. He rang the bell at the rectory of one of the Catholic churches. After having made known his state of mind and wishes to an ecclesiastic of the house, he received, it is said, this answer: ' We are very busy here and can't attend to you.'

" His third, and more successful application was made to the Sulpicians at St. Mary's Seminary, Baltimore. Here he was cordially received, duly prepared and admitted to that great Mother's bosom, so heroically sought for, so lovingly clung to." [1]

It is gratifying to observe in conclusion, that we have not been treading on barren ground, but on a field that is daily producing fruit, and that gives hope of more abundant harvests in the future. I may be permitted to give some statistics of conversions in the diocese of Baltimore. During the last five years, according to official returns, 3,500 converts, or an average of 700 each year, were received into the Church in this diocese. I have no means of obtaining any detailed information on the subject in regard to the other dioceses of the country. In several of them, no doubt, results at least equally encouraging have been attained. Assuming that the Catholic population of the United States is ten millions, should the proportion of converts to the Catholic population be as large in other dioceses as it is in Baltimore, the annual number of conversions throughout the land would exceed 30,000.

[1] *Reminiscences of Edgar P. Wadhams*, by Rev. Clarence A. Walworth.

It is difficult to overestimate the moral influence exerted by the accession of neophytes to the faith. They are a living argument of the attractive force and of the overwhelming claims of the Catholic religion on the conscience of mankind. For while we can hardly conceive any religious inquirer embracing the Church from human or temporal considerations, we know that many on entering the fold, are confronted by family and social ostracism, by pecuniary sacrifice, and sometimes even by the surrender of all hopes of political preferment.

Converts in their turn often become *converters* and missionaries on a limited scale. As men who acquire rich estates by their personal industry and exertions, set more value on their possessions than they who are born to wealth, so do converts usually appreciate the gift of faith more thoroughly than they who have inherited it from their fathers : and with a zeal that is born of charity, they ardently desire to make others share in their spiritual treasures.

CHAPTER XXIX.

CONGREGATIONAL SINGING.

A MONG the many agencies that may serve to awaken and foster a spirit of fervor and healthy religious enthusiasm throughout the members of a parish, the practice of congregational singing holds a conspicuous place. And, surely, there is no devotion that has a higher or holier sanction, or that appeals more forcibly to our reason and emotional nature than the chanting in unison of the praises of God by the people.

Choirs of angels and saints in heaven are unceasingly glorifying God by song. The Prophet Isaias thus describes the glorious heavenly vision with which he was favored before being consecrated for the prophetical office: "I saw the Lord sitting upon a throne, high and elevated: and His train filled the temple. Upon it stood the Seraphim. . . . And they cried one to another, and said: Holy, holy, holy, the Lord God of hosts, all the earth is full of His glory."[1]

"And I beheld," says St. John, "and I heard the voice of many angels round about the throne, . . . and the number of them was thousands of thousands, saying with a loud voice: The Lamb who was slain is worthy to receive power, and divinity, and wisdom, and strength, and honor, and glory, and benediction."[2]

[1] Isaias VI. 1–3. [2] Apoc. v. 11, 12.

At the birth of Christ, a multitude of the heavenly host was present, "praising God, and saying: Glory to God in the highest, and on earth peace to men of good will."[1]

"I saw a great multitude, which no man could number, of all nations, and tribes, and peoples, and tongues, standing before the throne and in sight of the Lamb, . . and they cried with a loud voice, saying: Salvation to our God, who sitteth upon the throne, and to the lamb."[2] "And I heard, as it were, the voice of a great multitude, and as the voice of many waters, and as the voice of great thunders, saying: Alleluia: for the Lord our God, the Almighty hath reigned."[3]

That it was customary for the children of Israel in the Old Covenant to sing the praises of God in concert, is evident from many passages of the Psalms and other portions of the Scriptures: "Come, let us praise the Lord with joy," cries out the Royal Prophet, "let us joyfully sing to God our Saviour. Let us come before His presence with thanksgiving, and make a joyful noise to Him with psalms. For, the Lord is a great God, and a great King above all gods."[4]

"Praise ye the name of the Lord, O you *His* servants. . . . Praise ye the Lord, for the Lord is good. Sing ye to His name, for it is sweet."[5]

"Sing ye to the Lord a new canticle: let His praise be in the church of the saints. Let the children of Sion be joyful in their King. Let them praise His name in choir: let them sing to Him with the timbrel and the psaltery."[6]

[1] Luke II. 13, 14.   [3] Ibid. XIX. 6.   [5] Ibid. CXXXIV. 1, 3.
[2] Apoc. VII. 9, 10.   [4] Ps. XCIV. 1–3.   [6] Ibid. CXLIX. 1–3.

"Sing to Him, yea, sing praises to Him : relate all His wondrous works." [1]

"Sing joyfully to God. Sing praises to the Lord on the harp, and with the voice of a psalm. Make a joyful noise before the Lord our King." [2]

Choral hymn-singing is approved even by the practice of our Lord Himself. Immediately after the institution of the Sacrament of the Eucharist, our Saviour and His disciples chanted together a sacred canticle : "And having sung a hymn, they went out unto Mount Olivet." [3]

St. Paul strongly recommends to his disciples the exercise of antiphonal devotional singing : " Be not drunk with wine, wherein is luxury ; but be ye filled with the Holy Spirit speaking to yourselves in psalms and hymns and spiritual canticles, singing and making melody in your hearts to the Lord." [4]

When Paul and Silas were imprisoned at Philippi, at midnight they " praying, praised God. And they that were in prison, heard them. And suddenly there was a great earthquake, so that the foundations of the prison were shaken." [5] Though " their feet were made fast in the stocks," their hearts exulted in apostolic freedom, and the very walls of the prison literally trembled at the sound of their voice.

That the faithful had the habit of singing hymns antiphonally in the primitive days of the Church, is manifest from the letter of Pliny to the Emperor Trajan : " They are accustomed," he says, " to assemble before daylight on a certain day, and to sing alternately a hymn to Christ as God."

[1] Ps. CIV. 2.   [3] Matt. XXVI. 30.   [5] Acts. XVI. 25, 26.
[2] Ibid. XCVII. 4-6.   [4] Eph. v. 18, 19.

Origen says: "We glorify in hymns God and His only-begotten Son, as do also the sun, the moon, the stars, and all the host of heaven. All these in one divine chorus, with the just among men, glorify in hymns God, who is over all, and His only-begotten Son."

So familiar were the people with the popular melodies of the Church that, according to St. Jerome, "they who went into the fields might hear the ploughman at his alleluias, the mower at his hymns, and the vine-dresser singing David's Psalms."

"Psalmody," says St. Ambrose, "is the blessing of the people, a thanksgiving of the multitude, the delight of an assembly of people, and a language for all. It is the voice of the Church, the sweetly-loud profession of faith, the full-voiced worship of strong men, the delight of the free-hearted, the shout of the joyous, the exultation of the merry. It is the soother of anger, the chaser away of sorrow, the comforter of grief. The Apostle commanded women to be silent in church, yet it becomes them to join in the common singing. Boys and young men may sing Psalms without harm, and young women without detriment to maidenly reserve. Psalms are the food of childhood, and even infancy itself, that will learn nothing besides, delights in them. Psalmody befits the rank of kings and of magistrates, and chorused by the people, each one vying with his neighbor in causing that to be heard which is good for all."

St. Augustine observes in one of his letters: "As for congregational psalmody, what better employment can there be for a congregation of people met together, what more beneficial to themselves, or more holy and well-pleasing to God, I am wholly unable to conceive."

The same Father tells us how tenderly he was moved on listening to the sacred melodies sung by the faithful in Milan: "How I wept in hearing Thy hymns and canticles, touched to the quick by the voices of Thy well-beloved Church! The voices flowed into mine ears and Thy truth distilled into my heart, whence the affections of my devotion overflowed, and tears ran down, and happy was I therein."[1] Again he says: "When I remember the tears I shed at the psalmody of Thy Church in the beginning of my recovered faith, and how at this time I am moved not with the singing, but with the things sung, when they are sung with a clear voice and modulation most suitable, I acknowledge the great use of this institution."[2]

Several Fathers and Doctors of the Church, including even Sovereign Pontiffs themselves, consecrated their talents to the composition of sacred poems. Ephrem Ambrose, Gregory Nazianzen, Methodius, John Damascene, Hilary of Poictiers, Gregory the Great, Gelasius, and at a later period, Bernard and Thomas Aquinas wrote canticles and anthems for the use of the clergy and people of their times.

In every age of the Church, the sects have made use of popular hymnody as a powerful vehicle for disseminating their doctrines and gaining proselytes.

At the beginning of the third century, the leader of the Gnostics composed religious verses of attractive melody, which contributed much to the popularity and diffusion of that heresy among the masses.

Arius was the author of engaging hymns embodying his errors against the Divinity of Christ. His followers

---

[1] *Confessions*, B. IX.   [2] Ibid. B. X.

23

were in the habit of congregating in places of public resort in Constantinople, on Sundays and festivals, and of singing these verses, which were so offensive to orthodox ears. St. John Chrysostom was so apprehensive lest the faithful should be seduced by the errors of Arianism, presented under the specious form of captivating melody, that he organized processional hymn-singing in the streets of the city, to counteract the efforts of the innovators.

Apollinaris, Bishop of Laodicea in the fourth century, wrote elegant verses for popular use, tinctured with his Sabellian errors against the Divinity of Christ. The people eagerly drank from this delicious stream of melody, many of them unconscious of the subtle poison it distilled through their veins.

Luther translated into the vernacular many of the old Catholic hymns, and wrote some original religious poems, which wielded an immense influence on the German mind, —an influence still felt in that country. Coleridge has said : " Luther did as much for the Reformation by his hymns as by his translation of the Bible." These verses were sung not only in the churches, but in the streets and fields, in the workshop, in the palaces of the rich, and in the cottages of the poor.

Marot's metrical translation of the Psalms, set to popular and devotional airs, became a formidable weapon in the hands of the Calvinistic leaders in France.

There is no doubt that the strong hold which Methodism took in the eighteenth century, and still retains on the lower and middle classes of England and America, is largely due to its soul-stirring hymnody, which appeals so forcibly to the religious emotions. It is said, that Charles Wesley accomplished as much in the cause of

Methodism by his hymns as John Wesley effected by his preaching. It behooves us to profit by the example of our adversaries.

If congregational doxology is sanctioned, as we have seen, by inspired writers of the Old and the New Testament; if it has the approval of Incarnate Wisdom Himself; if it has been so strongly commended by the voice of Christian antiquity, it must be ascribed to the fact, that the united song of praise strikes a responsive chord in the human heart, and satisfies a spiritual craving in our common nature. It is, in a word, an evidence that religious sentiment finds its fullest manifestation in sacred melody, and that the most overpowering expression of sacred melody is heard in the harmonious voice of the multitude.

Let us now, dear reader, briefly enumerate some of the principal spiritual blessings which a congregation may derive from the one act of celebrating the praise of God with song.

1°.—They are engaged in public prayer; for every hymn, or Psalm, or canticle that is sung, is a prayer of praise, of thanksgiving, or of supplication to God.

2°.—They are making an eloquent profession of faith; for how can a Christian proclaim his religion more openly than by standing up in the midst of the congregation, and announcing in a loud voice some truth of divine Revelation? Several years ago, on a Sunday morning, I entered the cathedral of Cologne, during a low Mass, and took a seat in the body of the church. The vast edifice was filled with a devout congregation, representing every station in life. I observed the officer and the private soldier, the well-dressed gentleman and the plainly clad laborer, ladies and domestics, young and old, priests and laymen, mingled together and singing in the vernacular, the popular sacred hymns of father-land. They seemed so absorbed in their devotional chant, as to be utterly oblivious of every thing around them. I said to myself: What a noble profession of faith is this!

I never attend a religious service in a German church without being charmed and filled with delight, on listening to the hymns so sweetly intoned by the whole congregation. Our German brethren have happily perpetuated this devout tradition of their forefathers.

3°.—By joining in sacred song, the people are preaching God's word, and often, though unconsciously, they touch the heart of some wayward soul that casually enters the church.

At the harmonious sound of religious melody coming from the fervent lips of sturdy manhood and innocent youth, the voice of the infidel is hushed, the scoffer hides his head in shame, and the rebellious heart is overpowered, yielding to the impulse of divine grace, even as the walls of Jericho fell before the shouts of the people and the trumpets of the ministers of God. Then, indeed, "the voice of the Lord is in power; the voice of the Lord in magnificence. The voice of the Lord breaketh the cedars: yea, the Lord shall break the cedars of Libanus."[1]

The joyous anthem of praise, or the tender notes of supplication, sometimes exert more influence in reclaiming a sinner than does the formal discourse from the lips of the priest. Monseigneur Dupanloup, Bishop of Orleans, was in the habit of delivering in his cathedral during Lent, a course of sermons, which attracted a large concourse of people. During the service, the congregation

[1] Ps. xxviii. 4, 5.

sang alternately with the choir the Psalm *Miserere.* The bishop relates that a gentleman, who for years had neglected his religious duties, was assisting at these services. At the close of the series of sermons, he called on the bishop and remarked to him : " Monseigneur, I have been filled with admiration at the eloquence of your discourses. You convinced my reason, but you did not move me to repentance. But when I heard the notes of the sacred Psalm resounding in your cathedral, my heart melted. I could no longer resist the divine impulse. I am converted."

4°.—By their example they are edifying their neighbor; for if a regular attendance at church edifies your brother by your mute presence, how much more do you encourage and sustain him by lifting up your voice and swelling the chorus of divine praise !

5°.—The law of charity and concord is diffused, "Psalmody," says St. Basil, " is tranquillity of mind, the arbiter of peace, the curb of tumultuous thoughts, the assuager of anger, the bond of friendship, the reconciler of enemies ; for what man can retain in his heart, enmity toward a brother or sister whose voice commingles with his own in giving praise to God?"[1]

6°.—The religious element in their being is quickened and aroused. They are better disposed to profit by a discourse after having taken an active part in a moving canticle, than if they had silently listened to an anthem from the choir. The words sung in unison, warm the heart and soften the ground for the seed of the Gospel.

" Give me the making of the ballads of a nation," said a very wise man, " and I care not who makes its laws."

[1] Proemium in Psalmos.

A national anthem has a magnetic effect in arousing a spirit of enthusiasm. When an English regiment hears *God save the Queen*, or a French corps, the *Marseillaise;* when a German squadron catches the strains of *Die Wacht am Rhein*, or an American troop, those of *The Star-Spangled Banner*, the patriotic spirit of the soldiers is suddenly and vehemently aroused. A devout hymn exercises a kindred sway on the religious mind. We may well imagine how the heart of Israel's children swelled with rapture and gratitude to the God of battles when, after their miraculous passage through the Red Sea, they rent the air with the majestic Canticle of Moses : " Let us sing to the Lord, for He is gloriously magnified. The horse and the rider He hath thrown into the sea." [1]

Nor can any one complain of this appeal to our religious feelings. Our emotional, as well as our intellectual, nature is a gift of God, and all the powers of our soul should be consecrated to Him.

7°.—Devout singing is the guardian of spiritual gladness and an antidote against melancholy : " Is any of you cheerful in mind ? " says St. James, " let him sing." [2] " Whensoever the evil spirit from the Lord was upon Saul, David took his harp and played with his hand, and Saul was refreshed and was better, for the evil spirit departed from him." [3] Saul was afflicted with the spirit of sadness, dejection, and despondency, which gave rise to envy, suspicion, and anxiety of mind. David by his harp appeased the tumultuous passions of Saul, dispelled his gloom, and refreshed his soul with gladness. If an unconscious instrument was so soothing to Saul, how

[1] Exod. xv. 1.   [2] James v. 13.   [3] I. Kings xvi. 23.

exhilarating to his spirits would have been a chorus of living voices chanting Israel's sacred canticles!

To sum up the advantages of congregational singing: It is a prayer; it is a profession of faith; it is a sermon; it edifies the neighbor; it conduces to fraternal charity; it is an incentive to fervent piety; and it contributes to joy of spirit.

The success of congregational singing depends, of course, on the personal exertions of the pastor. Without his leadership and steady coöperation, all the efforts of the people would be wasted. A zeal that is timid, faint-hearted, and spasmodic will not suffice. The rector should throw all the weight of his energies into the work.

The school is obviously the most appropriate place to inaugurate this exercise. Let some hours in the week be devoted to the study and singing of hymnody. The hymns and canticles can be afterward chanted at the low Mass for children, in the Sunday-school and Sodalities, in the devotions of the Month of May, in processions and benedictions of the Blessed Sacrament, and in other regular and occasional services throughout the year.

How soul-stirring the effect if, in the procession of the Blessed Sacrament, the voice of all the people resounded throughout the vault of the church, chanting the "*Lauda Sion Salvatorem*," like the children of Israel, who rent the heavens with joyful accents of praise when they carried the Ark from Silo; or like the great multitude that accompanied our Saviour in His triumphant entry into Jerusalem, and greeted Him with the cry: "Hosanna to the Son of David: blessed is He that cometh in the name of the Lord!"

The children could learn, also, the responses to the *Collects*, to the *Preface*, and to the *Pater Noster* at High Mass. They could study even the entire parts of a Requiem Mass, and assist in the chant of Vespers.

The words of the Third Plenary Council on this subject may be quoted here : " It is very desirable, in our judgment, that the rudiments of Gregorian chant should be taught and exercised in our parochial schools, and thus the number of those who can sing the Psalms increasing more and more, the greater part of the people, in accordance with the custom of the primitive Church,—a custom still prevailing in various places,—may understand how to sing Vespers and other offices with the ministers and choir."

Even if the pastor should have to depend on the rising generation for congregational singing, his efforts will be stimulated and cheered by the consideration that the children of to-day will be men and women in a few years.

But I see no reason why the grown members should not, from the beginning, take some active part in the congregational service. The exercise of joining in a devotional hymn, requires less effort than is commonly imagined. The ascent from speech to harmonious accents is not very arduous or remote.

A step will be taken in the right direction, if the pastor insist on loudness of voice and distinctness of enunciation in congregational *praying*. When the worshippers are taught to respond aloud and fervently at the recitation of the Rosary, the Litanies, and other prayers, the transition to fulness and fervor in singing will be easy and spontaneous.

The rudest people are capable of acquiring a knowledge of music, at least in its elementary form.

It is related in the life of Bishop Cheverus, of Boston, that he once paid a visit to the Penobscot Indians in Maine. On a Sunday morning, after a journey on foot of several days, when approaching the forest in which the Indians were assembled, he was filled with delightful surprise on hearing them singing in harmonious concert the royal Mass of Dumont. They had not seen a priest for fifty years, and their faith was kept alive by chanting in unison every Sunday the words of the sacred liturgy, which they and their fathers had been taught by the early missionaries of that country.

Surely the children of the forest are not gifted by nature or education with richer and more musical voices than an average American congregation. I can say with confidence that a general and hearty participation in the sacred anthems will result in bringing about a closer and more loving relation between the sanctuary and the nave; it will increase the attendance at church; and it will augment the piety and spiritual exultation of the worshippers.

Let no one infer from my warm advocacy of congregational music that my interest in our regular choirs is anywise abated, for I am deeply sensible of the important, if not indispensable, part they fill in our public worship. Some of the sweetest and most delicious moments of my life, are those spent in listening to the sublime Masses of the great composers.

Too much praise can hardly be bestowed on the zealous ladies and gentlemen who are consecrating their talents, and volunteering their services to Church music. Should they discontinue their labors, especially in our country churches, in which paid choirs cannot well be sustained, the sound of the organ, and the voice of melody would be hushed in many a house of prayer.

It is true, indeed, that some of our choirs, like all human institutions, are susceptible of improvement. But this circumstance should not diminish our gratitude to those that, year in and year out, have kept alive the sacred flame of heavenly song.

Let not our zeal for the establishment and development of congregational singing make us indifferent to the regular choir. There should be no conflict, but rather harmony between the two, for there is ample room for both.

To conclude : Let me indulge the hope that all of us may be inspired to labor assiduously for the growth and perfection of congregational song and worship by these majestic words of St. Thomas Aquinas :

> "Sit laus plena, sit sonora,
> Sit jucunda, sit decora mentis
> Jubilatio."

Sit laus plena—Let the full melody of praise burst forth from a united congregation. *Sit sonora*—Let the sonorous voice of manhood be joined to the treble of childhood. Let a jubilee of soul reign in our public services, joyous and decorous, that God may be glorified by the harmonious praises of His children.

CHAPTER XXX.

SICK CALLS AND FUNERALS.

THE visitation of the sick and distressed is the touch-stone of apostolic zeal and charity. A tender sympathy and solicitude for the afflicted were inseparably associated in the life of Christ with the preaching of the Gospel. Both duties were interwoven like threads of gold and silver in His public ministry. When asked by the disciples of John the Baptist, whether He was the true Messiah, He gave them this reply : "Go and relate to John what you have heard and seen. The blind see, the lame walk, the lepers are cleansed, the deaf hear, the dead rise again, the poor have the Gospel preached to them."[1] Never do we walk more closely in the footprints of the Prince of Pastors, never do we more nearly resemble Him, never are we more in touch with Him than when we bear the message of condolence to the house of mourning. "The Spirit of the Lord," says Christ, "is upon Me, wherefore He hath anointed Me to preach the Gospel to the poor, He hath sent Me to heal the contrite of heart."[2] The highest reward at His disposal is promised to those who discharge this duty ; and, as an additional incentive to its faithful performance, we are told to regard Himself in the person of the victim of sickness : " Come, ye blessed

[1] Matt. XI. 4, 5.   [2] Luke IV. 18.

of My Father, possess you the kingdom prepared for you from the foundation of the world ; . . . for I was sick, and you visited Me ; . . . for as long as you did it to one of these My least brethren, you did it to Me."[1]   He tells us by the mouth of the Apostle that the alleviation of human sorrow together with personal rectitude of life, is the very essence of Christianity : " Religion pure and undefiled with God and the Father is this : to visit orphans and widows in their tribulation and to keep oneself unspotted from this world."[2]

The priest should, therefore, like his Master, be an angel of mercy, as well as of truth ; a son of consolation, as well as of thunder.   A certain priest was once asked why he was so bold and vehement in denouncing sin in the pulpit, while he was so gentle in dealing with sinners in the confessional and in the home of sickness.   " Don't you know," he replied, " that when the Apostles received the power to preach the Gospel, the Holy Ghost came as a *rushing wind*, which filled and shook the whole house in which they were sitting, to denote the force and energy with which they should vindicate God's law ?   But when they received the power to forgive sins and to comfort the dying Christian, the Holy Spirit gently breathed on them, to intimate the patient tenderness which they ought to manifest toward the child of sin and sorrow."   In the house of God, the priest proclaims the doctrines of faith as a legislator ; in the house of mourning, he consoles as a father and friend.

Contrast the conduct of our Saviour in the Temple and in the stricken home of Lazarus.   In the Temple, He denounces the money-changers and, seizing a scourge, He

[1] Matt. xxv. 34-40.   [2] James i. 27.

drives them from the house of God. He sheds tears of sympathy for the bereavement of Mary and Martha. The lion in the Temple is transformed into a lamb at the tomb. The stern judge among the thieves becomes a comforting angel among the mourners, and the eye that flashed with indignation in the house of prayer, melts with compassion at the grave of a friend.

There is, perhaps, no duty of a priest's ministry so fruitful in the conversion of souls as the visitation of the sick and afflicted. To many, indeed, the sick room has been an ante-chamber of heaven. The atmosphere of physical disease or mental suffering, is most favorable for the growth of faith and virtue. It is a time most season-able for conversion to a life of grace and truth from a state of sin and doctrinal error. " Blessed are they that mourn, for they shall be comforted " by heavenly light and peace. Human respect and the passions of the heart lose their hold when death sends a warning, or when tribulation knocks at the door. It is then that God ploughs the heart to prepare it for the seed of repentance. " A grievous sickness maketh the soul sober." [1] When the ruler, mentioned in the Gospel, saw his son stricken down with a serious illness, he, no doubt, looked on this visitation as an unmixed calamity. In reality, however, as the sequel showed, this sickness was a blessing in dis-guise, for it proved to be the providential occasion of the conversion of himself, as well as of his entire family. Had his son not been taken ill, the ruler would not have consulted our Lord, and very probably he would have died, as he had lived, an unbeliever.[2]

[1] Ecclus. XXXI. 2.   [2] John IV.

Ignatius of Loyola, a gay and gallant soldier, wounded at the battle of Pampeluna, and lying a restless convalescent, thought little of the kingdom of God. To while away a weary hour, he asked for a romance. None being at hand, a volume of the *Lives of the Saints* was given him instead. "Why cannot I become what these true heroes were? I, too, can become a saint and, with God's help, I will." The result all know well. Sickness gave to the Church and to the world Saint Ignatius of Loyola and the great Society of Jesus.

Archbishop Audu, the venerable Patriarch of the Chaldeans, when attending the Vatican Council, related to me the history of his conversion. In his gay youth, he was bent upon the pleasures of the world. One day, while on one of his excursions in quest of enjoyment, he happened to visit a Chaldean monastery, probably to procure some refreshments. As he was entering, the keystone of the arch fell and severely crushed him. During his convalescence in the cloister, he devoted his time to pious reading, and so profoundly impressed was he with the instructions and the edifying example of the fathers that he left the sacred retreat a fervent Christian. He studied for the ministry and, finally, was elevated to the rank of patriarch.

The visit of the priest to the home of sorrow has nothing about it of an inquisitorial character. It is justly regarded not as a call of ceremony, but as one of genuine sympathy. He is received as an angel of consolation, and his words then spoken, are treasured up with special gratitude and affection.

St. Francis de Sales says that the sick chamber is a school of compassion for him who ministers comfort to the patient, and of loving patience for the sufferer. The priest is like Mary and John standing before the Cross in tender sympathy; the patient is, as it were, nailed to that Cross, sharing in the agony of our Lord's Passion.

When the pastor addresses his congregation from the pulpit, he is obliged to administer the same spiritual food to the hundreds before him. He may very reasonably expect that to many of them it may be neither palatable nor nutritious, and that some may even reject it as the children of Israel loathed the manna in the desert. There is no help for it. He cannot accommodate his sermon to the diversified tastes and capacity of his whole audience.

But the case is different when his ministry is exercised at the sick bed. His practical sense will at once suggest to him the line of instruction that is suited to the intellectual and moral condition of his patient, and his words of exhortation and solace will find a responsive echo in the breast of his afflicted parishioner.

> "Beside the bed where parting life was laid,
> And sorrow, guilt and pain by turns dismayed;
> The reverend champion stood: at his control,
> Despair and anguish fled the struggling soul;
> Comfort came down the trembling wretch to raise
> And his last faltering accents whispered praise." [1]

We are not, therefore, surprised at the number of conversions resulting from ministrations to the sick. The chaplain attached to the hospital of the French penal settlement of New Caledonia, to which the most hardened criminals are transferred, averred to a friend of mine that nearly all such convicts admitted into the hospital, die the death of the penitent.

Goldsmith's *Deserted Village.*

Thirty-five persons were received into the Church in a hospital in this diocese during a single year. Not many parish churches can reap so great a harvest during the same period of time. Conversions are not usually made in groups or battalions, but individually; and the reason is obvious. Every man is a world in himself. He has habits of thought, mental capacity, passions, prejudices, and temptations peculiar to himself, so that a chain of argument that would carry conviction to one hearer, might exert no influence whatever on another.

But while the pastor brings the peace of God to the invalid, the light shed on him radiates over the household. The members of the family are filled with gratitude toward their consoler, as Tobias and his family toward the angel Raphael. They are loud in his praise. The attachment that is then formed often endures through life, and not unfrequently some member of the household dates his conversion from one of these visits, for we readily believe those whom we have learned to admire and love.

The clergyman in charge of the Woodstock missions in this diocese, while journeying through the parish, was once called in to see an aged Protestant lady whose death was drawing near. Her friends had previously sent for their own minister, but he excused himself on account of the inclemency of the weather and of sickness in his own family. This message in their hour of sorrow, aggravated the wounds of their hearts. The worthy priest spoke to the dying woman such words of exhortation and comfort as the occasion suggested. The result of his casual visit was that the lady was baptized, and her reception into the Church was followed by the conversion of her aged husband and their son. I had the consolation of confirming at the same time, members of three generations belonging to this family. The son who was converted now resides in the old homestead, and is the father of eleven pious and devoted children.

Nor is the salutary influence of the pastor's ministration confined to the circle which he comforts by his presence. It is diffused throughout the neighborhood, as happened to our Lord when He visited the house of Lazarus. It is a significant fact, that, while many conversions resulted from the deed of mercy He then wrought, there are none recorded as having followed immediately from the Sermon on the Mount. The Gospel tells us that, when Jesus had ended His sermon, "the people were in *admiration* at His doctrine."[1] But His mission to the home of the afflicted sisters was far more fruitful. "Many, therefore, of the Jews who were come to Mary and Martha, and had seen the things that Jesus did, *believed in Him*."[2] The seed was sown by the sermon; the harvest was reaped by the miracle of compassion.

It is so in regard to the shepherd of souls. The people may admire him for the eloquence of his sermons, but they will love him for the eloquence of his beneficent acts. In silently making his daily rounds, like the good St. Francis, he preaches more forcibly than in the pulpit. The most intolerant enemy of Christianity never questions the orthodoxy of pastoral benevolence. By his diligent and assiduous care of the sick and sorrowing, by his repression of the demon of intemperance, by his healing of domestic quarrels, by his unostentatious help to the poor, by the odor of Christ which he leaves behind him, the priest becomes a tower of strength and a moral force

[1] Matt. VII. 28.   [2] John XI. 45.

24

in the whole neighborhood. He disarms prejudice, and while only a few may be at once converted to the faith, the observing portion of the community are won over to a higher esteem for his person, and to a better appreciation of the Catholic religion of which he is so bright an exemplar. " If all priests," they cry out, " were like that man, the Catholic Church would have few enemies."

Happy is the minister who when his course is run, can truthfully say with Job : " The ear that heard me, blessed me, and the eye that saw me, gave witness to me : because I had delivered the poor man that cried out ; and the fatherless, that had no helper. The blessing of him that was ready to perish came upon me, and I comforted the heart of the widow. . . . I was an eye to the blind, and a foot to the lame, I was the father of the poor, and the cause which I knew not, I searched out most diligently." [1]

It is not uncommon for a bishop when he announces his intention of promoting a priest to a more important field of labor, to receive petitions signed by leading Protestants, as well as Catholics, expatiating on the pastor's beneficent influence in the community and requesting that he may be allowed to continue with them. The picture which Chaucer draws of the model priest of his day, might be applied to any one of those to whom I have referred :

" Wide was his parish, and houses far asunder,
But he ne left nought, for ne rain ne thunder;
In sickness and in mischief to visite
The ferrest in his parish moche and lite
Upon his feet, and in his hand a staff."

I wish I could close with this edifying portrayal, but the medal has its reverse, the bright picture has its shades

[1] Job xxix. 11–16.

and backgrounds. "Not all who are of Israel, are Israelites; neither are they who are the seed of Abraham, all
children" of the promised inheritance.[1] There are some
anointed ministers here and there, happily few in number,
who do not adequately realize their grave responsibility in
the service of the sick, and who do not exercise toward
them the diligence and fatherly solicitude which their
sacred calling demands.

On the specious pretext, that sick calls at night are
often inspired by groundless fear, these clergymen are
reluctant to respond to such a summons, unless it is
accompanied by a medical certificate stating that the case
is urgent. When the messenger arrives, he is gravely
informed that the pastor is asleep, and does not wish to be
disturbed. "*Dormit Petrus.*" Peter sleeps while his Master, in the person of the afflicted patient, is in the toils
of death and struggling with the tempter. If after much
importunity the priest is aroused, he appears before the
messenger in an irritable frame of mind and expresses his
opinion, that the case is not of a pressing nature, and that
it could be safely deferred till the next morning. It is
true, indeed, that the ailment of the patient is frequently
exaggerated; but may not the pastor's indolent disposition
be, in some measure, responsible for the exaggeration?
The family are tempted to magnify the illness of the
invalid from the apprehension they feel that, if it is not
reported as very serious and critical, he may be deprived
of the ministrations of the priest.

In this unamiable mood, he approaches the sick
chamber, chilling both patient and attendants by his cold
and formal bearing. He performs the sacred rites in a

[1] Rom. ix. 6, 7.

forced and perfunctory way. His exhortation is without unction, his visit without comfort, his manner without composure, and he abruptly leaves, probably never to return, though the patient may survive for weeks or even months. Man's eternal destiny largely depends on the spiritual condition in which he is found at his last moments. That condition is, in no small degree, influenced by the ministrations of the priest; therefore, he shares in the condemnation of the dying sinner, if he makes no exertion to bring him to repentance.

God thus spoke to the Prophet : "Son of man, if when I say to the wicked : Thou shalt surely die, thou declare it not to him, nor speak *to him*, that he may be converted from his wicked way and live, the same wicked man shall die in his iniquity, but I will require his blood at thy hand."[1]

The medical adviser is prompt at the call of duty at all hours of the night. Surely, the physician of the soul should not be outdone in this respect by the physician of the body.

I am persuaded that one of the paramount duties of a priest is habitual kindness and patience toward every child of sin, sorrow, and suffering with whom he may be thrown. In repelling one that may seek our aid or counsel, in betraying impatience and irritability of temper, in using harsh or hasty language toward him, we may commit only a trivial fault. But we may be to him the occasion of a grievous delinquency. We may be the last plank to which the struggling sufferer tries to cling amid the waves of adversity, and when this final refuge is snatched from him, he sinks in the sea of despair. A

[1] Ezech. III. 17, 18.

severe rebuke, spoken perhaps inadvertently and without malice, has driven many a sensitive man from the Sacraments, and even from the Church for years, aye, for a lifetime.

Thank God, examples of ill-temper and negligence are very rare on the part of our devoted clergy. The few unfeeling and slothful ones only serve to bring out in bolder relief the lustre and heroism of the many who are deterred neither by a love of ease, nor by storms, nor by the fear of pestilence, from promptly and cheerfully devoting their life to the cause of suffering humanity.

After finishing the foregoing paragraph, I was visited by a worthy priest of the diocese. He informed me that, some time before last Christmas, he was requested to call on a Protestant young man who was suffering from an aggravated form of diphtheria. The family declined to send for their minister, being persuaded that, burdened as he was with a family, he would hesitate to expose himself to the danger of contracting the disease. The young man was then received into the Church, and since Christmas his mother, brother, and sister have, also, embraced the faith.

Lastly, while comforting others in their tribulations, the pastor is enlightening and instructing himself in the science of Christian philosophy. The home of affliction and mourning is the best school for the apostolic man. Every penitent is an object-lesson silently portraying some particular truth. In one the priest beholds the awful penalty of sin; in another he views the sublime example of Christian patience worthy of the Patriarch Job; in all he sees mirrored before him the vanity and brevity of human life. It is by making a spiritual diagnosis at the bedside of suffering that the physician of souls will most profitably learn how to instruct his congregation from the chair of truth on the solemn duties of life, and to instil into their hearts a genuine compassion for their afflicted brethren. His words will then have a vital force not easily acquired by the reading of books; for he is more impressed by what he sees than by what he hears.

> "Segnius irritant animos demissa per aurem,
> Quam quæ sunt oculis subjecta fidelibus, et quæ
> Ipse sibi tradit spectator." [1]

"From the fulness of the heart, the mouth speaketh." He readily makes others sensible of what he feels himself:

> "Si vis me flere, dolendum est
> Primum ipsi tibi."

Without a practical knowledge of the people's physical, mental, and moral ailments, a clergyman may be a fluent orator, but he will hardly be an effective preacher; for there is no true eloquence without zeal, no zeal without loving sympathy, no sympathy without the knowledge of distress, and this knowledge is best acquired by a personal visitation of his flock and a familiar acquaintance with their miseries.

Another opportunity for making a salutary impression on our separated brethren, as well as on members of the congregation, will often present itself on the occasion of funerals, especially in communities in which Catholics and Protestants have intimate social, family, and commercial relations with one another. In the presence of the angel of death, the human heart is profoundly moved by the

[1] Horace.

solemn voice of Religion, the scoffer is awed to silence, and sectarian preji lice is softened and subdued.

Some well-chosen remarks on the brevity and uncertainty of human life, on the never-ending duration of eternity, on the vanity of all things earthly, on the immortality of the soul, and on man's moral accountability to his Maker, will then appeal to the conscience more forcibly than at other times.

It is, also, a suitable occasion for alluding to the intermediate state in the life to come, and to the Catholic practice of praying for the dead. This consoling doctrine is at once suggestive of the soul's survival beyond the tomb, and of the hallowed communion by prayers subsisting between the living and deceased. It mitigates the sorrows of separation, and contains an implied rebuke to the dreary and despairing creed of annihilation after death. Though not in harmony with the religious opinions of a portion of the audience, a discourse on this theme, delivered amid the solemn funereal surroundings, cannot fail to commend itself to their reason, their sympathies, their yearnings, and to their religious sense. In a supreme moment like this, the "human soul naturally Christian" will assert itself. It will rise superior to the prejudices of education and to the traditions and conventionalities of popular creeds.

There are not a few devoted converts who can trace the first dawning of spiritual light on their heart to the revelation of this truth to them. An estimable lady of Richmond, belonging to an old Virginia family, related to me the history of her conversion. She lost an only daughter to whom she had been fondly attached, and her grief was intensified by the consideration that, according to her creed, death formed an insuperable barrier between them. When she casually learned the invariable belief of the ancient church on this subject, the announcement was to her a heavenly manifestation, it was a refreshing fountain to a thirsting soul. She soon after embraced the Catholic religion. Her son, who had served in the Confederate army, also entered the Church. He studied for the ministry, and became a zealous Paulist Father.

Without incurring the suspicion of betraying a polemical or controversial spirit, the pastor may also with propriety inform his mixed congregation that the practice of praying for the departed is not confined to the Catholic Church. It prevails, likewise in the Russian Church, in all the Oriental Schismatic Churches, as well as in a branch of the Episcopalian body, and is sanctioned by the Jewish, and even by the Mohammedan religion. The faith of the disciples of Mohammed is beautifully set forth by a British Poet in *The Veiled Prophet of Khorassan*, where the dying Zelica asks Azim to pray for her soul when she is dead :

> " Oh, live to pray for me—to bend the knee
>   Morning and night before that Deity,
>   To whom pure lips and hearts without a stain,
>   As thine are, Azim, never breathed in vain,—
>   And pray that He may pardon me—may take
>   Compassion on my soul for thy dear sake,
>   And nought remembering but my love to thee,
>   Make me all thine, all His, eternally !
>
> .   .   .   .
>
> Time fleeted—years on years had passed away,
>   And few of those who on that mournful day,
>   Were living still—when by a rustic grave,
>   Beside the swift Amoo's transparent wave,
>   An aged man, who had grown aged there,

For the last time knelt down—and though the shade
Of death hung darkening over him, there play'd
A gleam of rapture on his eye and cheek,
That brighten'd even death—like the last streak
Of intense glory on th' horizon's brim,
When night o'er all the rest hangs chill and dim.
His soul had seen a vision while he slept;
She, for whose spirit he had pray'd and wept
So many years, had come to him all dress'd
In angel smiles, and told him she was blest!" [1]

In some parts of the United States, the custom is observed of reading the prayers of absolution in English, after they have been recited in the language of the Liturgy; and there is no doubt of the good impression it produces on the congregation. I was informed by a venerable prelate from New Zealand, and by another from Cape Colony, that the same practice obtains in their dioceses with most edifying results. These prayers, authorized by the Church and consecrated by centuries of usage, abound in Scriptural allusions appropriate to the solemn occasion, and, when distinctly and reverently repeated in the vernacular, they command the attention of the hearers. They unfold to them the richness and hidden beauty of our Liturgy of which some of them, perhaps, never before had a glimpse; and they serve to convince them that our Ritual, when understood, appeals to the reason, as well as to the emotional nature, of man.

A priest of this diocese was recently called to perform the funeral service at the house of a deceased convert. All the attendants at the obsequies were Protestants, and they manifested a shy and reserved demeanor toward the

[1] See *"Die Jenseitige Welt"*—P. Leo Keel. *Fegfeuer*, p. 178. (*Purgatory*.)

officiating clergyman.   While he was reciting the prayers of the Ritual in Latin, they frowned on him, some of them even exhibiting marks of levity; but when he began to read the same in English, they listened with close and respectful attention.   And, finally, when he preached to them, they wept through compunction of heart:

"Truth from his lips prevail'd with double sway.
And fools, who came to scoff, remain'd to pray." [1]

[1] Goldsmith's *Deserted Village.*

CHAPTER XXXI.

Consolations and Rewards of the Priest.

THE life of a faithful missionary clergyman is one of
trials, vicissitudes, and habitual self-denial. He
makes an heroic renunciation of the pleasures of the flesh
and of the endearments of family ties. He is subject to
a life-long rule of discipline. Every day, almost every
hour, has certain duties marked out for him. He is
regarded as a public servant to whom the stranger as well
as the members of his flock, the unbeliever as well as those
of the household of the faith, may, regardless of his
personal inconvenience, have access at all times, to present
their grievances, to solicit his aid, or to invoke his counsel.

His labors resemble in kind, if not in degree, those of
the Apostle of the Gentiles. He is engrossed by the
financial management of the church under his charge; he
is preoccupied by the supervision of his congregation.
Every temporal or spiritual calamity that afflicts the
members of his parish is a source of concern and distress
to him. He can say with the Apostle: "Who is weak,
and I am not weak? who is scandalized, and I do not
burn?"[1]

And, then, how much he has often to suffer from the
calumnies of men who know him not, who are poisoned
by prejudice, and who are always disposed to view with

[1] II. Cor. xi. 29.

a sinister or suspicious eye his most harmless words and actions! With the same Apostle he can affirm: "We are reviled, and we bless; we are persecuted, and we suffer it; we are slandered, and we entreat; we are made as the refuse of this world, the offscouring of all even until now."[1]

Nevertheless, every apostolic man who has his heart in his work can truly declare with St. Paul: "I am filled with comfort; I exceedingly abound with joy in all our tribulation."[2] What is the secret of his consolation? What are those hidden springs that refresh his soul amid the incessant labors and sorrows of his ministerial life? What are those temporal recompenses and heavenly rewards which impart to him that serenity of mind, that joy of spirit usually reflected on his countenance?

In the first place, the devoted servant of Christ enjoys the glorious liberty of the sons of God. Unencumbered with superfluous means, and secure in the possession of a sufficiency, he has little concern about his future wants, which are few and easily supplied. He is free from the splendid misery of the rich man who is attached to his goods; who, instead of possessing his wealth, may be said to be possessed by it; who is full of anxiety about preserving and increasing his fortune, and saddened by the reflection, that he must one day part with it.

He is delivered from the tyranny of his passions, and is exempt from the gnawing anxiety and perplexities which harass those that are burdened with the care of a growing family. He has no chains to bind him to the earth; but, like a traveller untrammelled by baggage, he

[1] I. Cor. iv. 12, 13.   [2] II. Cor. vii. 4.

is equipped for his long journey whenever it may please his Master to summon him to a better world.

Another source of joy and consolation to apostolic workmen, is the sense of Christ's abiding presence with them, and of the special providence with which He watches over them.   It is a significant fact, that, in the very first discourse which our Saviour delivered to the Apostles after He had made choice of them, as well as in the very last words He addressed them before His Ascension, He particularly exhorts them to be without solicitude and to trust in Him, in view of His continual care of them.

Before sending them on their mission, He tells them that the more they endure, the more they will be like Him ; that they should have no dread of the contradictions and hostility of men ; that they are not to fear them who kill the body, and are not able to kill the soul ; that a hair of their head will not be disturbed without God's permission ; that, if they are loyal to Him and to His Gospel, He will plead for them before His Father in heaven.   The parting sentence He utters to them on earth, is this : "Behold I am with you all days, even to the consummation of the world."

What repose and contentment, what confidence and security, do not these words inspire !   If a soldier in battle is cheered by the consciousness, that the eye of his commander is upon him, how much more is the soldier of Christ encouraged by the consideration, that his Divine Captain is invisibly at his side, upholding and sustaining him in his daily labors and conflicts !   Not only is the minister of the Lord supported, like all just men, by God's providential watchfulness over him, but he is also com-

forted by the sacramental presence of Christ in the holy
Oblation, which is a privilege personal to himself.   How
amply is he compensated for the surrender of family and
kindred and for the loss of friends, by the daily companion-
ship of his Master, whose intimate and loving friendship
he enjoys in the Sacrifice of the Mass and in his visits to
the Blessed Sacrament!   In the celebration of the Sacred
Mysteries, he is favored with a spiritual refreshment and
a hidden light from heaven which enable him to endure
the toils and to meet the emergencies of the day.   This
celestial Bread, like the food which nourished the Prophet
Elias in the desert, gives him strength to renew every
morning the journey of life, till he reaches the true Mount
Horeb.

The edifying priest will have, also, an inexhaustible
fund of interior delight in the testimony of a good conscience.   The joy of a good conscience is a perennial feast.
He who possesses an upright conscience, has the kingdom
of God within him, the kingdom of peace and tranquillity.
He is not disquieted by the storm of words that rages
around him ; for the unfavorable judgments of men weigh
lightly with him who acts from rectitude of motive, and
who covets only the approval of Heaven.

St. Paul says : " Now the end of the commandment is
charity from a pure heart, and a good conscience, and an
unfeigned faith."[1]   In other words, the object or aim of
our ministry is to nourish the virtues of faith, hope, and
charity in the hearts of the people ; and a living faith, a
genuine love for our brethren, and a pure conscience are
the three elements that render our ministry acceptable to
God.

[1] I. Tim. I. 5.

How happy is the servant of Christ, when he can say with the Apostle: "Our glory is this, the testimony of our conscience that in simplicity of heart and sincerity of God, and not in carnal wisdom, but in the grace of God, we have conversed in this world; and more abundantly towards you."[1]

The mutual love subsisting between the spiritual Father and his children in Christ is the strongest and most hallowed sentiment that can sway the human breast. It is the fountain of the noblest and purest joy. This bond of heavenly fellowship was a subject of pious exultation to the Apostle. In writing to the Corinthians, he says: "We are your glory, even as you also are ours in the day of our Lord Jesus Christ."[2]

There is no rational pleasure more elevating and enduring than that which springs from the consciousness of rendering good service to others. So keen was the satisfaction which St. Paul experienced in the sanctification of souls, that he exclaimed: "I most gladly will spend and be spent myself for your souls: although loving you more, I be loved less."[3]

St. John speaks of the gladness which filled his heart when he learned that his disciples were advancing in virtue: "I have no greater grace," he says, "than this, to hear that my children walk in truth."[4] Such, also, is the gratification which the zealous pastor feels when a sinner is reclaimed, when he observes that the confessional and altar-railing are more than usually frequented, and that the congregation assembled in church on the Lord's-Day is marked by an increase in number, and a more earnest devotion.

[1] II. Cor. I. 12.　　[2] Ibid. I. 14.　　[3] Ibid. XII. 15.　　[4] III. John I. 4.

He derives immeasurably more delight on beholding his flock grow in holiness under his pastoral care, than the millionaire enjoys from his accumulating wealth, or the husbandman from his abundant harvest; because when the riches and the crops will have perished, the souls whom the shepherd had helped to redeem, will be a glorious aureola around his brow. He can address his children in the words of the Apostle: " My dearly beloved brethren, and most desired, my joy and my crown." [1]

The satisfaction that the priest experiences from his deeds of benevolence to his charge, is much augmented by the lively sense of gratitude which they manifest toward him. An earthly ruler can demand of his subjects the tribute of their money; but he cannot extort the golden coin of heartfelt affection which the flock freely and cheerfully pay to their pastor.

The children of the parish love him. They instinctively run after him as their spiritual Father, as the one who brought them forth in the Sacrament of Regeneration, who nourished them with the milk of heavenly knowledge.

The adults who have preserved their religious and moral integrity, bless him as the visible angel-guardian who has guided their steps in the path of truth and righteousness.

The penitents show their gratitude for him as a loving pastor who rescued them from the thorny road of vice, and bore them back after their wayward wanderings to their Father's house.

The poor look on him as their benefactor from whose steps they were never repelled, and whose hand was ever open to succor them.

[1] Phil. iv. 1.

The sick trust in him as their spiritual physician, assuaging their pains by his heavenly ministrations and words of sympathy.

The sorrowing and disconsolate cherish him as their consoler, lightening the burden of their heart.

The whole congregation revere and honor him as a guide and friend who breaks to them the Bread of Life, preaches to them the words of salvation, solves their doubts, and heals their dissensions.

Nor is this devotedness of the people confined to mere sentiment. They are eager on every occasion, to testify their loyalty by self-sacrificing deeds. Many a true pastor can affirm of his flock what Paul said to the Galatians : " You despised not, nor rejected ; but received me as an angel of God, *even* as Christ Jesus. . . . For I bear you witness that, if it could be done, you would have plucked out your own eyes, and would have given them to me." [1]

There are few passages in Holy Scripture so touching and pathetic as that which describes the parting of Paul from the clergy of Ephesus, when, before embarking, he knelt down and prayed with them on the shore, and when they wept and embraced him, " being grieved most of all for the word which he had said, that they should see his face no more." [2] Not less loved is the devoted pastor, nor less lamented, when called to another mission, or summoned to his eternal reward.

This reciprocal affection between the Christian ambassador and his people, is one of the strongest incentives to life-long toil, privations, and self-renunciation. " Where there is love, there is no labor, or if there is labor, the

[1] Gal. IV. 14, 15.   [2] Acts XX. 38.

labor is loved." [1]　Love is stimulated by obstacles.　It surmounts every difficulty, smoothes every path, sweetens every toil.　It was the intensity of this fatherly attachment that prompted the Apostle to say: " I wished myself to be an anathema from Christ for my brethren who are my kinsmen according to the flesh."　It was this attachment that made him endure with joy, stripes and persecution, shipwreck and imprisonment.

But the vital principle of happiness to the minister of Christ, is the assurance of an eternal recompense.　The kingdom of heaven is promised by our Lord chiefly to four classes of persons:

1°.—To those that have endeavored to lead a blameless life, and that have sincerely repented of the faults and transgressions they may have committed: " Who shall ascend into the mountain of the Lord, or who shall stand in His holy place?　The innocent in hands, and clean of heart, who hath not taken his soul in vain, nor sworn deceitfully to his neighbor." [2]　" Blessed are the clean of heart, for they shall see God." [3]

2°.—To those that have voluntarily renounced the world, and consecrated themselves to His service: " Behold," said Peter to Jesus, " we have left all things, and have followed Thee; what, therefore, shall we have?　And Jesus said to them: Amen, I say to you, that you who have followed Me, in the regeneration, when the Son of man shall sit on the seat of His majesty, you, also, shall sit on twelve seats, judging the twelve tribes of Israel. And every one that hath left house, or brethren, or sisters,

---

[1] " *Ubi amatur, non laboratur, aut si laboratur, labor amatur.*"—St. Augustine.

[2] Ps. XXIII. 3, 4.　　　　　[3] Matt. v. 8.

or father, or mother, or wife, or children, or lands for My name's sake; shall receive an hundred-fold, and shall possess life everlasting." [1]

3°.—To those that have exercised a spirit of practical charity toward the poor and afflicted : " Come, ye blessed of My Father, possess you the kingdom prepared for you from the foundation of the world. For I was hungry, and you gave Me to eat; I was thirsty, and you gave Me to drink; I was a stranger, and you took Me in; naked, and you covered Me; sick, and you visited Me. . . . As long as you did it to one of these My least brethren, you did it to Me." [2]

4°.—To the fearless herald of the Gospel, whose life is in harmony with his teaching : " Every one that shall confess Me before men, I will also confess him before My Father who is in heaven." [3] And the Apostle says : " If thou confess with thy mouth the Lord Jesus, and believe in thy heart that God hath raised Him up from the dead, thou shalt be saved. For with the heart we believe unto justice ; but with the mouth confession is made unto salvation." [4]

Now, does not the blessed hope of the zealous missionary rest upon each and all of these four titles? Has it not been his constant aim to live in righteousness and innocence, and to implore God's forgiveness every morning at the foot of the altar for his daily offences and negligences? Did he not renounce the goods and pleasures of this world when, at the altar, he solemnly took the Lord as " the portion of his inheritance? " Is not a good part of his daily life spent in relieving the wants, and in

[1] Matt. xix. 27–29.
[2] Ibid. xxv. 34–40.
[3] Ibid. x. 32.
[4] Rom. x. 9, 10.

assuaging the sorrows of the poor and afflicted? And is it not his special mission, and habitual practice to proclaim Christ, and to vindicate His honor?

O Brothers in the ministry! if a grateful country erects monuments to her statesmen and soldiers who defended her in the halls of legislation, or on the field of battle against foreign or domestic foes, surely, the Lord of hosts will amply reward you, the confessors of the faith, who have wielded the sword of the spirit, which is the word of God, in upholding the integrity of the Christian Republic, and in vindicating her sacred laws against the assaults of her enemies. For if God rules as a God, judges as a God, punishes as a God, He also rewards as a God.

How few of those that fought for their country, have had their names inscribed on the roll of fame! How many a brave captain, who displayed the genius of a Napoleon, the fortitude of a Washington, and the iron will of a Wellington, has fallen on the field of battle, "unwept, unhonored, and unsung," because there was no chronicler to record his martial deeds!

God is not thus unmindful of the soldiers of the Cross. The village pastor, whose preaching was unheralded by the press and unheard outside his humble church, whose good deeds were unseen by men, will have his golden words and works written on the imperishable pages of the Book of Life. For if Christ would not suffer the fragments of material bread to be wasted in the desert, He will certainly not permit the living bread of truth and charity to perish. It will not only nourish those to whom it was dispensed, but, like the Royal Prophet's prayer, it will return to the bosom of the dispenser, and fill him with spiritual strength and consolation.

If God said to Abraham, the father of His chosen people: "I am thy Protector, and thy reward exceeding great,"[1] He will not be less bountiful in his benedictions to the spiritual father of the Christian family whom he has begotten in Christ, and nourished with the food of the Gospel.

If the Apostle declares that a crown of glory is laid up for those who "have fought a good fight, and have kept the faith," how much more brilliant a crown is reserved for the faithful shepherd who has not only preserved the faith in his own breast, but has also planted it in the heart of others! "He that shall do and teach," says our Lord, "he shall be called great in the kingdom of heaven."[2]

St. Paul declares that his dear Corinthians, who were then the objects of his pastoral solicitude, would be his crown and his glory in the life to come. More exultant and radiant with joy than any Roman conqueror entering in triumph the imperial city was Paul, when he ascended to the heavenly Jerusalem, enriched with the treasures of good works, and greeted by that host of redeemed spirits whom he had made captive to his Master.

We are equally assured that those blessed souls whose conversion and sanctification the faithful disciple of Christ had promoted on earth, will lend additional lustre to his glory in heaven.

When the zealous and devout pastor contemplates his spiritual children who will have persevered to the end, has he not reason to exclaim with the Apostle: "What is our hope, or joy, or crown of glory? Are not you in the presence of our Lord Jesus Christ at His coming?"[3]

[1] Gen. xv. 1.   [2] Matt. v. 19.   [3] I. Thess. ii. 19.

Your happiness will be mine, because it will be shared by me. When you abound with merits, I shall superabound with joy. Your virtues will enhance my reward. Your glory will encircle its rays around my brow. For if "children's children are the crown of old men, and the glory of children are their fathers,"[1] my glory will be augmented by your salvation. Let this thought be an inspiration to us all in striving to multiply the number of the elect.

We know that there are degrees of rank among the angelic choirs, and we have the testimony of the Apostle that there are, also, grades of celestial glory among the saints in heaven : "One is the glory of the sun, another the glory of the moon, and another the glory of the stars, for star differeth from star in glory."[2]   And may we not, without presumption, assign the highest degree of beatitude to those God-like men, such as Benedict, Francis of Assisi, the Apostles of nations, and the fervent missionaries, whose hearts glowed with the seraphic fire that inflamed and illumined the Christian world, and who, like the angels on Jacob's ladder, ascended to receive light from above, and descended to communicate it to the children of man?

Even in this life they possess the hundred-fold of "the peace of God which surpasseth all understanding," and in the life to come they shall inherit the beatitude promised by the prophet : "They that are learned shall shine as the brightness of the firmament, and they that instruct many unto justice, as stars for all eternity."[3]

Blessed are they who, with an upright heart, have announced the glad tidings of salvation.   To them Christ

---

[1] Prov. XVII. 6.   [2] I. Cor. xv. 41.   [3] Daniel XII. 3.

repeats what He declared in His last discourse to His disciples: "In My Father's house there are many mansions. If not, I would have told you, that I go to prepare a place for you. . . . I will come again and will take you to Myself, that where I am, you also may be. . . . Amen, amen, I say to you, that you shall lament and weep, but the world shall rejoice; and you shall be made sorrowful, but your sorrow shall be turned into joy. . . . I will see you again, and your heart shall rejoice, and your joy no man shall take from you."[1]

Another Evangelist holds out the same consoling promises of honor and happiness, made by our Redeemer in different words: "You are they who have continued with Me in My temptations: And I dispose to you, as My Father hath disposed to Me, a kingdom: that you may eat and drink at My table in My kingdom: and may sit upon thrones, judging the twelve tribes of Israel."[2]

As ye have partaken of My sorrows on earth, so shall ye share in my joys in heaven. As ye were my co-laborers here, so shall ye be co-heirs and co-judges with Me hereafter. You will recline with Me at My everlasting love-feast, which will delight without surfeiting. "You shall be inebriated with the plenty of My house, and shall drink of the torrent of pleasure."[3] The Venerable Bede and other Fathers of the Church, commenting on these words of our Saviour, declare that the judicial power and glory pledged to the Apostles, were not to be restricted to them, but would be extended to all apostolic men that were to succeed them.

[1] John xiv. 2, 3; xvi. 20, 22.   [3] Ps. xxxv. 9.
[2] Luke xxii. 28-30.

As we cannot fathom the depths of God's mercy **and** loving kindness, neither can we comprehend the immensity of the heavenly reward that is promised us, because it will be measured not by our merits, but by His infinite love. "Eye hath not seen, nor ear heard, *neither hath it entered into the heart of man,* what things God hath prepared for them that love Him."[1]

The glimpses of celestial glory vouchsafed to Peter, James, and John, to Paul and Stephen should serve, as they are intended, to stimulate in us a yearning for the blessed kingdom that awaits us; just as the glowing description of the messengers sent by Moses to survey the Promised Land, inflamed the Israelites with renewed zeal to take possession of their destined country.

Let us, therefore, like the Apostle, glory in our tribulations, "knowing that tribulation worketh patience; and patience, trial; and trial, hope; and hope confoundeth not."[2] Let us not be disheartened by labors, remembering that "the sufferings of this time are not worthy to be compared with the glory to come, that shall be revealed in us."[3]

---

[1] I. Cor. II. 9.   [2] Rom. v. 3-5.   [3] Ibid. VIII. 18.

INDEX.

AARON, called by God to the priesthood, 32.
Addison, 194, 247.
Alaska Missionaries, 123.
Alexander the Great, 59, 234.
Alfred the Great, 221.
Algar, Joseph, 297.
Allies, 246.
Allison's History of Europe, 198.
Alma Mater's pride in her sons, 49.
Alphonsus, St., 30, 87, 158, 214.
Alumni, advice to, 65.
Ambition, a magnanimous sentiment, 53.
Ambrose, St., Archbishop of Milan, 25, 141, 244, 353.
America, the rising generation the hope of, 315.
American authors write in too much haste, 206.
   Christian mothers, 319.
   Civic institutions, 263.
   People reverence Christian revelation, 324.
   Youth, education of, 330.
Americans a reading people, 175.
Angelic choirs, degrees of rank among, 390.
Angelo's (Michael) sublime conceptions, 201.
Annihilation after death a despairing creed, 375.
Anselm, St., 52.
Anthem, national, magnetic effect of, 358.
Anthusa, Mother of St. John Chrysostom, 316.

Antiphonal devotional singing in primitive days of the Church, 351.
Antony, St., 185, 234.
Apelles' answer to criticism, 190.
Apollinaris, Bishop of Laodicea, wrote elegant verses for popular use, 354.
Apostasy—St. Paul and St. John lament and denounce, 29.
Apostles aggressive, 334.
   Called to the service of God, 21.
   First and last words of our Saviour to, 381.
   Christ manifests His predilection for, 3.
   How chosen, 21.
   Not deficient in theological knowledge, 166.
Apostles of nations will have highest degree of beatitude, 390.
   Privations endured by, 120.
Apostolic workmen have Christ's abiding presence, 381.
   Zeal, 335.
Arians sang in public resorts in Constantinople, 354.
Arius, author of engaging hymns, 353.
Athanasius, St., of Alexandria, victim of persecutions, 181.
Audu, Archbishop, Patriarch of Chaldeans, 366.
Augustine, St., Bishop of Hippo, 221.
   Ascribes conversion to a sentence of St. Paul, 185.

393

MEPKIN ABBEY
1098 Mepkin Abbey Road
Moncks Corner, S.C. 29461